Invitation
to Catholicism

Beliefs + Teachings + Practices

Alice Camille

ASSISTING CHRISTIANS TO ACT

PUBLICATIONS

Invitation to Catholicism
Beliefs + Teachings + Practices
by Alice Camille

Edited by John Van Bemmel and Gregory F. Augustine Pierce
Cover design by Tom A. Wright
Typesetting by Desktop Edit Shop, Inc.

Cover Illustration: *Pentecost,* painted by a Westphalen Master in
the fourteenth century. From the slide collection of Jean Mor-
man Unsworth.

Excerpt from *Community and Growth* by Jean Vanier, tranlation
© 1979 Jean Vanier, second revised edition © 1989 Jean Vanier.
Used with permission of Paulist Press. www.paulistpress.com.

Scripture quotations are from the New Revised Standard Version of the Bible, copyright © 1989 by the Division of Christian Education of the National Council of the Churches of
Christ in the U.S.A. Used with permission. All rights reserved.

Published by: ACTA Publications
             Assisting Christians To Act
             4848 N. Clark Street
             Chicago, IL 60640-4711
             773-271-1030
             www.actapublications.com

Library of Congress Catalog Number: 2001094296

ISBN: 978-0-87946-227-7

Printed in the United States of America by McNaughton & Gunn, Inc.

Year: 15 14 13
Printing: 7 6 5

Contents

Acknowledgments

Writing a book can be rather lonely work—like hiking the Grand Canyon without someone along to share the wonder and discovery of the journey. Happily, I was not alone in my journey through this book. My sister-in-law Susan Hancock Pedergnana agreed to be my "Protestant" reader, pointing out any obscure Catholic ideas I might have used without definition. My neighbor and long-suffering friend, Erin J. Boulton, was willing, as a recently professed Catholic who loves the church, to be my RCIA reader. My sister Evelyn Mautner also read every page and e-mailed me daily to assist and encourage me. (She also offered to leaflet all the cars in the supermarket parking lot with a free chapter, to boost sales.) Without Susan, Erin and Evie, this book would have been written in a vacuum. Thanks also to my fellow religious writer Paul Boudreau, who was my "computer guy" throughout, as well as fact-checker and heresy-spotter.

Dedication

To my parents,
Evelyn and Theodore Pedergnana,
from whose generous love and fidelity
I learned my faith.

Introduction

All stories begin somewhere. This one has its beginning at the deathbed of a friend. He was well loved and gentle in spirit, regarded by all as a wise and holy person. In his final illness, he told the story of his journey toward God. It surprised many of us who thought we knew him thoroughly.

My friend had been brought up in the country by parents who were indifferent to organized religion. While he was still a small boy, a neighbor offered to take him to church along with her brood, and so it was that he was introduced to the God of Christianity. It was not a highly influential encounter. What mattered to him more was the kindness and welcome of the neighbor and her family.

As a young man, my friend began to travel, first around the country and then around the world. He was astounded by the vastness of the world, the immense variety of human experience and culture. He was attracted in particular to the ways the people of many lands seek the face of their God. In order to understand this phenomenon, he decided to participate in it, immersing himself in each people's language, culture and worship. He became fluent in many tongues and sympathetic to the common yearning soul of humanity. He prayed in Arabic, kneeling on his prayer rug in mosques. He contemplated among Buddhists, attentive to the gong of his bowl. He wore his prayer shawl at the Western Wall in Jerusalem, reciting Hebrew texts and rocking back and forth with rabbis. He was very serious about each experience, respectful of every tradition he encountered.

But from each religious expression, he came away convinced that he could be only a visitor. His own spiritual home eluded him. He dabbled here and there among the congregations of the United States and finally shelved the religious quest altogether, moving to Utah to tend bar at a ski lodge.

As so often happens, once we stop our determined effort to find God, God finds us. My friend overheard coworkers at the lodge talking about visiting a monastery down the road a ways. A Catholic monastery, complete with cowled monks! In the heart of Utah this seemed unlikely, so my friend decided to have a closer look. On the weekend, he drove to the monastery and asked for a room. Left alone with his thoughts, he found the experience restful and clarifying, so he made plans to visit again. This became his habit for months and years to come.

Eventually he developed a relationship with one of the monks, Father Patrick. Each time he came to the monastery, he would meet with the monk and volley questions at him—about God, Jesus, the Catholic church, and the absurdity of knowing anything for sure about the spiritual world. He'd seen it all, studied it all, and it was all the same. There was no way to know God, ultimately. "It's no use," he would tell the monk each time, feeling the despair in his words.

One day, my friend came to the monastery as usual, and asked to see Father Patrick. Word was sent to him that Father Patrick would not meet with him any more; there was no purpose to it. My friend had built up a fortress with his questions, and no answer the monk had to offer would penetrate it. There was nothing left to say.

My friend panicked, sending word back that he would go away and leave the monk alone if only he would meet with him one more time. Just once more. In the end, Father Patrick agreed and came to the small, bare sitting room where guests of the monastery were received.

The monk entered the room and said not a word. Kneeling down, he took off my friend's shoes and socks and kissed his feet with great tenderness. Then he stood up, bowed to my friend and left in silence.

My friend burst into tears. Suddenly his heart opened and he understood, beyond words, the answer to all his questions. He had encountered the love, compassion and humility of Christ, and knew his long search was over. That Easter he was baptized and received into the Catholic church.

Coming to the crossroads
For my friend, nothing could have been more strange and

2

unsought than the idea of joining the Catholic church. From the outside, Catholicism can seem foreign and complex, a step backward into the Middle Ages or onto another planet. Most of what non-Catholics know about the church comes from two sources: Hollywood (saints preserve us!) and ex-Catholics. Practicing Catholics are some of the quietest believers on earth, but ex-Catholics are usually ready to talk your ear off about why they don't practice their former faith.

To be sure, former Catholics often have very good reasons why they found the church wanting. Chief among these reasons is how they were treated (and perhaps mistreated) by the primary representatives of the church: parents, clergy and religious personnel, teachers at the parochial school, and other church members. Those wounds can take a long time to heal, and sometimes that healing has to take place in another community altogether. The church may be "the communion of saints," according to its creed, but even saints are sinners, prone to errors in judgment, foolishness and lapses in love. One of the great mysteries of Christianity is the call to forgiveness, and the church is not excluded from those who need to be forgiven and to seek forgiveness.

Many who pick up this book may find themselves at a crossroads of sorts. Perhaps you are like my friend, looking for God or a community of faith or answers to questions you can't even form in your mind. Or maybe you love someone who is a Catholic and you want to understand what that identity means to him or her. Some of you may be sifting through some unfinished business with the church, trying to understand what went wrong and what may still be right about the religion you left behind. Others may be lifelong Catholics who are looking for a way to get a sense of the "big picture" of Catholic belief. You've been on the inside for so long that it's hard to see the forest for the trees.

This book may serve as a topographical map of the terrain of Catholic belief. Unlike a catechism, it won't be full of doctrine and dogma and official pronouncements. For the last word on every subject of that nature, the *Catechism of the Catholic Church* has already been written. What I offer here, as a lifelong believing Catholic, is a sense of what I find beautiful, joyful and good about Catholicism. It's the side of Catholic belief that doesn't appear much in news magazines and movie scripts. It is, I hope, a presentation of the church that demonstrates how a thinking person in the twenty-first century can embrace Catholicism without compromising reason. Furthermore, as a person deeply committed to a life of integrity and meaning, I want to present Catholic Christianity as a courageous choice that enlivens and supports the quest for fulfillment and true freedom.

If life has become unsatisfying, empty or desperate for many, it is because we seek answers that the world cannot give. As a professor at Princeton University observed not long ago, more and more children are being raised in homes that are "fatherless, godless, and jobless," the acknowledged formula for both depression and crime. If more of us are looking for a sense of love and belonging, something greater than the dollar to worship, some meaningful work for our hands, what we seek can be found in yielding to the image in which we are made: to the God who created us to be more than slaves to the clock and to our physical needs.

What's in this book

The organization of this book has a lot to do with the twenty years I've spent as a religious educator in parish work, campus ministry, and especially with the formation of adults who wish to enter the Catholic church formally through the Rite of Christian Initiation of Adults (RCIA). Each chapter ends with a set of questions for personal or group use, as well as suggestions on how to apply this topic to real living. Sometimes one good question is worth a whole essay, so even if you're reading this alone, scan the questions to see if one of them has your name on it.

The first chapter, on mystery, attempts to lay out basic ideas that religious people—Christians and then Catholics in particular—take for granted. It includes some of the "primary colors" with which we paint reality. For those with no formal religious experience or those who have had only a secular exposure to religion, this may be especially helpful.

The next three chapters focus on the Trinity, as revealed through the Hebrew and Christian scriptures, better known as the Old Testament and New Testament of the Bible. The Bible is, hands down, the most important book you'll ever read, and I can't emphasize too strongly the need to develop a relationship with this book. But because it's large and old, and because many of us have learned to be afraid of its complexity, many lifelong Christians have yet to sit down with it personally. So I present a Cliff Notes-like version of it, with the hope that it will lessen your fear and increase the longing to go further in your spiritual search.

Chapter Five is about the church. From writing a children's textbook on this topic I've learned that a whole book is not enough to cover what has evolved through twenty centuries of living and countless volumes of theologizing. So this single chapter is only Sandbox Theology 101, as my seminary teacher used to say. It gets you in the door—but once there, you're on your own.

The next three chapters are about the sacraments, and although they may seem like old hat to veteran Catholics and voodoo to those raised apart from the church, the approach here is not simply "seven sacred signs" but how to *live sacramentally.*

The last four chapters include topics that people ask questions about the most: prayer, Mary, morality, and the afterlife. An appendix including basic prayers used by Catholics and others can be found at the end.

Why I'm writing this book

There are hundreds of books in print right now about Catholicism, ranging in style from scholarly tomes to trendy little outlines. Many are written expressly for RCIA groups or Catholics returning after some time away or practicing church members looking for an update. One more volume in that sea of information might not seem significant, unless it's the one that finds you.

Rather than defending the need for still another book on

this topic, let me explain why I wrote *Invitation to Catholicism*. Let's go back to the beginning of this introduction, to the deathbed of my friend. He lived the last twenty-five years of his life as a thoroughly happy, jubilant Roman Catholic. He was, frankly, the best advertisement for the church that we cradle Catholics who knew him had ever seen. He spent every year of his post-baptismal life in exuberant evangelization for the sake of Christ. This cause inspired his living, as well as the lives of everyone around him. And it illuminated his dying, so that all that remained in his last hour was his breathing and the light of Christ.

Beyond the loss of someone I loved, all I could think of in his final hours was how dearly I want a death like his. Such a death, I feel sure, is available to all of us and is intended for us as surely as we take in our first breath. But as Flannery O'Connor, Southern writer and notorious Catholic, insisted, "The creative work of a Christian's life is to prepare his own death in Christ." Far from being macabre, this statement is as matter-of-fact as the idea that we are what we eat. We weave the future out of the frayed elements of the past, and we create all our tomorrows out of what we do with the precious bits of today. The spiritual quest is not a hobby or a luxury; it is our destiny. Sometimes it may seem that we just don't have time to find God or get our spiritual act together. But the truth is that time is not given to us for any other reason.

I hope that the time you spend here will not be wasted. May God bless you on your journey.

One

Room for Mystery

The word mystery used to be huge, evocative of worlds and possibilities that lie hidden to us. But contemporary use of the word has shriveled it to where it's no mystery at all. It now means hardly more than "whodunit," as in there's a body-on-the-floor, a weapon-in-the-lake, and three suspects-to-choose-from. Mystery as a genre has shrunk the concept down to manageable size, where we can tame it if only we pay attention to the clues and don't get seduced by the attractive stranger with the iron-clad alibi.

Mysteries of this kind are meant to be solved. These mysteries are really no more than facts that have yet to come to light. Mystery, in the popular sense, is a temporary state of ignorance, easily resolved by the clever person in the trench coat.

We treat mystery this way, I suspect, because of the scientific revolution. What was once the terrain of mystery—cosmic forces, star-embedded skies, the power of the elements, the wonder of the human mind, the ruthless dominion of disease and death—are now problems we are solving or have yet to solve. Mystery is a condition easily remedied by the clever person in the lab coat. When mystery becomes interchangeable with mere ignorance, then knowledge is the tool that will bring it under our control.

One can read articles that seek to explain love as a chemical response or heroism as a biologically comprehensible decision. God and religion have long ago been tossed into the dust bin of useless notions. The appeal of mystery in its former meaning—something that is at bottom patently incomprehensible but about which we can learn more and more—seems to challenge the foundation of scientific inquiry itself.

How science meets religion

Science is not the natural enemy of the spiritual quest, though some fundamentalist approaches to religion have viewed science with great misgivings. Science is a noble enterprise, with its many fruits laid at the service of humanity. All of us are beneficiaries of its gifts, in this generation more than in any other. But science will fail us if we view truth through the lens of scientific inquiry alone. What science cannot offer is an answer to the *why* questions that most humans start asking at the age of two. A child asks her father why the ocean is blue, and her dad rattles off a twenty-minute exposition on the properties of light and water and the workings of the eye and brain. Having proven his thesis, he finishes with great satisfaction, but the child stares at the restless body of water before her and asks again, "But why blue?"

Or why is there an ocean, or a father and child, or anything, instead of nothing? Why time, space, history? Why being of any kind? Why the ability to ask why? Why an asker of any question, and a universe answering or mutely refusing an answer? Here we enter the realm of protoscience, or philosophy. Why does a woman suddenly miscarry a healthy child, seemingly without medical cause? Even if science attempts a response, the reply is meaningless in the arena of grief. "But why has this happened to my child, to me?" the woman asks. For this, chaos theory or statistical probability has nothing useful to offer.

When it comes to the problem of human suffering and the reality of evil, nothing that science or philosophy has come up with can make these two disappear for good. All over the globe, from the rising of the sun to its setting, people are asking questions that cannot be answered with a pill or a theory. And they may carry the questions in their hearts for all of their lives.

The spiritual quest

The enterprise of religion has been around a long time. It does not preclude or exclude scientific discovery or science-born truths, though many speak as if it did. The goal of religion is not to take things apart to see what makes them tick, but to see

8

beyond the pieces to the Maker of the whole. If the goal of science is human knowledge, the endpoint of religion is knowing and being known by the One who is and was and is to come.

The distinction between science and religion is critical, because to attempt to use religion in place of science—or vice versa—causes intellectual or moral schizophrenia. Many people of the twenty-first century who reject the religious enterprise see it in conflict with the truths of science. They feel compelled to make a choice between the two, and the educated mind finds it hard to vote against intellectual freedom.

To those who feel such a conflict, relax. Nobody is asking you to turn off your brain. What is needed is to activate another faculty entirely: the living spirit within you.

Religious truth does not challenge scientific knowledge, any more than it attempts to trump historical truth, mathematical truth or the inquiry systems of any other discipline. As theologian William Herr has noted, if a thing is true, it has to be compatible with faith. Religious truth, particularly as it applies to the Old and New Testaments, addresses the matters of meaning and purpose and direction that exist beyond or beneath the questions that other disciplines ask. The story in Genesis about the Garden of Eden does not seek to address the dating of dinosaur bones or the beginning of the human race. The story of the Great Flood was not written as a historical record of a "perfect storm." The idea of the Israelites wandering forty years in a desert that could be crossed easily in a short period of time is not about having a poor sense of direction. And the theological concept of Trinity is not a math problem of how three equals one under certain circumstances. Religious truth is broader than temporal, tangible fact. To grasp the difference, we may look to the ancient discipline of myth making.

A word about myth
Popular usage has it all wrong about myth. We use the word to dismiss something as patently false: "That's a myth." On the contrary, a myth encapsulates truths about the human condition that lie deep beneath the surface. Its domain is the presentation of those elements of human reality that are not simply

historically true—true for some particular person, place or moment in time—but universally true: true about people, life, the way things are everywhere and in every age. Mythological truth is most naturally presented in storytelling and poetry. Here human experience is communicated not as a means of historical record keeping but to advance human self-understanding: This is what human beings have done or are capable of doing. This is how it is, and how we are.

Of course it must be said that not all we learn by means of myth is true. A lot of myth making depends on the person, people or culture behind it. Think about the personal myths you carry around from your family of origin, the proverbs you were taught to guide you through life. You may have heard simple prejudice pronounced as fact: "Those kinds of people are like that." Or paranoia presented as truth: "Watch your back. People are not to be trusted." You may have also imbibed the American myth, the inner story of a people that is still evolving its themes: "Hard work will be rewarded" or "Anyone can grow up to be president."

Myth making travels a long, winding road from Homer's epics and Aesop's fables to the parables of Jesus to the American dream. Although it is a dynamic and creative avenue of human truth, it does not nail us to the floorboards of predestination but presents us with decisions for us to make with our freedom. It leaves room for mystery.

God as mystery

Religious mystery is not for solving, as we have said, but rather simply for acknowledging. "Be still, and know that I am God" (Psalm 46:10). God alone is God, an infinite, eternal and therefore incomprehensible Other from the perspective of finite, mortal, limited humanity. When it comes to reality, we are sitting in the cheap seats, and what we can see from here is humble compared to the vastness of God's timeless, limitless perspective. Just grasping the reality of our mortality teaches us not simply about ourselves but about God. What we are, God is not. And what God is, we are not. God is maker, and we are made; we are creatures before the Creator.

Isn't it surprising how few people live as though this were true? We often live as if we believe we are God: titans with limitless energy who will never die, with no needs, in total control of the flow of events. Mortality is a fact we don't even consider until illness or disability strikes, a loved one dies, or we hit the wall of our own limitations. Somewhat clinically, theologians call these experiences of our mortality "teachable moments." When we suffer, suddenly our inner atheist gets religion, big time.

When we do respect the mystery of God, however, we also honor our own human nature. We know who God is and who we are. The freedom of this knowledge presents the possibility of unspeakable cooperation between what we can do and what God can do. The first step in acknowledging the Sacred, then, is embracing humility by facing who we are. The second is using our freedom to learn who we can become.

A new way of seeing

Opening the window on mystery offers a new way of seeing and interpreting the world around us. Most people who "get religion" of some kind don't lapse into visions, at least not right away. A sense of the God-embedded nature of things comes upon us in a more organic way. In fact, the natural world is the best place to begin to understand the presence of God-with-us, since creation was God's first utterance. God's desire is not to remain hidden from the created world but to be known by it and through it.

In light of this, we discover that we can approach the infinite God through the finite world. This leads to an important tenet of Catholic belief: Common things hold sacred realities. "The world is charged with the grandeur of God," as Jesuit priest and poet Gerard Manley Hopkins wrote. If you want to know about the majesty of God, stand among the Rocky Mountains and look around. If you want to know God's beauty, gaze over the edge of the Grand Canyon. If you want to know God's abundance, travel the lush farms of the heartland of America. If you want to know the awe-inspiring power of God, go to Death Valley when the high winds are blowing. The God who created

11

these marvels contains all these possibilities within the divine imagination.

We also learn about God through certain signs and symbols that have been given to us through the tradition of believers. These common things—bread and wine, water and oil—teach us about the life that God offers us in every ordinary moment of our days. God uses ordinary items for divine purposes. And each of us, out of the ordinariness of our lives, is invited to become aware of ourselves as children of God, living stones built into a new temple where God chooses to dwell (1 Peter 2:5).

The Catholic way of seeing extends beyond the recognition of God's self-revelation in the wonders of creation and in common, ordinary things. We also see one another as the revelation of God. The story of Jesus who was both human like us and divine Son of God affirms this way of seeing. We are urged to see Christ in every person, to uncover the divine face in the lowliest and most unexpected face of all (Matthew 25:40). Our use of sacramental signs, as in baptism, Eucharist, and the anointing of the sick, expands our appreciation of the sacredness of all times, places and persons. The vision of God's holy presence in all that is—what we can call the sacramental worldview of Catholicism—goes beyond our moments of ritual to all the hours of human existence and experience. (We will explore the meaning of the sacramental worldview in more detail in Chapters Six to Eight.)

A new language

It used to be said of a person who accepted a creed or joined a church that he or she had "had a conversion." That is still true, although the word *conversion* implies more than the formal acceptance of a creed or a church. Religious conversion means making a formal assent to a new way of "seeing" and involves, for Catholics, baptism and a profession of faith, which is an affirmation of the God we know as Trinity and of the community we know as church. But that is only the first step of conversion. The fuller meaning resides in turning over the whole of ourselves to God.

Our understanding of conversion is rooted in the Judeo-Christian tradition. The Hebrew word for conversion is *t'shuvah* or "turning." It involves turning away from the self and toward God. It does not imply a negation of the self but an orientation to "right relationship" between God and ourselves. Giving to God what belongs to God reveals our rightful identity: not as servants of the world but as the beloved of Love itself.

Another word that influences our understanding of conversion is the Greek word *metanoia*, which means "a change of heart." Since the books of our scriptures are written in Hebrew and Greek, the insight of key phrases in these languages helps us to grasp more fully the meaning behind our use of the words. "Change is never the same," as the old irony goes, and conversion means we can't go on being the same once we have professed that God is in charge and we are not. The earth moves under our feet when we profess faith in God. Everything changes, and that includes us.

Theologian Bernard Lonergan has identified five aspects of conversion in our lives: religious, moral, conversion of the head, conversion of the heart, and a social dimension of conversion as well. After religious conversion (we've made the assent; we have been "still" long enough to know that God is God), we find that our language has changed. We no longer ascribe events to luck or chance but to grace or providence. We no longer speak cynically but with hope. We no longer look for the bad news and the gossip but put our hope in the unrelenting good news of the gospel.

Next, we face the challenge of moral conversion. That means what it sounds like: Our lives have to change in keeping with our words. Moral conversion means practicing what we preach. If God is sovereign, if God rules, then God's ways take precedence over our inclinations to do otherwise. The scriptures contain the Ten Commandments from the Law of Moses (Deuteronomy 5:6–21), nine Beatitudes from the teachings of Jesus (Matthew 5:3–11), and all kinds of good advice to use as guidelines on how to live. More will be said about moral conversion in Chapter Eleven.

Conversion of the head and heart, or intellectual and affective (emotional) conversion, accompany this process. We usually think of events happening in a linear way, but conversion follows its own route, so don't expect to check these off your list in a straight line. Think of these five aspects of conversion as spokes on a wheel rather than a ladder to climb. We probably won't conquer them one by one, but rather we will return to each over and over as our life in faith deepens.

Intellectual conversion is the movement away from superstitious or rigid thinking about religion. Just as we didn't learn everything about life by the age of thirteen, so we have not learned everything there is to know about God in Sunday school, religion class, or up to the present moment. Graduating from parochial school or finishing the RCIA process won't teach a prospective believer all there is to know about God, any more than getting a Ph.D. in theology will. The search for God and knowledge about God is a lifelong process. We have to keep learning, even if it means asking uncomfortable questions and upsetting our smooth system of beliefs now and then. Life itself, with its unsettling turns, is a great promoter of intellectual conversion.

Conversion of the heart, or affective conversion, is the process of unlearning most of what our hearts have learned so far in life. It is the softening of hearts made hard by broken dreams, betrayals of trust, lack of forgiveness and experiences of sorrow. Affective conversion is making ourselves vulnerable again to love, forgiveness, compassion and trust. It's a darn fool thing to do, by worldly standards. But to one who is wandering the wheel of conversion, it is the only way of becoming more like the One in whose image we were made and long to be. We become like children again, trading in our world-weary hearts of stone for hearts of flesh (Ezekiel 11:19).

Even as we till the soil of moral, intellectual and affective conversion, however, we have to contend with one more thing: social transformation, or what Lonergan calls "socio-political conversion." The other forms of conversion seem rather personal and private, but mature Christianity is not a private matter. The gist of socio-political conversion—and it's every bit the mouthful it implies—means no less than the transformation of

14

our relationship to all the structures around us. Many of the systems that support our lives—political, economic, professional—are tainted with the same corruption (known as sin in religious language) that has touched our personal lives. Just as we must surrender to the grace that frees us interiorly from the effects of sin, so we also have an obligation to commit ourselves to the transformation of society as well.

"Getting religion," we can see, is not enough. It is not the end of the story of conversion, only the beginning.

A *language beyond words*

Think of the words that shape reality as our culture defines it: democracy, progress, upward mobility, freedom, individuality. People undergoing the effects of religious conversion find themselves with a whole new vocabulary for the description of reality. Sin (missing the mark of love), grace (God's endless presence and supply of help) and salvation (not being lost to the control of sin but rescued for unending joy) are three of the handiest words to keep in your front pocket after religious conversion. They will help you to understand what is happening to you—but don't expect them to play well with family or friends who have not shared your experience. Sin, grace and salvation tell the whole story, but only for those who have "arrived."

But in addition to religious words we Catholics have the language of ritual, which we use to communicate the same understanding. Why ritual? The Reformation of the sixteenth century, which resulted in what we today call Protestantism, asked this question critically. At that time, the church was divided over many serious issues, one of which was the way in which God seeks to be made known among us. Martin Luther and others insisted that the authority of God's word is spoken among us *sola scriptura*, "only in scripture." Anything beyond that was of human origin and therefore carried less authority. Although some mainstream Protestant denominations today, such as Episcopalians and Lutherans, employ a great deal of ritual in their worship similar to that of Catholics, many other denominations rely almost exclusively on the proclamation of scripture and the sermon as the center of their gathering.

15

The authentic expression of Catholic Christian faith continues to hold that God is known in many ways, including the incarnational approach of ritual. To incarnate means to "enflesh" the abstract, to "embody" what is spirit. In ritual, we incarnate what we mean by our very actions, as when we put a hand on our hearts to pledge loyalty to our country. The celebration of the Mass is evenly divided between a ritual of scripture and one of sacrament, expressing the same truth in two ways: in story and in symbol. God is made known to us in the readings from the Old and New Testaments as well as in the bread and wine, which we hold in faith to be the body and blood of Christ. The seven sacraments of the church are all ritual encounters with God's presence and grace. In our formulaic greetings ("The Lord be with you." "And also with you.") and in our ritual gestures (making the sign of the cross over ourselves, the bending of one knee known as genuflection, sharing the sign of peace with a handshake or hug), we give witness to our common faith with our whole person and share that witness with one another.

Ritual language and gesture, of course, are no alien observance in our society. We observe proper rites in our stadiums, courtrooms and classrooms, as well as in the ordinary greetings we exchange on the street. Ritual is a natural and orderly way we honor people and events and convey meaning in our lives. Birthday parties, a toast, observance of holidays and anniversaries, and the habitual way in which we begin every day suggest that the role of ritual is both useful and beneficial.

Ritual, above all, helps us to remember. We are fragile beings, and a lifetime gives us a lot to hold in our memory. We want to make sure we don't forget the important people and the crucial events and places that have shaped who we are and where we are going. If ritual helps us to find our keys by putting them in the same place all the time, won't it help us to remember more ultimate things, like why we are here and what we are striving to become?

The need for community
People on a religious quest will often ask this question of

Catholics: Why do we need the church? Can't I find God on my own? The short answer is, of course, you can. God isn't hiding from us, to be found only in a church. You can find God on a mountain in Tibet, on the worst street in a city near you, or even in an obnoxious neighbor. If you're looking for the Judeo-Christian God in particular, you can buy a Bible and read it to get the basic story. You can buy books of church teaching called catechisms, or use the vast variety of prayer books, or become a hermit in the desert. In all these ways and more, you can have an authentic experience of the God of Moses and Jesus.

But if you understand anything from all that activity, you will seek a church community promptly. Christian faith is a communal enterprise. We are all in this together. The community of church isn't an obligation but a gift. It is part of the process, and in some ways it is the crux of the matter. "For where two or three are gathered in my name, I am there among them," Jesus told his followers (Matthew 18:20). By gathering followers, traveling with them, and sending them out only in pairs, Jesus formed a community before the word *church* was ever spoken. Christianity is not do-it-yourself enlightenment. It entails authentically becoming the people of God.

We can read everything the Bible has to say about love, peace, justice, forgiveness and joy, but if we aren't living that out in a community of faith, then we are just cruising the surface of our religion. If we profess our faith privately to God but don't declare it publicly within the community, what does our profession mean? If we give our testimony under a bushel basket, how does that light become useful and profitable? Faith, we Catholics come to understand, is not really a private matter at all. It has to be publicly spoken, shared with others, and supported by others in a common mission. The mission of Jesus' disciples is to go forth and bring the gospel to the "ends of the earth" (Acts 1:8). The "ends of the earth" generally refers to an area larger than a backyard, one's own family, a geographical neighborhood, or even a parish community.

That's why *church,* as Catholics define it, is larger than a local congregation. Even a parish is not a large enough arena in which to live out our faith. The church is a community of *faith,* not just a community of _truths._ It is a lighthouse for the sake of the whole world. That is not a modest vision; it takes the high-visibility witness of a worldwide community to shine that light to the ends of the earth.

Did someone say witness?

There is a figure in popular culture that comes to mind when we hear words such as "witness" and "testify." He's the lonely guy who stands in the park on top of an overturned crate and shouts Bible verses to the amusement or annoyance of passers-by. He's a gutsy fellow, if somewhat negative and unappealing in his overall message: Repent or be destroyed!

There are variations on this stereotype of religious witness. There are the people who ring your doorbell and want to have the "salvation chat" with you. There are the nice young people who wear ties and want to share their ideology on the street. There are the people who would be grateful to sell you a rose at the airport. None of these approaches are what the Catholic church promotes as part of its witness.

Testimony, in the Catholic sense, is once again an incarnational event. It happens in the daily witness of your life, in the way you live out your commitments to family and friends. It means fidelity to your spouse, tenderness and attentiveness to your children. It has to do with the honest day's labor you present to your employer, the just way you deal with your employee. Testimony is reflected in keeping God (and not money) at the center of your attention. It is rendered in a lifestyle that is simple and suitable. It shines out in the way you speak, act, vote and relate to others. And it is never so powerful as in your relationship to the poor.

Catholics believe in a God who is known in the _real presence._ This is the term we use to describe the reality of Christ's true presence in the Eucharist. Bread and wine are not only a memorial meal for us, a remembrance of things past. We believe that Christ continues to be with us in a very real way in the Eucharist, and we incorporate Christ into our flesh and into our lives when we share in this meal. In fact, the eucharistic hosts that remain from the Mass are reserved in the tabernacle of

18

every Catholic church to remind us that God is also truly present in the world in Christ's Body, which is the church.

In a similar way, we become the witnesses of this real presence wherever we go. We are the bread of life for a hungry, restless world that has needs—material and spiritual—that are not met. In our love, in our compassion and especially in our joy, we testify to the reality that Jesus lives, our God is real, and the Spirit of God dwells within our world and is available to anyone who reaches out in faith and hope.

A return to mystery

This overview of the Catholic perspective will have been familiar to some and a bewildering drive-through for others—full of unfamiliar language, ideas and landscape. The rest of this book will offer more opportunities to encounter these same ideas again at greater depth. Although getting the facts straight is helpful for a solid foundation of faith, it would contradict the nature of divine mystery to suggest that "getting the skinny on God" is desirable or even possible. Trying to define love or uncover the dimensions of joy might prove equally fruitless. God, like love and joy, can be known only in the experience.

The information provided here may help foster that experience. But acquiring information about faith is not the same as having it and living it, and the entire enterprise can be deceptive if faith is seen as an end in itself. Through a prayerful, reflective consideration of the Questions to Explore at the end of each chapter, you may productively spend more time with each chapter's material. If you are part of a faith-sharing group, articulating your own questions or stories related to the themes of each chapter may be clarifying. The questions provided are only suggestions; other questions you may come up with may have more personal relevance to you. In the same way, the Faith Responses suggest possible ways of incorporating the chapter's idea into your lives, but you or your group might find more meaningful ways to integrate the material.

Questions to Explore

1. Describe the kinds of truths with which you are comfortable or uncomfortable. Why do you find it hard to deal with "truths" that are not scientifically verifiable?

2. What were the myths, proverbs or sayings that were central to your upbringing? What have been the effects of these truths on your life?

3. Does humility seem like a virtue or a character flaw to you? Describe how your feelings about humility affect your relationship to God.

4. How have you experienced God in the created world? What are your personal ways of encountering the Divine? What are your symbols or names for God?

5. Who are the people who have revealed the face of God in your life? Describe how they did it.

6. Considering the five aspects of conversion discussed in this chapter (religious, moral, intellectual, affective, socio-political), which ones sound easy to you? Which are more challenging? How have you already dealt with some of them?

7. Describe some secular rituals that are meaningful to you. Are you generally comfortable or uncomfortable with ritual? Why?

8. Describe your personal history with the Catholic church or with churches in general. What was positive about it? Negative? What would you hope for from a community of faith?

9. What are some of your deepest convictions? How do you witness to your convictions in your daily life?

10. Where and how do you experience the real presence of God in the world?

Faith Response

1. Start a journal to accompany you as you read and interact with this book. You may want to answer some of the end-of-chapter questions or note phrases and ideas that concern you as you read along. You may also want to record your faith experiences with some of the Faith Response exercises.

2. In response to this section on mystery, make two columns. Write at the head of one, "I Know God Is God Because…" and jot down any evidence, personal or theological, that you can think of. At the head of the other, write, "I Know I Am Not God Because…" and present the evidence for that statement. Compare the two lists. What do they teach you about humility and the nature of God?

3. Draw a conversion wheel according to the five aspects of conversion considered in this chapter: religious, moral, intellectual, affective, and socio-political. Describe a few ways you are being called to respond to each of these avenues of conversion in your life right now.

4. Be still and know that God is God. Spend some time in the silence of a church, park or some favorite place where you feel calm and at peace. Pray for the gift of humility and its freedom to live as a child of God. Still your body, your mind, your heart. Imagine yourself pressed to the heart of God and listen to the God's warm heartbeat of tenderness. What is God saying to you?

Two

God: The Story

We believe in one God,
the Father, the Almighty,
maker of heaven and earth,
of all that is seen and unseen....
—Nicene Creed

Make a list of everything you believe about God. This list may be brief or extensive—depending on the role religion has played in your life or how much you may have read or thought about God. If you were raised in a Judeo-Christian environment, your list may contain statements like "I believe God created the world" and "I believe God is all-powerful and all-knowing." You may further state that you believe God is good, merciful, loving and the just judge of the universe. You may believe God has certain expectations for human beings to live up to and future rewards or punishments to mete out after we die.

If your life has been affected by the Christian story, you may include these kinds of statements in your list: "I believe that Jesus is the Son of God" or "I believe that God is revealed as the Trinity of God the Father, the Son and the Holy Spirit."

By making this simple list, you have been engaged in the enterprise of theology. When we talk about God and start to uncover our basic system of belief, we are doing the work of theology. Theology may sound like a dry, highbrow discipline reserved for specialists of the "sacred science," but it is actually a much plainer and more common activity than that. We are doing theology when we decide which sources are legitimate teachers of God's nature or will: Do we accept the Bible, the Koran or the Bhagavad-Gita as revelation of God? Does the revelation of God's truth reside within the story of the Jewish people only, or does the gospel of Christianity tell us even more?

Does the tradition of the Catholic church add something useful or necessary to our understanding of God? Is it possible that our own experience can be a source of divine revelation?

Far from being an elitist discipline, theology is something even children are comfortable considering. Ask any child to draw a picture of God and you may be surprised with the results. Psychologists have done crosscultural studies of children from various religious traditions and found that most children have a very clear sense of who God is. Part of the theological world of children is shaped, certainly, by their training and the beliefs they have absorbed from their parents. But others are more individualistic, bordering on the mystical. A six-year-old girl explains that Jesus comes to her and stays with her as she sleeps: "It makes me feel special." A young boy says with authority, "God sits in the sky and eats cabbage." This may be a minority view, but it's a definite if halting step down the road of theology.

A formula for belief

When we make lists of things we believe about God, we are forming the basis of a personal creed. *Credo* is the Latin word for "I believe." The early church community formed many creeds to express what it understood to be true. In one of the letters of the New Testament, for example, we find this early "sure saying" about Jesus: "If we have died with him, we will also live with him; if we endure, we will also reign with him… (2 Timothy 2:11–12).

Within the first centuries, the Apostles Creed (based on the teachings of the apostles, the earliest leaders of the church) became a well-known summation of what Christians believe. It has a trinitarian structure, which means it is organized around statements about the three divine persons: God as creator of the world, Jesus as savior of humanity, and the Holy Spirit as inspirer of the church. (See the Appendix for the complete text of the Apostles Creed.) From this creed, later church councils drew up the Nicene Creed, which is the official profession of faith that many Christians use today. It is the creed Catholics profess during the Mass. The Nicene Creed is based on the trinitarian format of the Apostles Creed, but it has been expanded to include certain precise and clarifying phrases intended to counter the prevailing heresies of the fourth century. We will be looking at the Nicene Creed paragraph by paragraph in the following chapters, and it is printed in full in the Appendix.

For the moment, we are focusing on the first four lines of the Creed, the part concerning God the Creator, which appear at the head of this chapter. Whole books have been written about just the first line of the Creed, "We believe in one God," so what is said here can be only a brief summary of the theology contained within the creed. Let's consider the word "one" to begin with. Among the unique contributions of the Hebrew story was the revelation of God as one, which is called monotheism. The first Hebrews were nomadic people like many of the tribes that inhabited the region we now call the Middle East. The neighboring cultures worshipped a variety of local spirits, and early Hebrews most likely saw their God as one among many, though certainly the only God worthy of their allegiance. Eventually, through generations of experience and prophecy and reflection, they came to believe that there is only one true God, not a pantheon of rivaling deities. The worship of lesser local gods was seen as foolish and even blasphemous: "Hear, O Israel: The Lord is our God, the Lord alone. You shall love the Lord your God with all your heart, and with all your soul, and with all your might" (Deuteronomy 6:4–5).

Because we hold in our hands today the Bible that begins with the book of Genesis, we get the sense of monotheism as a given. "In the beginning" only one God is on the scene, creating everything in six days. The books of the Bible were not written in their present order, however, nor were they composed by one hand. Actually, a careful reading of Genesis reveals several strands of theology developed somewhat independently of one another. For instance, two creation stories are presented, one in chapter 1 and the second in chapter 2. In the first creation story, God creates the earth from plants to animals to humanity—the man and woman becoming the pinnacle of creation. In this version, the first couple is created simultaneously. Yet in the second creation story, a man is created for the garden before the birds and animals, which are then created in the process of finding the man a suitable helper. When none is found among the animals, a woman is fashioned as the final movement of creation.

This example of the two creation stories is but one that scholars point to as they unravel the various origins of scripture. The consensus of Catholic scholars today is that four main schools of theology are represented in the first five books of the Bible. The first school believed in a powerful, remote God who could spin a universe out of nothing and then retire to a regal distance, like the Creator of chapter one of Genesis. The second school envisioned God as a more personal, accessible deity who cared enough about the loneliness of the first human to personally bring creature after creature to him until a suitable partner is found. A third school of theology saw God as concerned with minute matters of worship and ritual, as in the long descriptions of the ark of the covenant and correct sacrifices found in Exodus chapters 25–30. The fourth school was very interested in spelling out and maintaining God's law, as much of the book of Deuteronomy exemplifies.

Eventually these four strains of theological tradition, and perhaps many more, were compiled to form a cohesive theology for the Israelites. The many competing religious factions at the time of Jesus—not to mention among present-day Christians—reveal the tensions that by necessity reside within a complex but shared view of the one God.

Our relationship with God

One of the features of the Apostles Creed is its personal assent to faith. "I believe in God," it begins. The Nicene Creed starts with the bold phrase, "*We* believe," making this an affirmation of the whole church. By professing this creed, we join our personal allegiance to the historical and present community of the people of God. The communal nature of the creed underlines the communal nature of Christian faith. Our personal assent to the God we profess unites us to the whole church, to Christians everywhere, to those who have lived faithfully in past ages and to those believers yet to come. Together, all of us believe in this same God.

And who is this God we believe in, this "one God" the ancient Hebrews came to know as the *true* God who exposes the falseness of idols and demands complete allegiance? The Old Testament traces the story of a people intrinsically intertwined with their emerging sense of relationship with this God. Just as our personal experiences lead us to an awareness of God that can be individual and distinctive (does God eat cabbage?), the Hebrew story is about learning, often through trial and error, what God's will is for the world.

Consider for a moment how crucial our understanding of God's will is to our understanding of ourselves. To theologians, the question "Who is God?" is immediately related to the question "Who am I?" If God is the creator of all that is, then I am God's creature, which puts me in immediate, subordinate and natural relationship with the Divine. If God is just judge of the universe, as many theologies hold, then I am one to be judged, which places me in a relationship of respect, obedience and perhaps a deep sense of awe of God. If God is love, as the evangelist John proclaims, then I am beloved (1 John 4:16) and feel love, joy and gratitude in response. If God to me is an uncaring, distant force or a vengeful angry giant, these same characteristics likewise create a sense of who I am and what I do in response.

The ancient Hebrews understood God's nature in many ways. They perceived a world full of good things, but they also saw a world tarnished by evil and suffering. What could they learn about God from these separate and sometimes clashing realities? Much of the early part of Genesis is a theological grappling with these issues: God is the source of creation and its goodness but human decisions against goodness lead to suffering. How could a creature choose what is contrary to the will of the Creator? The power to choose must have been granted by God. This gift of freedom makes humanity like God in the one pivotal sense that we too can "create" the world, for good or ill, in which we live. Being made "in the image and likeness of God," as we are, we can still fail to choose the good consistently and show ourselves to be quite unlike our Maker.

27

The sin of more

The first sin to enter the world has been variously described as pride, disobedience or even lust by those who use the stories of Genesis as a guide. Catholic theologians prefer the term *concupiscence*, or the "desire for more." In a perfect world, paradise by all accounts, Adam and Eve sought still *more* than they had (see Genesis 3). The sin of wanting more afflicts the world still. It is the parent of every serious evil, causing wars and violence, greed and injustice, infidelity, envy, addiction. It adds bitterness and sorrow to every cup.

Instead of freely entering into a grand cooperation with our Maker, humanity chose the bondage of concupiscence and its restless longing after more. That bondage, called original sin, led humanity further and further from God's dream for us. After causing a rift in our friendship with the Creator, we brought about the same fracture among ourselves, as we see in the story of Cain and Abel (Genesis 4). The rupture widens in the account of Noah and the ark, where we are finally separated even from the creation that God put into human hands for caretaking (Genesis 6–7). With the benevolence of creation grown hostile, our alienation from God's desire for us is nearly complete. By the time of the story of the Tower of Babel (Genesis 11), we can no longer even speak to one another and our original human unity is altogether lost.

Theology might have ended there, on a dreadful note, if not for the emergence of one who dared to enter into a personal relationship with his Maker again. The story of Abraham officially begins the Hebrew story and—in a real sense—the hope of Christians as well.

God makes a promise

Abram (whom God later names Abraham, meaning "ancestor of a multitude of nations") is an ordinary sort of man who is led to do an extraordinary thing. He is born in the land of Ur (present-day Iraq) and taught to reverence the gods of that place. He is, like most of us, content to accept the religion he inherits and not to ask too many questions. But Abraham hears a call from an unknown God to go on to the land of Canaan. This new

God makes promises that go against conventional wisdom. If Abraham leaves his kin and his country, this new God will give him both land and heirs to fill it! This is especially intriguing since Abraham is childless. In a culture that valued women only for the children they bore, Abraham has been married many decades to the same woman who has borne no children. What is most striking about the situation is that Abraham chooses to remain loyal to Sarah despite this fact. The culture would have supported his taking a second or third wife, at the very least. Abraham reveals something unusual about himself in his loyalty to Sarah and reluctance to marry again. This trait of faithfulness makes him a good choice to become the keeper of God's promise.

The stories of Abraham and Sarah take up a good part of Genesis (12–22). Abraham walks with God, sometimes trusting a lot but sometimes showing some hesitation, as when he lies about Sarah being his wife in order to protect himself (Genesis 12:11–13). Yet Abraham is perceptive enough to know a divine visitation when he receives one and comfortable enough in his relationship with God to dicker over the fate of Sodom and Gomorrah (Genesis 18). Though he loves his son Isaac, his overriding loyalty to the God who gave him this son makes him even willing to sacrifice Isaac if commanded to do so. The God of the promise, however, does not require such a sacrifice (Genesis 22).

Abraham's relationship to the God of the promise is familiar to all of us who have sought to know God's will for our lives. God makes us promises that are contrary to the conventional wisdom of our world, for God asks us to abandon trust in our own strength and in the tangible securities of money and control. We who buy insurance on everything from house and car to health and life find the idea of "trusting in the Lord" a little unnerving. Just how far am I expected to go with this trust-in-God business? Is "blessed assurance" going to take care of me when I'm ill or old? Won't I be simply foolish if I make decisions based on my faith rather than on the hard, cold numbers in my bank account? We have to remember, however—as Abraham discovers over and over again—that the journey of faith

29

isn't taken in a day and isn't over in one act. Although rare people like Francis of Assisi do walk away in a heartbeat from everything they own, most of us relinquish our trust in worldly supports much more gradually and only as our confidence in God's promise is proved again and again.

Abraham learns to surrender completely to the One who called him on his journey. The lineage of Abraham moves forward through history, as God promised. Isaac's son Jacob receives the name Israel, meaning "struggles with God," from a night of wrestling with an angel and imparts it to God's chosen people ever after (Genesis 32:24–30). The great-grandchildren of Abraham leave their promised land during a generation devastated by famine and go as refugees to Egypt. At first they are welcomed warmly, but soon they grow too numerous to be trusted by the local citizens. Egypt then enslaves the Israelites, and the story of Exodus begins.

A God who saves

The Bible may seem like a huge book, but the story of God and humanity can be told in four words: We sin; God saves. The Bible merely supplies the details to this basic truth. When the people of Israel are enslaved in Egypt, only solid trust in God can deliver them to freedom. Once again God chooses a personal emissary, this time Moses, to accomplish the divine plan.

Until now, the people of Israel have related to God as "the God of the promise." Now they will find a new way to speak about God that will define their relationship for all time: The God of Israel is the "God who saves." Captive in a foreign land, they long for liberation. Moses, a Hebrew adopted by Pharaoh's daughter (Exodus 2), is an unlikely choice for liberator. He has few ties to his heritage and little knowledge of his people's God. But salvation history—the story of God's saving plan for humanity—is full of unlikely people becoming the perfect instruments for God's purposes.

Moses doesn't meet the God of Abraham in Egypt. As the story unfolds, Moses is forced to flee Egypt after he murders an Egyptian for mistreating a Hebrew. He assumes a new life as a shepherd in the wilderness (Exodus 2–3). Near the mountain of

30

God, called Horeb in some theological strands and Sinai in others, Moses sees a bush on fire but not consumed. Approaching it, he receives the call to cooperate with God's plan to save the people of Israel. As fearful as one might expect, Moses expresses several objections to God's idea, objections that God overrides fairly quickly. So Moses surrenders to God, returning to Egypt to confront Pharaoh and to free God's people (Exodus 3–4).

Ten plagues and many miracles later, God parts the Red Sea and leads the people into the freedom of the desert (Exodus 5–15). Now what? Because human beings are not simple creatures, the story of God's relationship to Israel doesn't end here, with gratitude and praise for the rescue. Not long after, the people are dissatisfied again. The sin of *more* has crept in and they begin again their gripes and laments, which will last for roughly forty years. Liberation is fine, but thirst and starvation are even more immediate realities that consume their attention. Now that Moses has become their shepherd, he is going to tend this new flock for the rest of his life, interceding for them with God all the way to the promised land.

Moses receives a renewal of the promise (which is called a covenant) between God and the children of Abraham. The original covenant, or pledge, between God and Abraham was sealed in fire (see Genesis 15). The sign of acceptance of this renewed covenant is the circumcision of the flesh of every adult male (Genesis 17). This covenant mediated through Moses is then forged in law. Moses receives the Ten Commandments on the holy mountain, commandments designed to bring God's people into conformity with God's original will and desire and to protect them from the tyranny of sin (Exodus 20).

The long journey described in the book of Exodus (*exodus* means "the road out") is the road each of us must take in order to achieve liberation from the tyranny of sin and to embrace the freedom of God's people. Every person's story is about learning and relearning, severing and then mending the ties that unite us to God's desire for us.

Think of the ways you may have been in need of liberation along the path of your life: from relationships, jobs, habits or influences that denied your full humanity. There may be factors in your life right now that keep you from being the person you long to be: debt that chains you to a soul-deadening career; old friendships with people who affirm you in values you no longer hold; personal habits that waste your time, energy and resources. Your personal exodus may seem like a very long road out, but the God who saves does not intend to leave even one human spirit languishing behind bars. When you and I are ready for freedom, God is ready to send a liberator to part the sea and show us the way.

Even though Israel's exodus to the promised land takes forty years and is not without battle scars, they make it. When the people of Israel arrive at last at the Jordan River, Moses is one hundred and twenty years old and ready to die. The people cross the river into the promised land under Joshua's leadership. Will the attainment of this land bring a final peace between God and the children of Abraham? You may have already guessed the answer.

Judges, priests, prophets and kings
Even during the time of Moses, it was challenging to govern a nation like Israel. Moses appointed a series of judges (in Hebrew, an elder or governor, including a military leader) to help him govern the people. This system of governance continued in the Israelites' new homeland.

The priesthood, founded under Aaron, Moses' brother, was a cultic or ritual office that had as its function the mediation of peace between God and the nation. The priests maintained holy equipment (for example, the Ark of the Covenant, a mobile altar of sacrifice containing the tablets of the Law and other sacred items) and holy places (such as the shrines that sprang up wherever the people encountered the divine presence). In generations to come, the main arena of the priests would finally be within the Temple at Jerusalem.

Prophets were active as well during this period. Prophets came out of left field, officially speaking. While judges were appointed by the people after Moses died and priests had to be born of the lineage of Aaron, prophets were God-appointed individuals who often challenged the leaders and in general caused a great deal of unrest by saying what people didn't want to hear. Prophets often argued for sweeping changes in the way the Israelites did business, and people are notoriously reluctant to change. As *nabi* (Hebrew, meaning "mouthpiece of God"), prophets had great personal authority but often risked their lives in speaking out against established authority.

Judges, priests and prophets did not hold mutually exclusive offices, nor do these titles suggest precise descriptions of what leaders actually did. Joshua was a judge, but he acted mostly as a military leader (see the book of Joshua). Deborah was a judge and prophet who was known both for her arbitration and military prowess (Judges 4). Samuel was a judge and prophet, but it is as prophet that he is chiefly important to salvation history (1 Samuel). Elijah and Elisha functioned as "pure" prophets, with no other office to support their authority (1 Kings, 2 Kings).

Spiritual leadership and its authority has always been an issue for sincere seekers in religion. Who speaks for God in our world? Which church or leader has the authentic message? Discernment, the art of seeing how God is acting in the world and in our lives, is an issue we will cover in Chapter Eleven. Discernment is important because the voices that claim to speak for God are many. We can turn on the television or radio at any hour and hear strong, sometimes compelling evangelists who interpret world events according to a "word from God" they have received. Since these messengers "from God" do not always agree, only some of them—perhaps few of them—are authentic. Like ancient Israel, we need guidance and insight when those who claim to speak for God are in conflict.

The one kind of leader the people of Israel didn't have—for a long time—was a king. This was a deliberate decision, since Israel was established as a theocracy, a nation ruled by God. "One nation, under God" was no mere sentiment for a people who had served under Pharaoh for bitter generations. They knew that any human who represented the Divinity as a monarch did was suspect and that any human leader could lead them into sin.

A king of Israel

A nation with no king may be a spiritually advanced idea, but it can lead to diminished esteem in the eyes of other nations. For Israel to take its place among the nations that surrounded it required a recognized leader. The people press the prophet Samuel to supply a king for the nation, to select someone pleasing to God. Samuel brings their request to God, and God warns once again that the people are rejecting divine ways for human (1 Samuel 8:4–9). Samuel tells the people that having a king will lead to wars, oppression and injustice, but they refuse to listen and receive Saul as the first anointed king of Israel.

Saul fulfills the forecast exactly. He is a great military leader at first, and the people admire his appearance and strength; they take great pride in him before the nations. But eventually Saul overreaches his position, disobeying God's injunctions. His relationship to God and rightful authority are broken (1 Samuel 15) and he devolves into madness, all Israel suffering with him.

But God does not abandon the people to the consequences of having a king. Samuel is prompted to seek and anoint the next king of Israel. It is David, the youngest son of Jesse (1 Samuel 16). Though David will not rule for some time to come, God's plan for liberation is already in the works.

The story of David assures us that there is nothing we can break that God can't mend—even when we make decisions apart from the will of God, as Israel did in its desire for an earthly ruler. God proves time and again that we will not be abandoned to the consequences of our actions, like punished children who are going to "get what's coming to them." Salvation history is contrary to the idea of predestination, the belief in a fixed path that destiny inexorably follows. Nor do we believe in the railroad-track theory of human fate: Swing the switch one way, and we ride in safety to heaven; swing the switch in the opposite direction, and the train flies off the tracks to certain destruction. If we abandon God's desire for our happiness and take another track, the "God who saves" will most certainly move quickly ahead of us to give us another chance to have a change of heart and be saved.

David's kingship-in-the-wings is God's second chance for

Israel. After many battles, David wins over for his kingdom both the northern tribes of Israel and the southern tribes of Judah. He establishes Jerusalem as his capital and unites all of Israel for one great generation of peace. David is so full of love for God and fidelity to God's law that God makes yet another covenant, this time with the house of David. David's lineage will never be forsaken and his kingship will endure forever (2 Samuel 7).

Though David is the greatest king Israel will ever know, even he is a man of flesh, capable of sin and betrayal. His adultery with Bathsheba and the murder of her husband is forgiven (2 Samuel 12–13), but the intrusion of sin into his reign leads to the eventual downfall of Israel. His son born of Bathsheba, Solomon, will be renowned for his wisdom, but even Solomon will be unable to hold the kingdom together.

The Temple rises, the kingdom falls

The Temple at Jerusalem was originally David's idea. Because he felt guilty that his own palace surpassed God's house in greatness (2 Samuel 7), David meant to honor God with a magnificent dwelling place, much grander than the Tent of Presence that currently held the Ark of the Covenant. It fell, however, to Solomon to actually construct the Temple, which in its design was extraordinary in every detail (1 Kings 5–6).

A dwelling place for God is an uneasy proposition from the start. Once human beings create a place to encounter God, it is easy to imagine in time that God is confined to that space and can be ignored otherwise. The elaborate rituals surrounding the Temple sacrifices and the creation of a Holy of Holies (a hidden place for the ark that even the priest could visit only once a year) made God seem *less* accessible rather than *more*. Solomon himself seems to find no moral or civic conflict between the construction of the Temple and additional shrines for his foreign wives' various gods. As the nation of Israel fractures definitively into the northern kingdom of Israel and that of Judah to the south, the people likewise fracture into mumbled allegiances to many idols. The unity of the nation, under the God who is One, is ended after a relatively brief time.

The fragmentation of the kingdom of Israel is very much like the tearing of our lives by our loyalties to the "many gods" we strive to serve. Life gets complicated as we try to please our parents, our children, our employers, our friends and society's image of who we are supposed to be. Do you define success in terms of what your parents always wanted for you? Do you risk your relationship to spouse and children to accumulate enough overtime to get your kids into the best schools? Do you do whatever the boss wants, even if it's illegal or immoral? Do you drive the car that makes people jealous, or color your hair and have surgery to maintain the lie of youth in a culture that worships deception over truth? Idol worship isn't simply an ancient biblical sin. It is alive and well in our efforts to serve, for their approval or favor, the many who wield power around us.

Israel's worship at too many altars leads to moral and political deterioration. Successive kings inhabit the thrones of the north and the south. A few are faithful to the God of Abraham, but most are driven by greed and lust for power. Prophets arise to challenge their rule, but court-appointed prophets likewise support the king in his decisions and blur the sense of who speaks for God. A half-dozen prophets, including Isaiah and Jeremiah, warn the kings and their citizens that they will lose God's protection if they refuse to honor the covenant. Eventually the northern kingdom is overrun by Assyria (722 B.C.) and the southern kingdom is taken by Babylon (587 B.C.). The children of Abraham are sent into exile, their Temple destroyed, their kingdom in ruins. Is this the end of the story? Can the relationship between God and this people be salvaged?

A new covenant coming

The prophet Ezekiel has a vision in which God's glory departed from Jerusalem (Ezekiel 10). But the word of God comes to him on the heels of that vision, proclaiming a new covenant in place of what was lost:

> I will give them one heart, and put a new spirit within them; I will remove the heart of stone from their flesh and give them a heart of flesh, so that they may follow my statutes and keep my ordinances and obey

them. Then they shall be my people, and I will be
their God.

—Ezekiel 11:19–20

Other prophets see beyond the renewal of the covenant.
Not only will the people of Israel be restored, but the covenant
they enjoy with God will be extended to all the nations of
earth:

[God] shall judge between the nations,
>   and shall arbitrate for many peoples;
they shall beat their swords into plowshares,
>   and their spears into pruning hooks;
nation shall not lift up sword against nation,
>   neither shall they learn war any more.

—Isaiah 2:4

Though the children of Israel might languish in exile, God
does not abandon the covenant made with them. And as the
prophets proclaimed, God's desire goes further: to the end of
the ancient enmity between nations, to a time of peace not
unlike the world God once created. This exile will end, a new
nation and Temple will be built on the ashes of the old. Still
other oppressors will come, culminating in the empire of Rome
sprawling across the known world and overtaking Israel in 63
B.C. But the story of God and God's people is far from over.

A covenant with God is a very serious thing, and God is
remarkably creative about preserving it even when we are friv-
olous with it. It is God's way to preserve what is in danger of
being lost, to save what seems hopeless, to re-create and heal in
the path of destruction and pain. We can make a big mess of
our lives from time to time, but the God who formed worlds
out of chaos cleans up after us when we are ready to return to
the divine will with our whole hearts. Whatever lies in your
past, don't be afraid. God can bless the barren desert and make
it bloom.

God of the seen and unseen

Looking back, salvation history is not such a tangled skein of long ago names and places as we may have thought. The characters and events in the Old Testament are not so foreign after all. We too struggle to live in fidelity to the God we are only beginning to know. Like the people of ancient Israel, God's will is often clearer to us than our will to follow it. Yet the Bible is not simply a mirror in which we find ourselves and recognize our weaknesses. It is a storehouse of wisdom and a revelation of the hope that is ours. After all, if God can bring salvation out of the likes of Abraham, Moses and David, then there is hope for you and me as well.

The Nicene Creed expresses in one compact sentence the sum total of our understanding of God through the Hebrew story: "We believe in one God, the Father, the almighty, maker of heaven and earth, of all that is seen and unseen." It is somewhat easy for us to profess faith in a God who is the source of life (Father in the sense of progenitor), sovereign (almighty), and maker of all that is (heaven and earth). The tricky part is believing in the God of the "seen" and the "unseen." That is what Abraham had to do, leaving his kin behind, relying on promises that could have been illusions. That is what Moses had to do, trembling before Pharaoh, or what David, the boy anointed to be king, had to hold on to during many long nights in hiding. All actors in salvation history have to believe, ultimately, not just in what they see and know to be true but also in what they don't see but hope for.

Prophet and priest, leader and follower, all have to put their trust in the God they can't see, the future they can't be sure of. Only through faith can we accept our own place within salvation history and enter into relationship with the God of the seen and the unseen.

Questions to Explore

1. Look at your list from the previous chapter of things you believe about God. Compare them with the knowledge of God that the people of Israel gain on their exodus journey as God's people. What is missing on your list? Add any additional beliefs you have to your list.

2. How do you demonstrate in your daily life that you are a monotheist, a believer in one God? Are there other gods that vie for your attention and allegiance? Who or what are they? *. ego*

3. How do you answer the question: Who is God? How does that answer affect your self-understanding as you respond to the question: Who am I?

4. How does the sin of wanting more (concupiscence) influence your life? How does it shape the society we live in? *every day media*

5. Give examples of promises that have been kept or broken in your life. How does the image of God as the perfect promise keeper affect your understanding of the life God desires for you?

6. Describe a time you or someone you know was saved from danger or oppression. How does the image of a divine savior affect your relationship with God?

7. Name the mentors, leaders or holy people who have influenced you. What did they teach you about yourself? About God?

8. Where do you go to encounter God? How do "sacred places" limit or expand your idea of where God can be found? *nature running*

9. God renewed the covenant with Israel many times throughout salvation history. Has God extended a personal covenant to you? Describe how.

10. Consider things you believe in that you can't see—such as love, friendship, the future. What helps you to believe in them?

Faith Response

1. Try your hand at writing a creed. You can use the Apostles Creed as a model, or invent your own formula. You may want to use the list of things you believe about God as a reference. Post this where you can reflect on it and compare your day-to-day life with your profession of faith.

2. How many conflicting "strains of theology" exist within you? Is God distant or familiar, a friend or a feared authority, or all of the above? Try to isolate the different ideas about God that co-exist within you. Then try to identify their source: your parents, Sunday school, a teacher, the Bible, a friend, something you read or experienced.

3. Identify the ways that concupiscence (the desire for more) has a grip on your life. Choose one way you resolve to free yourself from its tyranny and turn that part of your life consciously over to God. You may want to pray daily for the courage to resist, or you might ask someone to pray with or for you.

4. Write a personal covenant between you and God, for your eyes only. Write what you want and hope for from your relationship with God. Describe too how your life should change as God's beloved. Return to this covenant often. Consider how you might need to rewrite or expand it as you grow in your relationship with God.

Three

Good News: Jesus and the Gospels

...We believe in one Lord, Jesus Christ,
the only Son of God,
eternally begotten of the Father,
God from God, Light from Light,
true God from true God,
begotten, not made, one in being with the Father.
Through him all things were made.
For us and for our salvation
he came down from heaven:
by the power of the Holy Spirit
he was born of the Virgin Mary, and became flesh.
For our sake he was crucified under Pontius Pilate;
he suffered, died, and was buried.
On the third day he rose again
in fulfillment of the Scriptures;
he ascended into heaven
and is seated at the right hand of the Father.
He will come again in glory to judge the living and the dead,
and his kingdom will have no end....
—Nicene Creed

Consider the face of Jesus. Hebrew law prohibited making images of God, but Christianity has had no such prohibition in regard to Jesus. We have many ways of representing him. Think about images of Jesus that you have seen in painting, sculpture and stained glass. Which is the face of Jesus that reveals his nature most profoundly for you?

For many people, the idea of Jesus leads immediately to the cross—either an image of the crucified Jesus or of the empty cross—as a symbol of triumph and resurrection. For others,

Jesus is understood most readily as the Child of Christmas, the incarnation or God-made-flesh, the God willing to become one of us so that we can share in the divine life. In between those two images are many others familiar to us: Jesus teaching the crowds, healing the sick, raising the dead, walking on water or calming the storm; Jesus feeding the multitude with a few loaves, breaking bread with his friends one last time. We have representations of Jesus as the good shepherd, as the stranger knocking at the door of our hearts. We see him carrying his cross with resolution and love or lying still in the arms of his anguished mother, as in Michelangelo's *Pieta*.

God is mysterious and unseen, but Jesus seems to have many faces and seeks to be known. This is no accident, because the story of Jesus in the gospels is, in fact, the revelation of what God is really like. Jesus comes into our midst, breaking into time and history as the revealed face of the Divine.

The recognition that Jesus is the very revelation of God, like the Hebrew understanding of God in the early scriptures, evolved over time. The Nicene Creed expresses the doctrine, or official church teaching, that was formulated in the fourth century to counter heresies concerning Jesus. The two basic heresies about Jesus are: 1) Jesus is God but not really human. His humanity is a mirage that God uses to teach us a few things about how to live. Jesus' birth, life, death and resurrection were, therefore, staged. 2) Jesus is human but not really God. He is a superior human being, so perfectly obedient that God adopts him as a favorite son among the human race. To call him Son of God is like saying we are all children of God, only Jesus shows us how to do it right.

The consistent understanding of Christianity and the doctrine of the Catholic church, however, holds that Jesus is truly God and truly human. These two natures are full and entire: Jesus is "true God from true God," *born* of a woman into the world as a human being but *begotten* of God. In John's gospel, written near the end of the first century, John presents "Jesus B.C.," the preexistence of Jesus as the Word of God before the world began:

In the beginning was the Word, and the Word was

with God, and the Word was God. He was in the beginning with God. All things came into being through him, and without him not one thing came into being.... And the Word became flesh and lived among us, and we have seen his glory....

—John 1:1–3, 14

Theology, as we have seen, is not a static business of gathering "the facts," but a fluid process that builds upon what has gone before and joins it with what is presently understood. John was building upon a tradition within the Hebrew writings known as Wisdom literature, which includes books such as Proverbs, Sirach, Wisdom and Ecclesiastes. The Wisdom writers constructed their understanding of God apart from the Temple authorities, often writing as Jewish scholars away from their homeland, influenced by the wisdom literature of other cultures. They believed that God could be known and served through a life lived wisely and well, that foolishness and sin went hand in hand. And they taught that Wisdom, God's companion in creation, participated in the making of the world according to wise principles that could be understood by meditating on creation itself. In this passage from Proverbs, Wisdom speaks:

Ages ago I was set up,
   at the first, before the beginning of the earth....
When [God] established the heavens, I was there,
   when he drew a circle on the face of the deep,
when he made firm the skies above,
   when he established the fountains of the deep,
when he assigned to the sea its limit,
   so that the waters might not transgress his
     command,
when he marked out the foundations of the earth,
   then I was beside him, like a master worker....

—Proverbs 8:23, 27–30

John's gospel identifies Jesus, the man born into history, with the divine Word of God spoken in creation, the Wisdom

43

of God that creates all the wonderful patterns of the universe. Jesus is the Son of God who participates in the very life of God in a way that is unique. We are all *created* by God; Jesus alone is *begotten of God.*

Why do Christians consider the dual natures of Jesus—truly God, truly human—the centerpiece of their theology? The idea that Jesus can save us depends on the Hebrew idea that God is the one who *saves*. Jesus is savior precisely because he is one with God's nature. But Jesus saves *us* precisely because he is one with us and met every challenge of human living without ever breaking covenant with God.

What does it mean to you that God once walked in the rain, rejoiced at the beauty of a starry sky, wept at the loss of a friend, hungered for bread, hoped for rest? The distant gods that ancient religions served had no sympathy for the human condition. They were feared and had to be appeased. But a God who knows what it's like to be born poor, raised in obscurity, misunderstood by parents, betrayed by friends and deserted in suffering—even to the point of humiliation and death—is a God who is very close to *our* reality. That is a God who can be called upon with the intimate address of Brother, a God who is a companion in our darkest seasons, a God who is friend even when we are friendless.

Telling the story

The Nicene Creed relates the facts about the historical Jesus rather baldly: He was born of a woman named Mary. She is described as a "virgin," which is intended to underline the divine origin of Jesus, who was conceived by the power of the Holy Spirit. Mary is among those individuals in salvation history whose personal cooperation with God advanced God's saving plan. Her unique contribution to the Christian faith will be explored in Chapter Ten.

The creed refers to the birth of Jesus and then moves to his crucifixion under Pilate, suffering, death and burial. His ministry and teachings, which are the subject of the greatest part of the gospels, are not mentioned. Although the bulk of the creed is about Jesus, most of what is professed about him concerns what scholars call "the Christ of faith." His identity as Lord and Son of God, his resurrection and return to God, his future coming in glory to judge the world and establish the final reign of God are all statements that believers accept in faith. It is Jesus, *the Christ of faith* and not simply *the man of history,* in whom Christians place their hope.

Telling the story of the historical Jesus is not a straightforward task, as some movies have made it seem. Consider how someone might set about relating the story of your life. They may begin by interviewing people who know you, family members and friends. They may dig out your old yearbook, find a yellowed newspaper column about you, review your resume, visit places where you have lived and worked. Because the story they will tell depends on the reliability of human memory, holes might appear in the story, conflicts may surface, and parts of the sequence may be wrong. People may remember things as better or worse than they were. Your mother may make you sound like a hero. Quotations from you will be embellished. Is the final product, then, your life story or not?

Originally, the followers of Jesus who encountered him in some way after the resurrection fully expected him to come back shortly to establish God's reign on earth. They told the story of his life and good works—especially the details of his death and return to life—to share the good news and prepare others for his return. They didn't write anything down at first, because in the days well before the printing press not much was written down unless it had to last beyond a generation, and no one thought the story of Jesus would require that.

Paul of Tarsus, the first major missionary of the church, was the first to write about Jesus, between A.D. 40–60, and that decision was a function of his management style. As a traveling community-builder, the only way to keep in touch with the churches he left behind was to write them letters. He could hardly have imagined that one day those letters would become part of the sacred scripture of his faith. A convert to the faith after the time of Jesus, Paul was not an eyewitness to the life of Jesus and has little to say about the man of history. Instead, he confines his writing to the Christ of faith.

Not until the original followers of Jesus were being put to death did it seem necessary to put the story in writing. The oral tradition about Jesus, scholars believe, was first organized into a manuscript of the sayings of Jesus. This source of sayings has been dubbed "Q," for *quelle*, the German word for "source." No manuscript of sayings survives, but there is enough internal evidence of such a source within the existing writings about Jesus to support the "Q" hypothesis.

After the martyrdom of Peter and Paul around the mid-60s A.D., and because Jesus' imminent return had not materialized, disciples got serious about writing down the story of Jesus so that it would survive for future generations. Little did they suspect that their writings would last two millennia and more.

The secret of Mark

Mark's gospel, likely written between A.D. 60–70, is credited to John Mark, an early companion of Paul's. His gospel, distinguished by its brevity, gets right to the adult Jesus and his mission, beginning with the ministry of John the Baptist. (There is no infancy narrative or story of the birth of Jesus in Mark). Wasting no time in getting to the heart of the matter, Mark proclaims in his first sentence, "The beginning of the good news of Jesus Christ, the Son of God." Although Mark states the identity of Jesus clearly from the beginning, scholars call the unfolding of this identity "the Marcan secret." Throughout this gospel, whenever someone presumes to know who Jesus is, Jesus orders that person not to reveal him. The demons of the possessed shriek his name, and he silences them. People are cured, and Jesus commands them not to tell anyone about it. After the miracle of the calming of the storm, his followers are in wonder. "Who then is this," they ask (4:41), "that even the wind and the sea obey him?" The question remains unanswered through the gospel of Mark.

Some of his contemporaries apparently thought that Jesus was the reincarnation of John the Baptist, whom King Herod had beheaded. Others thought he might be Elijah, the prophet whose return was popularly anticipated at the start of Israel's new ascendancy as a kingdom. When Jesus asked his disciples

46

if they knew who he was, Peter guesses that he is the Messiah. *Messiah* is Hebrew for "anointed one." (The Greek word for anointed one is *christos*.) Many Jews were anticipating another king like David to come and revive Israel's fortune as a nation. Since both kings and prophets were anointed to leadership, it is not entirely clear what Peter intended by attributing this title to Jesus. But after Peter speaks, Jesus again orders his disciples not to tell anyone about him (8:27–30).

When Jesus refers to himself in Mark's gospel, he uses the phrase "Son of Man." "One like a Son of Man" appears again in the scriptures that deal with the end of the world. These are called apocalyptic writing, from which the last book of the Bible gets its name, Apocalypse, or Revelation. In the Old Testament as well, the prophecies in the book of Daniel contain references to the Son of Man, a powerful figure who is to come at the end of time to judge the world (Daniel 7:13–14). Other nonbiblical writings further describe the Son of Man as a terrifying figure who closes the present age and ushers in the age to come. In Mark, it is by this name only that Jesus wishes to be known.

One day Jesus takes Peter, James and John aside, leading them up a high mountain. This event echoes the ascent of Moses on God's mountain. Jesus' appearance changes gloriously, and a voice from heaven calls him "my Son, the Beloved." Though the disciples have seen something wondrous, Jesus forbids them to speak of this "until after the Son of Man has risen from the dead" (9:2–7).

Later, as Jesus passes by, a blind beggar shouts out (10:47), "Jesus, Son of David, have mercy on me!" And the people call out their hosannas "to the one who comes in the name of the Lord! Blessed is the coming kingdom of our ancestor David!" (11:9–10). The identification of Jesus with the awaited Messiah of God grows stronger, and yet he remains silent about his identity. He refuses to declare by whose authority he is teaching when the priests, lawyers and elders challenge him (11:27–33).

Toward the end of Mark's gospel, however, Jesus warns his disciples not to fall prey to false messiahs and false prophets who will appear before the final coming of the Son of Man (13:21–27). When Jesus is taken into custody and asked point-blank by the high priest, "Are you the Messiah, the Son of the Blessed One?" Jesus answers forthrightly, "I am" (14:61–62).

Thus is the Marcan secret unleashed, and the assembly of priests and elders clearly consider Jesus' reply blasphemy. He is condemned to death for daring to claim this identity. Dragged before the Roman authorities, Jesus is asked by Pilate if he is the king of the Jews, but to this he cryptically replies, "You say so" (15:2). He is crucified with this charge hanging over his head: "The King of the Jews."

Upon his death, a nearby centurion declares, "Truly this man was God's Son!" (15:39) What was not obvious to the religious leaders and elders is now clear even to a pagan foreigner. The secret of Mark is laid bare to the world: Jesus the anointed one is the Son of God.

Mark's gospel invites us to wonder who Jesus is for us. Is our faith in Jesus a "secret" that people would be surprised to learn? Who do we expect Jesus to be for us: a not very relevant religious figure of the past or the vital Lord of our lives? Is the name of Jesus something we call out when we pray...or when we swear? In the end, who Jesus is for us is revealed by our actions and not just by our words. We may call Jesus "Lord" with our lips but deny him with our lives.

Matthew and the kingdom

When the writer of Matthew sat down to write his gospel, it is clear that he had Mark as well as the Q sayings in hand. Much of Mark's gospel is duplicated in Matthew and Luke, but up to fifty percent of Matthew's material is unique to Matthew. Since the apostle Matthew was the inspiration for the gospel, his own recollections may contribute to the additions. The final edition of the gospel itself was probably written by a later Jewish Christian, around the year A.D. 80. His goal is to argue, from the tradition of Matthew grounded in the Old Testament, the case for faith in Jesus. This gospel quotes the Old Testament extensively—the intended audience is undoubtedly Jewish—in defense of the teachings and actions of Jesus.

Mark's gospel, you may recall, began with John the Baptist. Matthew begins with Abraham; that is, with a "genealogy of

Jesus the Messiah, the son of David, the son of Abraham." Matthew wants to establish the Jewishness of Jesus head-on, so he presents the lineage of Jesus in numerical sets of fourteen. There are fourteen generations between Abraham and David, fourteen between David and the exile to Babylon, and fourteen between Babylon and Jesus. Fourteen is the numerical value of the name David according to Hebrew numerology, so Jesus is presented as the everlasting king of the house of David, the one God promised would reign according to the covenant with David. As debaters go, Matthew does not intend to be subtle.

The story of Jesus begins with an infancy narrative that centers on Joseph as the main actor, for it is through him that the lineage of Jesus has been traced. Joseph is led, through a series of dreams, to participate in God's saving plan. He is told not to despise Mary for being found pregnant before their marriage but to accept her as his wife and become the guardian of the child Jesus, whose name means "God saves." He is also led to take the mother and child to Egypt before Herod comes to destroy him in the slaughter of the innocents and later to return when the threat is past. Joseph's character imitates that of another dreamer named Joseph, whose story is told in Genesis 37–50. That earlier Joseph, too, went to Egypt against his will, and his people were brought out of Egypt under the protection of God. Through this second Joseph, Matthew portrays the birth of Jesus as a new cycle of salvation for Israel. Once again, in a way still to be revealed, God is shown to be the God who saves.

Joseph is called "son of David" (1:20), and the theme of Davidic kingship abounds in Matthew. The kingdom or reign of God that Jesus comes to establish is, of course, not the sort the people were expecting. Instead of inaugurating a new era of glory for Israel and Jerusalem, Jesus has come to announce a reign of bread and seeds, dragnets and coins, to use some of the images from his parables about the kingdom. The kingdom is mentioned nearly fifty times in Matthew's gospel, and each time the image is given another twist. What is this reign Jesus proclaims so urgently? The meaning of the kingdom is uncovered slowly throughout Matthew's gospel.

John the Baptist first announces that the reign of God is near and demands repentance (3:2). Shortly after he baptizes Jesus, John is arrested and Jesus takes up his message, saying, "Repent, for the kingdom of heaven has come near" (4:17). When Jesus preaches his famous Sermon on the Mount, another visual reference to the authority of Moses, he promises the kingdom to the poor and the persecuted (5:3–11). He equates it with God's "righteousness" (6:33). Those who live according to God's justice are already living in the kingdom.

Jesus is presented in this gospel as a supporter of the law and the commandments. He teaches that the reign of God belongs to those who keep the commandments faithfully, but he defines "faithfully" as exceeding the performance of many religious leaders (5:17–20). Jesus is clear that entrance into the kingdom is not about being merely religious—those who say "Lord, Lord" may not enter, unless they do God's will (7:21–23). Even though John the Baptist may be a great prophet, even the least in the kingdom is greater than he is (11:11). The keys of the kingdom are not given to the great and powerful but to the likes of a poor fisherman like Peter (16:19). Greatness in God's reign will be measured in terms of humility, and those who want to be great should become like children (18:1–4; 19:13–14). The rich are going to find the kingdom hard to buy into (19:24).

Clearly, the kingdom is not what people have been expecting. If the miserable bottom of society is *in* and the established leaders are *out*, you can imagine that Jesus' message did not sit well with the people in power. The kingdom he announces is not the one they are waiting for.

When the leaders of the people challenge Jesus, he replies they should be able to tell he is operating under God's authority by the fact that he casts out demons. A kingdom divided cannot stand, but "the kingdom of God has come to you" when the demons fall (12:25–28).

What Jesus proclaims remains "unhearable" to the people. He continues to teach in parables—the word means "to compare"—short stories that have two or more meanings side by side. The disciples are permitted to receive "the secrets of the kingdom of heaven," but those who will not accept God's reign will hear only the apparent side of the story (13:10–13). Chapter 13 of Matthew's gospel contains many parables about the kingdom. Jesus tells several stories about sowing seeds to reveal the responsibility of the hearer to cultivate the message Jesus brings. He compares the kingdom to a mustard seed, which is small and yet sufficient. The reign of God is also common, like a woman leavening bread, and hidden, like a treasure in a field. If someone were to find the kingdom, like a rare pearl, it would be worth spending all that one has to purchase it. The kingdom is also like a dragnet that pulls up the good along with the bad, sorting them out in the end. Training for the kingdom means being flexible enough to draw upon the value of what is old and what is new, like a householder with many items in store.

After teaching all of these parables, Jesus asks the disciples if they understand what he has said. They answer, "Yes," but their actions later belie their words. The kingdom sounds mysterious, if not contradictory. How can it be common like yeast, yet rare like a pearl? How can it be hidden, and yet found?

And just when we think the kingdom sounds benign and pleasant, it takes a harsh turn. The violent will take it by force and bear it away, Jesus says (11:12). The parable of the slave who is forgiven his debt and refuses to forgive his debtor comes to a bitter end (18:23–35). This warning is echoed when Jesus teaches his disciples to pray. (See the Lord's Prayer in the Appendix.) After the petition, "Your kingdom come," is a timely request to be forgiven in the same measure we forgive. Jesus also includes a plea, knowing how frail humans are, that we be spared the time of trial and the approach of evil (6:9–13).

The reign of God, when you come down to it, sounds patently unfair by human standards. No matter when you sign on to it, you receive the same reward, even if you come in on the tail end and someone else has been with it from the beginning (20:1–16). The last are first and the first are last, and only the last are going to be happy about this. The mother of James and John doesn't get the message, which is why she asks Jesus to allow her sons to be first in his reign (20:20–23). We begin to understand that the kingdom Jesus proclaims is not a place but a *way of seeing,* one that turns protocol, tradition and conventional reality upside down. If we want to be part of it, we have to find a new way of seeing and valuing the world around us.

When Jesus arrives in Jerusalem at the end of his ministry, he enters the Temple and, in the very teeth of the authorities, makes his final proclamations about the kingdom. There his teachings becomes fierce: Tax collectors who collaborate with the Romans and prostitutes who disobey the laws of God are entering the kingdom ahead of the religious leaders of the community! Jesus threatens the authorities openly, declaring that the kingdom will be taken from their jurisdiction and given to those who bear its fruits, even though they are the most unlikely people imaginable. The leaders want to arrest him, but they are afraid of his popularity (21:28–46). Jesus further states that the poor example of the leaders prevents others from attaining the kingdom, and for this he curses them, Hebrew-style, with a series of "Woe to you!" refrains (23:13–39). And with that, Jesus exits the Temple.

Privately, Jesus assures his disciples that the good news of the kingdom will be "a testimony to all the nations" before the end of time (24:13–14). That time is unknown, however, so he warns them to be alert and prepared, like the bridesmaids with their lamps or the servants with their talents (25:1–30). The closer Jesus gets to his final hour and the cross, the more urgent the images of the kingdom become. We come to understand that the kingdom is not just an invitation to a nice banquet but an ark that will enable us to escape the coming destruction. After his resurrection, Jesus appears again on a mountain in Galilee and makes clear once and for all his relationship to God: "All authority in heaven and on earth has been given to me," he tells his disciples. His kingdom is now established.

The reign of God as Jesus describes it is a pretty demanding way of looking at the world. Seeing as God sees means owning a vision that turns contemporary values upside down. To share this vision will cost a great deal: power, material wealth, the esteem of others. Those who want to sign on as citizens of the kingdom might look like fools before the very people they most want to impress. Some, like the rich young man (19:16-22), might find themselves turning away at the gates of the kingdom, sad because they have many possessions they are not ready to surrender.

God's people in Luke

The kingdom is for everyone (handwritten)

Luke is often identified as a Greek convert of Paul's. He wrote both his version of the gospel and the Acts of the Apostles. Writing roughly around the same time as Matthew, Luke uses stories from Mark and sayings from Q, as Matthew does. Still, about sixty percent of Luke's material is his alone. Some have speculated that Mary, the mother of Jesus, may have been one of his sources, since he develops her character more than any other gospel writer. Certainly in his story Luke is sensitive to the presence of women and may have been influenced by women disciples.

Luke's Jesus is forgiving + compassionate (handwritten)

Since Luke is Greek, he is not interested in telling the story of Jesus from the perspective of the Old Testament. He is writing to Greeks like himself, and he wants to share with them the story of a Jewish rabbi who has something to say to the world outside of Judaism. Like his teacher Paul, Luke is pushing the envelope on the story of Jesus, which is not just for Israel anymore.

The descendents of Abraham saw themselves as God's chosen people. Luke doesn't disagree, but he offers an enlarged view of who the people of God can be. Just as Isaiah had a vision of all nations coming to worship Israel's God (Isaiah 2:2–4), Luke believes Jesus came to offer God's saving plan to the whole world. This is why Luke develops another genealogy for Jesus that goes all the way back to Adam—and from there, he says simply, to God (3:23–38). All children born of Adam and not simply those born of Abraham have an equal stake in the story of this savior. Jesus is going to be much more than "the king of the Jews."

The story in Luke's gospel begins with two unlikely conceptions: one by a very old woman and one by a young virgin girl (1:8–38). The fact that the story is told through the activity of women and not men is typical for Luke. In God's new chosen people, women are equal citizens with men. God will bring

53

the saving plan about through the participation of these two women. Poor Zechariah, a priest and the husband of Elizabeth, has his mouth sealed throughout the process. It's as if the angel doesn't trust the priest with the same information given to the women!

The story also begins in the context of the reign of Caesar Augustus and the governorship of Quirinius (2:1–2). These details are added not for historical accuracy but to give the story a worldwide arena. Luke places the story of Jesus in the Roman Empire at large, as big a setting as he could imagine.

At the birth of Jesus, the shepherds are among the first to welcome him (2:8–20). They were wild, scruffy and largely unpopular individuals. The fact that Jesus' birth is announced to them first reminds us that he comes for the poor and outcast. When Jesus begins his ministry, he will read first from the scroll of Isaiah, announcing good news to the poor (4:16–21).

After the birth of Jesus, his parents take him to the Temple and the baby is heralded twice: once by Simeon the holy man and the second time by Anna the prophet (2:21–38). This establishes a pattern in Luke: Most events will contain both a male and female actor. Healings, references in teaching stories, and followers of Jesus all come in matched sets of male and female. Even the appointment of the Twelve is followed soon after by the report that women also traveled with Jesus and supported him out of their own means (8:1–3). And Jesus will befriend women and receive them as his students, a practice that challenged the conventions of the day (10:38–42).

It is not long before this acceptance of "outsiders" gets Jesus into trouble. During his first teaching in Nazareth, he mentions two stories about prophets who championed foreigners over Israelites. It nearly gets him killed (4:23–30). He even heals the slave of a Roman centurion, a favor to the occupying forces (7:2–10). When Jesus embraces Samaritans, however, it makes things even worse. The Samaritans, long-time enemies of the Jews, were even more despised than the Romans. Yet Jesus tells stories that have Samaritan heroes (10:29–37) and cures the Samaritan leper (17:11–19). Still, Jesus does not neglect his own people. When a leader of the local synagogue approaches Jesus about his sick daughter, Jesus does not hesitate to help the girl (8:40–56).

Jesus also shows an interest in sinners and forgives sin with the authority reserved only to God (5:17–26; 7:36–50). Every time he forgives someone, the religious leaders are more upset than when he heals someone. The power Jesus wields threatens them on all levels. Jesus insists in Luke's gospel (as in Matthew's) that the kingdom will be for "the poor, the crippled, the lame, and the blind"—those who were largely regarded as sinners by law-abiding folk (14:12–24). Such people, marked for their sins with suffering, were unlikely candidates for salvation. Yet Jesus includes them, even prefers them, to the powerful and self-righteous. When the leaders grumble at his poor taste in companions, Jesus tells them stories: of the shepherd who comes for the lost sheep, the woman who seeks the lost coin, and the father who forgives his lost son (15:1–32). What Jesus is announcing here is nothing short of revolutionary. God is not looking for perfect children but rejoices in forgiving repentant ones!

Jesus is even depicted in Luke as a lawbreaker. He frequently cures people on the Sabbath or acts in a way that was forbidden by the letter of the law (6:1–5; 6:6–11; 13:10–17; 14:1–6). His response to those who object is simply that the Son of Man is lord of the Sabbath. Jesus claims authority not equal to but greater than that of Moses. He is not disturbed when the hemorrhaging woman touches him, leaving him ritually unclean according to law (8:43–48), nor does he refrain from touching a leper (5:12–13). Purity of heart is more important to Jesus than ritual purity (11:37–41).

Luke is _not_ concerned with showing Jesus as a miracle worker in command of the forces of nature. Jesus doesn't walk on water in Luke, for example, as he does in other gospels. But Luke _is_ interested in showing Jesus as a miraculous healer. Perhaps because Luke himself is, according to tradition, a physician, he records more healings than any of the other gospels. For example, his is the only gospel to record not one but two instances where Jesus raised someone from the dead—a son and a daughter, naturally (7:11–15; 8:49–56).

When the time comes for Jesus to be handed over for execution, he is passed from Pilate to Herod and back to Pilate, highlighting again that this story is for the Greco-Roman world as well as for the Jews. Simon of Cyrene, another outsider, shoulders the cross for Jesus. Women accompany him along the way of the cross, for he always stood by them. He forgives those who are putting him to death and even, while on the cross, rescues one last sinner. Inclusive to the end, Luke mentions the Roman centurion who acknowledges his innocence, as well as a Temple leader who is generous and brave enough to see to the burial of Jesus (23:1–56). In Luke, women followers first discover the empty tomb, but only Peter believes the "idle tale" of women and follows up on their report (24:1–13). Despite his long ministry of inclusion, many of Jesus' followers still didn't get it: The kingdom in Luke is for *everyone.*

The issues Luke raises are not archaic but in fact sound remarkably contemporary. Building bridges of communication and respect between old enemies is the cornerstone of diplomacy in our times. Allowing women to share as full partners in human endeavors is a task yet to be completed. Justice for the underprivileged is still a dream, and the healing of bodies and spirits an endless mission. Compassionately responding to political and personal enemies, divisive social issues, economic injustice and worldwide suffering is *the* measure of discipleship under Luke's terms.

John, the gospel of glory

Toward the end of the first century A.D., someone decided to write yet another gospel. (Actually, gospels continued to be written into the second century, but they did not gain canonicity, which in this case meant being accepted into the authorized collection or canon of scripture.) John's gospel got into the Bible, even though his is very different from the other canonical gospels. Mark, Matthew and Luke are called synoptic gospels, that is, they share a common view or general perspective. But ninety percent of John's story is told nowhere else in the gospels. It is difficult to imagine that he had no access to the other versions or their sources by the 90s A.D. Scholars presume

56

that he deliberately determined to say something new about Jesus and from a much different perspective. He intended his gospel to be not just another rendition of the story of Jesus but an advanced theological reflection for those who already knew the story.

Who is this John? Could he be the same writer who calls himself John in the book of Revelation and the author of the three letters attributed to John? Both of those assumptions are quite unlikely. Nor is he the same John who was an apostle of Jesus, unless that man lived to be extremely old. What most scholars are willing to assert is that the gospel writer was a follower of the apostle John or inherited his traditions. There is also a character in John's gospel who is referred to only as "the beloved disciple." It is hard to imagine the author referring to himself that way, but a disciple might well have referred to his teacher in that manner.

If Mark's gospel starts abruptly with the ministry of Jesus, and Matthew's begins with Abraham, and Luke's with Adam, John has them all beat by starting with Jesus as the Word of God who existed with God from all eternity! This cosmological beginning lets us know right away that this book is more about the Christ of faith than about the historical Jesus. Perhaps John felt enough had been said about the Jesus of history and more needed to be said about his significance for all time.

Jesus looks and feels different, in John's story. If the synoptic gospels show us the Jesus of justice and compassion, John's gospel shows us mostly the glory and full authority of the divine Son. Jesus doesn't do much teaching in John—he never tells even one parable. Jesus doesn't do much curing—three cures as opposed to a dozen or more in the other gospels. There are eight miraculous events in John, and most of them are rather sterile in emotion compared with the synoptics. The miracles of Jesus in John are not compassionate acts but "signs" that indicate his authority.

Why would the writer of John choose to tell the story this way? Why would he present Jesus as the resolute Lord of History who marches to the cross without shedding blood and tears in the garden of Gethsemane first? Some suggest that John's gospel was written in a time of persecution for Christians, and perhaps the author intended to remind his audience that their Lord was an unflinching example of fidelity to God's will and mission. Certainly John's gospel is more concerned with the theology of Christ's divinity than with his humanity.

Jesus is a commanding figure in John. John the Baptist hails him as "Lamb of God" and "Son of God" as soon as he sets eyes on him (1:29–34). Andrew, a disciple of the Baptist, decides to attach himself to Jesus at once. But first he seeks out his brother and explains that he has "found the Messiah" (1:41). It doesn't take long—usually just one encounter—for people to figure out who Jesus is. No Marcan secret would last long around the charismatic rabbi that John is describing.

The first section of John is often called the "book of signs" (chapters 1–12). The miracle at Cana is the first of seven signs that reveal Jesus as the Son of Glory. He turns water into wine, just as Christians will celebrate the transformation of wine into blood at every Eucharist (2:1–11). Yet only in John's gospel is there no story of bread and wine at the final supper. John rearranges the familiar details and speaks only in terms of signs as he transforms the occasion of the Last Supper into the story of the washing of the feet (13:1–15). The eucharistic meal is therefore defined as a call to active service and not simply a remembrance of things past.

Jesus also challenges the Temple authorities from the beginning, not at the end of his ministry as in the other accounts. Jesus cleanses the Temple before the end of chapter two, not only chasing out the money lenders and their animals as in the other versions, but by beating them out with a whip (2:13–22). This is no gentle Jesus, not the friendly healer we are used to!

Like Luke, John is concerned to show that Jesus comes for those beyond the house of Israel. The dialogue between Jesus and the Samaritan woman at the well shows him respectful of a woman who is a foreigner (and also a sinner by popular definition). Jesus is even willing to exchange theology with her, and as a result of this conversation she is converted to faith and brings the whole town to meet him (4:1–42).

58

The second sign of Jesus' ministry is in the healing of an official's son. The father and his household come to believe in Jesus, but compared to the mass turnout by the woman in Samaria, this response by Israelites is not rousing (4:46–54). The next sign, the curing of a paralyzed man, results in outright hostility. Because it occurs on the Sabbath, public opinion begins to turn against Jesus at this early stage. The fact that Jesus continues to refer publicly to God as "my Father" does nothing to ease the situation (5:2–18).

The fourth sign makes Jesus a little more popular. He multiplies loaves of bread and feeds five thousand people. For this, they want to make him king and call him a prophet, since both Elijah and Elisha, prophets of the ninth century B.C., were able to multiply food for the hungry (6:15). Jesus then walks across the sea ahead of his disciples, performing the fifth sign (6:16–26). But ultimately it is bread that gets Jesus into the most trouble. His "bread of life" speech is considered blasphemous. Who exactly is he claiming to be? After this troublesome teaching, even many of his followers turn away.

The healing of the man born blind is the sixth sign of John's gospel. It makes the religious leaders incensed, partly because it was accomplished on the Sabbath and partly because it was accomplished at all. The scene is as close to comedy as one can find in John: the leaders running around like ants on an anthill, interrogating the man once blind then his parents, and then the man again, hoping to learn something to use against Jesus. Eventually, in a rage they drive the man from the Temple. Jesus indicates that this man, who has professed faith in him, sees better than the leaders, who remained steeped in their blindness (9:41).

The raising of Lazarus from the dead is the seventh sign in John and the point at which the leadership actively plots to put Jesus to death. A man with the authority to raise the dead is too powerful to challenge and must be eliminated (11:1–53). Indicative of their obstinate blindness, it never dawns on them that perhaps he is from God after all.

Jesus has arrived at the hour of his glory. The crucifixion is not to be misunderstood as some terrible mistake, a tragedy of

59

betrayal, but a deliberate decision that the Son makes to achieve glory according to God's plan. Jesus has taught his disciples many ways to consider his identity: "I am the bread of life" (6:35). "I am the light of the world" (8:12). "I am the gate" (10:9). "I am the good shepherd" (10:11). "I am the way, and the truth, and the life" (14:6). "I am the true vine" (15:1). Overall, he has invoked the phrase "I am," which is the unspeakable name of Divinity, as God first spoke it to Moses. Jesus has also said, "The Father and I are one" (10:30). There is no margin for misunderstanding when the relationship is that close. Jesus knows who he is.

Judas never betrays Jesus with a kiss in John; he wouldn't dare. Instead, Jesus identifies himself for his accusers, and they fall down under the power of his words. He hands himself over because it is his decision to do so, not because anyone could lift a finger against the Lord of Life (18:11). Jesus is so frank with the high priest that a guard slaps his face for insolence (18:19–23). Jesus stands before Pilate as a peer, one sovereign speaking to another, and they have a conversation about the nature of power and authority. It is hard to imagine that Jesus is going to his death, their discussion is so dignified. Pilate clearly wants to release Jesus, but cowardice prevents him from doing it (18:28).

In John, Jesus does not cry out from the cross in the pain of abandonment, nor does he offer forgiveness or surrender his spirit in the softer ways of the other passion accounts. Jesus discharges his mother to a disciple, speaks to fulfill scripture, and offers the final words, "It is finished." One who has been attentive to the gospel of John knows that it is not Jesus who is finished. Rather his mission is now fulfilled (19:26–30).

How are we to respond to the portrayal of Jesus in John's gospel? He is not "Jesus our brother" as we've grown used to him, not a warm and caring face of God. He is rather the embodiment of God's will being achieved "on earth as it is in heaven." Should we be intimidated by a Lord who follows the divine will so unswervingly, while we haltingly feel our way, far from perfection? If the majesty of John's Jesus makes him seem alien to us or distant, however, the conviction he demonstrates compels us to pick up our cross once again and quit whining about the inconvenience and hardship. The lesson of John is that our personal agenda must be set aside "for the greater glory of God" if we are to follow Jesus.

Who do you say that I am?

Mark, Matthew, Luke and John give us their testimony about who Jesus is, what he did and taught. What does it all mean: the birth, life, death and resurrection of Jesus? That he is the Son of Man, Son of God, Messiah and King of Glory? That he will come again in glory and reign over a kingdom that has no end?

The story of Jesus portrayed in the four gospels is one of increasing urgency. The discipleship modeled there is not presented as a "religious preference" or a popular "spirituality." It is a call that requires a personal response on the part of each of us in both word and action. The gospels were never intended to be a manual in wisdom teachings or a source of moral guidance. They were an attempt to help us formulate an answer to the question, "Who do you say I am?" (Matthew 16:15). As C. S. Lewis, the popular Christian author, wrote:

> A man who were merely a man and said the sort of things Jesus said would not be a great moral teacher. He would either be a lunatic—on a level with the man who says he is a poached egg—or else he would be the Devil of Hell. You must make your choice. You can fall at his feet and call him Lord and God. But let us not come with any patronizing nonsense about his being a great human teacher. He has not left that open to us. He did not intend to.

Questions to Explore   — Godspell — Jesus Christ superstar

1. Name some portrayals of Jesus in art or movies that are most meaningful to you. What do they tell you about who Jesus is for you?   w/ children around

2. Of the four gospels, which expresses the Jesus you most want to follow? (You may have to sit down and read each one again before answering, but what better use could you

Luke

61

make of your time?) Explain what attracts you to this portrayal of Jesus.

3. What does Jesus teach us about God that is new or different from what you understand from the story of God in the Old Testament? *loving + compassionate God*

4. Which idea requires more faith from you: that Jesus was a human like you are or that Jesus is the unique Son of God? Explain your response. *& how do you explain this*

5. Write one sentence describing the Jesus you meet in each of the four gospel versions. How does each "Jesus" support or challenge your faith?

6. Consider the "secret" of Jesus' identity in Mark. Which of the names or titles of Jesus—Messiah, Lord, Son of Man, Son of God or others you have heard—are most revealing of who Jesus is to you? *"I am"*

7. Which parable about the kingdom or reign of God in Matthew's gospel helps you to understand its significance most clearly? What does it mean to you to pray "Your kingdom come, on earth as it is in heaven"? *my God's kingdom to earth.* *& it is our resp. to help bring*

mustard seed (small but significant)

8. Luke envisions a "new Israel" in which the poor, the disabled, the sinner and the outsider are all equal members of God's people. How do you see that vision being lived out, or not lived out, in the church today? Cite examples. *Pope*

9. What does the gospel of John add to your understanding of Jesus that you receive from the synoptic gospels? *Euch meal → Extends to service*

10. The longest section of the Nicene Creed (given at the beginning of this chapter) is about Jesus. What insights do you have from the Creed about who Jesus was? What does this mean for your daily life? *Following God's plan*

Faith Response

1. What do you believe about the humanity of Jesus? What do you believe about the divinity of Jesus? Make two lists,

one for his human nature and one for his divine nature. Don't write what you are *supposed* to believe but what you *really* believe. How near or far are your beliefs compared to those in the Creed?

2. Compose a list of all the names and titles of Jesus that you know: Messiah, Son of God, Prince of Peace, etc. Which names make it easier for you to approach Jesus in prayer? Which make Jesus seem more remote to you? Make a collage of pictures from magazines that illustrate the many faces and identities of Jesus for you.

3. Try praying or meditating in the presence of different images of Jesus throughout the week. Find a cross or crucifix in your church, a favorite statue, a stained glass window, a portrait, your own drawing or sketch. Note how the various representations of Jesus affect your prayer.

4. Read one of the gospels from beginning to end, or all of them if you have time and desire. If certain passages seem new or particularly meaningful for you, copy them down and reflect on them for a while. You may want to memorize a particular verse that is important to you. Perhaps you can have it calligraphied or otherwise displayed where you can let its "good news" penetrate your life.

Four

Spirit and Fire

...We believe in the Holy Spirit, the Lord, the giver of life,
who proceeds from the Father and the Son.
With the Father and the Son he is worshipped and glorified.
He has spoken through the prophets....
—Nicene Creed

So let's talk about the Holy Spirit. At first glance, this could be a short conversation; what is there to say? Of the three members of the Trinity, the Holy Spirit is the most elusive. Our tradition calls God "the Father" and Jesus "the Son of God," but the Holy Spirit is...what? A dove? A tongue of fire? A paraclete (advocate)? In trying to capture the Holy Spirit, we find we have closed our hands on air.

God the Father, the first Person of the Trinity, stands outside of history and yet can be known from within it. We only need point to creation in order to have much to say about God the Creator. God is the source of life and beauty, majesty and wonder. God is powerful and also mysterious, generous and also to be feared. We have the testimony of the Hebrew and Christian traditions to add to the conversation—stories about the God who promises and saves and who above all loves us.

In the same way, we find it easy to talk about the Word, the second Person of the Trinity, who through the incarnation became the man Jesus. Unlike God the Father, Jesus stands within human history and has no fewer than four official "biographies" in the Bible to refer to for details about his life and thought. Whereas God is pure spirit, Jesus became flesh and blood. Though God is mysterious, Jesus was revealed for all to see. God is all-powerful, yet Jesus was vulnerable for our sake. Artists have been rendering the image of Jesus for two millennia, and he has become easy for us to picture.

But the third Person of the Trinity poses problems for us. If

65

the predominant act by which God the Father is known is cre-ation, and the primary act of Jesus is his death and resurrection, then the act by which the Spirit is known is what takes place on Pentecost—the great arrival of missionary courage to the disciples depicted in the second chapter of Acts, in which a rush of wind and flame are all that is seen. The Spirit, people of Christian faith believe, is not *of* history and yet acts *within* it, within *us*. So if we look outward to creation to know God, and into history to know Jesus, we must look within ourselves to know the Spirit. That is, in a way, the most hidden and difficult place to look for anything.

What is spirit?

In time, every one of us comes to terms with the death of a person we love. The parent who cared for us, the spouse we chose, the child we bore, the brother or sister who companioned us, the friend who knew us perhaps best of all—these are subject to the same mortality that will extract its wage from us. When someone we love dies, at first it may seem we are left with nothing. But then gradually it becomes clear that we have been bequeathed something very precious that no one can take from us: The spirit of the one we lost lives on in us.

This spirit isn't a ghost. It isn't the disembodied presence of the one who has died but a vital essence of what this person's life was all about—what he or she held true and valued. We remember what made our mother laugh, and it makes us laugh till the tears come. We remember the fierce way our brother looked when he saw children mistreated, and we are moved to step in wherever children are abused. Our grandmother's afghan warms us with the memory of her gentleness and pride in our achievements. We feel comfort and strength just pulling it around us. Our friend loved flowers, surrounding the house, the yard and herself with them. We linger over the flowers every spring now, and see them as we never did before.

Spirit is more than memory. It is the past joining with the present to create new life within us, so that nothing that has gone before is really lost and no death is really final. When I carry the largest watermelon from the farmer's truck into the family kitchen, like my grandfather did every summer amid the squeals of the children gleeful for its sweetness, my grandfather's generosity and love of surprises lives on among all of us.

Spirit in the Hebrew tradition

It first must be said that Trinity—the threeness of God who is nonetheless one—is a Christian idea that is not shared by Jewish tradition. God is *one* according to Jewish theology, which does not embroider this idea any further. Christianity agrees that God is one, but advances this oneness in the doctrine of Trinity without finding any contradiction in it. Can three be the same as one? In Christian understanding, the answer is yes, even though the arithmetic falls under the category of mystery. We don't know how three persons "reside" within one God, but chalk up the confusion to being finite creatures trying to understand an infinite identity!

So in the most technical sense, we have to acknowledge that the Holy Spirit, as Christians speak of it, is not mentioned in the Old Testament. But the Spirit, as early Christians understood it, certainly had its precedent in the Hebrew story. The spirit of God is communicated by the biblical word *ruah*, a Hebrew word meaning the movement of air, wind or breath. God breathes into the clay in the second creation story and Adam comes to life (Genesis 2:7). God takes back the divine breath and all creatures return to dust (Job 34:14–15). The breath of God is understood to be the life-force, the thing that animates matter and imparts to the creature something of the nature of its creator.

The spirit of God does more. In many books of the Old Testament the spirit of the Lord rushes upon someone and causes that person to grow wise, speak prophecy, develop leadership charisms, display superhuman strength, or exhibit abilities beyond what mortals can do, such as healing the sick or raising the dead. There are even moments (see 1 Samuel 19:20) when people seized with the spirit of the Lord fall down in prophetic frenzy and display ecstatic speech, much like the phenomenon of "speaking in tongues" that the Christian church later displays.

67

The spirit or breath of God is sent forth to bestow instruction, guidance, fruitfulness, justice and liberation on the nation or on individuals. The prophet Isaiah describes the sixfold gifts of God's spirit as wisdom, understanding, counsel, might, knowledge, and fear of the Lord (Isaiah 11:2). That last gift, fear of the Lord, is better translated as reverence or awe in the presence of God's wonders.

Identifying the divine life or essence as breath makes sense, since early people recognized the close connection between breath and life: People who stop breathing lose the vital spirit that keeps their bodies going. Also, a person's spirit could be shared with another, just as the spirit of God could be communicated at God's will. The spirit of the great prophet Elijah was given to Elisha his follower in double portion, which made Elisha's career twice as remarkable as his master's had been (2 Kings 2:9–15). Evil spirits could also come over a person or nation, causing violence or even war.

The relationship between this understanding of spirit and the later development of angels and demons who represent the powers of divinity and darkness, respectively, is not clear. But like our understanding of participating in the spirit of those we love, it is the *experience* of spirit that leads us to find ways to *speak* of it.

Spirit and Trinity in the Christian tradition

Certainly the Spirit of God as Christians use the term owes something to the *ruah* or "breath" of the Old Testament. Since the New Testament is written in Greek, the word used to describe the Spirit is *pneuma*, which becomes in Latin *spiritus*. None of these words should be confused with the Greek philosophical concept of soul, however. Body and soul as dual realities within a person would have been a foreign idea to the Jews, who became the first Christians. They saw human life as intrinsically incarnate, as flesh animated by God's breath.

The birth of Christianity took place in a century that had seen a great development of interest in the world of spirit. The Pharisees, a class of educated Jews who took their religion very seriously, believed in the existence of angels and spirits, a full-fledged afterlife, including the resurrection of the dead and a final judgment of rewards and punishments. This theology was rejected by the ruling party of Sadducees, who controlled the Temple, but we all know that an idea doesn't have to be orthodox to be popularly accepted.

This interest in extra-human reality is what makes our Christmas story so colorful. The angel Gabriel, dreams, visions, the star of Bethlehem and the heavenly host all make an appearance in the infancy narratives. And then of course there is the virgin, overshadowed by the power of the Holy Spirit, who conceives the son Emmanuel, "God-with-us" (Luke 1:35). Although God's spirit is often called "holy" in Hebrew tradition, never before has the proper name Holy Spirit been used in quite this way, as a distinct personality within the Divinity

But be careful here. Dealing with a mystery like the Trinity, it is easy to fall off the fine line between honoring God as Three-in-One and simply accepting a three-headed God. Maybe we say as little as possible about Trinity because the more we say the easier it is to separate God into three distinct pieces. The Holy Spirit does not exist apart from God the Father or God the Son. (This isn't like the executive, legislative and judicial branches of our own government, which often seem to work in ignorance of one another!) God has been revealed as Creator, Redeemer and Sanctifier. But the God who creates, saves and makes holy is *one* God.

Theologians create more mental furniture for the Trinity by calling it "unity-within-community," a model for what the church should be. Some have also used the names "Lover," "Beloved," and "Love Itself" to speak of God's triune nature, focusing on the intimate relationship of these realities. But whatever we arrive at in the end, we haven't nailed down God's nature—not by a long shot, and not ever.

The Spirit as dove

John the Baptist is the next person to speak of the Holy Spirit in the gospels. He minimizes his role in the story of salvation by admitting that his baptism is only with water: "But one who is more powerful than I is coming.... He will baptize you with the Holy Spirit and fire" (Luke 3:16). John's pronouncements always have a lot of pizzazz. This baptism of Spirit and fire does not sound like a modest blessing but some very serious fireworks. Jesus, of course, will live up to all of his advance press and more.

When Jesus does make an appearance near the waters of the Jordan, he insists that John baptize him—not for the remission of sin or as a sign of repentance but to please the one Jesus calls "Father." And God is pleased: The Spirit of God, we are told, descends like a dove upon Jesus (Mark 1:10; Matthew 3:16; Luke 3:22; John 1:32). This scene, with its unusual image of God as dove, gives us the primary symbol by which the Spirit is depicted in art. The dove was a biblical creature often cited for its serenity and gentleness, a symbol of peace, the bird whose failure to return to Noah's ark marked the receding of the waters (Genesis 7:12). This last event probably led to the dove image at Jesus' baptism—the end of the reign of sin and its destruction had arrived in Jesus. Harmony between heaven and earth would be restored, and the waters of death would recede before him.

When we see the Holy Spirit likened in devotional art to a harmless dove, however, we should not be fooled. The Spirit is not a gentle force by any means! That small "bird" is the "dead end" sign for the effect of sin in our lives. It is a brick wall beyond which death itself is helpless to go.

The Spirit as our advocate

Jesus doesn't receive the Holy Spirit only for himself. He also promises it to those he leaves behind. The Spirit will be given to those who ask God for this gift (Luke 11:13). In John's gospel, Jesus calls the Spirit by the name Paraclete ("advocate"), a term used for the defender of an accused person in court. Perhaps this term echoes a similar usage in the book of Job. "I know my Vindicator lives!" Job declares, faithfully and hopefully, as he stands accused of sin because of his misfortunes (Job 19:25). From within the depths of misery and sin, we all need this Advocate to speak on our behalf.

The Advocate, Jesus promises, will teach his followers

everything they need to know (John 14:26). The Advocate is also called the Spirit of Truth, who cannot come unless Jesus first takes his leave of them (John 15:26, 16:7). When Jesus returns to his followers after the resurrection, he breathes on them and says, "Receive the Holy Spirit" (John 20:22). In this holy breath, Jesus imitates the action of his Father in creation, infusing his disciples with his own divine life.

We have talked of the Holy Spirit as the God we find not by looking out into the world or into history but within our own lives. It is a great consolation to think we have an Advocate who speaks for us from the depths of our hearts. Especially when circumstances in our lives leave us speechless or prayer is hard to find, we believe our Vindicator lives and that the Spirit of God is within us and will guide us to truth.

The sign of the cross

Just before Jesus is lifted up in his final ascension or return to God in glory, he gives his followers one last command: "Go therefore and make disciples of all nations, baptizing them in the name of the Father and of the Son and of the Holy Spirit" (Matthew 28:19). This command becomes the church's mission statement for all time: to carry the good news of Jesus to all the corners of the world. This statement also becomes the most recognizable blessing in the church, which Catholics have incorporated into the sign of the cross (see Appendix).

The sign of the cross is a simple gesture. With the left hand on the heart, we trace the image of a cross over ourselves with the right hand: "In the name of the Father" (touching the forehead), "and of the Son" (touching the middle of the chest), "and of the Holy Spirit" (crossing widely over the shoulders, touching first the left, then the right). We profess ourselves followers of Jesus by making this gesture of his cross over our body, claiming its saving action for our lives. The sign of the cross, the great Trinitarian blessing of the church, begins and ends every Catholic act of prayer, including Mass. By this gesture, we profess our faith in God—known through Jesus as the loving Father and active in our lives today through the power of the Holy Spirit.

Look for crosses in Catholic places. They are atop every Catholic church and altar, carried in processions, kissed on Good Friday (the day of Jesus' death), and used in blessings during every sacramental moment (see Chapters Six to Eight for more on the sacraments). You will find a cross on almost every Catholic grave marker. From the first moment of our life in the church to our final resting place, the sign of the cross marks us as followers of Jesus. Everywhere we go, we bear this sign of our mission to bring the good news of the God who creates, saves and renews our world.

Pentecost alight

Near the end of John's gospel, Jesus breathes on his chosen ones and imparts the Spirit to them (John 20:22). It is a peaceful, quiet scene. Luke tells the story differently. In his Acts of the Apostles, we hear the story of the disciples gathered in an upper room, praying up a storm (Acts 2). They've been there for weeks, since Jesus was crucified, and even though they know he was raised from the dead and have seen him with their own eyes, they are still behind closed doors. They had witnessed Jesus ascend to heaven forty days after Easter (Acts 1), yet now they're uncertain about what to do next. So they've been praying for guidance. And praying. And praying.

Pentecost should serve as a warning to us all: Don't pray unless you really mean it:

> And suddenly from heaven there came a sound like the rush of a violent wind, and it filled the entire house where they were sitting. Divided tongues, as of fire, appeared among them, and a tongue rested on each of them. All of them were filled with the Holy Spirit and began to speak in other languages, as the Spirit gave them ability.
>
> —Acts 2:2–4

The disciples stumble out of the closed room into the street. They begin to proclaim the story of the gospel to anyone who will listen. And the people *have* to listen, because the citizens from many lands in Jerusalem for the Jewish feast all hear what these Spirit-crazed folk are saying, each in his or her own language! Here's where the story gets really interesting. Because no one can figure out how this multiple-language event can be happening, they decide that the gospel proclaimers must be drunk. "This can't be real—therefore there must be something wrong with *you*" is the brunt of their argument.

Peter, however, playfully insists that it's too early in the morning for them to be drunk. Pentecost, with its wild winds and remarkable manifestations of power, eventually wins over the crowds. Three thousand people are baptized into the message of the disciples that day. And then *they* start praying and the church is born.

So what happened to the Spirit?

The Acts of the Apostles records many instances where Peter, Paul or one of the other disciples teaches a crowd and the Spirit descends on them, just as it did at Pentecost, with a release of gifts, especially that of speaking in tongues. In Paul's letters to the Gentile or non-Jewish communities of Christians he established in his years of missionary travel, he speaks often of the outpouring of the Spirit. At first it's a great surprise to Peter and others that the Holy Spirit would be given to Gentiles. Isn't the good news of Jesus Christ just for the people of Israel? Paul's many successes among the communities outside of Israel eventually persuade the leaders in Jerusalem that a mission to the Gentiles is the will of God. After all, if the Spirit is going to the Gentiles, shouldn't the church follow?

Paul urges the communities of faith to cling to the unity and peace that the Spirit gives them. Even when the Spirit metes out its gifts differently to different people, one person is no more favored than another. Just as the body has many parts that rely on one another, so the members of the church, endowed with distinct gifts by the Spirit, need one another (1 Corinthians 12).

The "gift of tongues" causes perhaps the most trouble of the Spirit's gifts. People accepted the idea that one person might have a clear gift for leadership and another for teaching. But arguments arise about the place of the gift of tongues within the community. Does it mark people as more "in the Spirit" than those who do not speak in tongues?

Adding to the confusion is the observation that the gift of tongues appears to have two distinct expressions. One is the complete clarity of language that those in the streets experienced at Pentecost, a kind of unscrambling of the Tower of Babel effect (see Genesis 11). The other is the phenomenon of glossolalia, an unintelligible speech that seems to be a communication between the deepest self and God. Paul writes primarily about glossolalia in his letters. He himself has the gift, but he does not find in it a matter for boasting. He places it among the lesser gifts, saying it is not something that marks one for particular greatness within the church (1 Corinthians 14). Paul puts the whole debate in context at the start of his beautiful poem on love: "If I speak in the tongues of mortals and of angels, but do not have love, I am a noisy gong or a clanging cymbal" (1 Corinthians 13:1).

Some denominations within Christianity, most notably the Pentecostal congregations, practice the gift of tongues within their public worship and in personal prayer today. Among Catholics, those who speak in tongues are known as Charismatics, a movement that was revived in the church in the 1960s. They hold "Life in the Spirit" seminars and embrace a fervor not unlike the tone we gather from Paul's letters. Among Charismatics, the gifts of healing—both body and spirit—are promoted, and other gifts are encouraged through regular prayer meetings and Charismatic-style Masses.

Pentecost today

The Holy Spirit is given to the church for all ages. Jesus said he would not leave us orphans and would send his Spirit to companion us to the end of time (Matthew 28:20). Since we believe in the God of the promise, we know we can count on that.

The Catholic church teaches that grace operates within the life of every believer. *Grace* is another term for the activity of the Holy Spirit in the world. We've all seen the world-weary bumper stickers that proclaim, in so many words, that bad things "happen." Well, grace "happens" too, though not in such a passive way. Grace—the active presence of God in the world—is available to each of us, giving us the courage and strength to transform the bad things of this world into God's glory.

Consider the story in John's gospel of the man born blind (John 9). Everyone around Jesus, disciples and enemies alike, wants to use the man's blindness to say something about the presence of evil: in the man, in his parents, or in Jesus himself for healing him. Is the man in the grip of sin? Is Jesus operating under the power of the devil? Jesus brushes all of this aside when he says simply that the man "was born blind so that God's works might be revealed in him" (John 9:3) We too, through the power of grace, can see the suffering, hardship and even the sin that is born from our weakness as an opportunity to bring about and reveal God's glory. Nothing can happen to us, no matter how terrible, that God cannot transform through the power of grace. We are reminded of this every time we look at the cross. Could anything worse than this come to a human being? Yet God took the cruelty and humiliation of the cross and made it the source of mercy and hope for all people.

In the same way today, the alcoholic who determines to stop drinking and seek the support of a group like Alcoholics Anonymous is surrendering to the power of grace. So is the person who finds the courage to leave an abusive relationship, the co-worker who dares to speak the truth at the risk of unpopularity in the office, the couple who finally says no to the call of materialism and embraces "downward mobility" to free themselves for service, the child who rejects the pressure of peers to try the latest drug, and the person who chooses to let go of a long-standing grudge in favor of peace in the family. Grace is always available, but it doesn't operate in a passive or automatic way—and certainly not against our wishes. We have to bend our will in the direction of Pentecost and let the wind of the Spirit take us from there.

The church mediates the grace of the Holy Spirit through its sacraments, but grace operates outside of the church as well. The Holy Spirit is free to work as it pleases. Does the Spirit still work in miraculous ways as the New Testament testifies? Yes.

The gifts of leadership, missionizing, teaching, prophecy and healing are still available to us, just as the gift of tongues is still heard in the world. If we don't see it as often or as visibly as it seems to have occurred in the first century, that is not the fault of the Spirit. If you want to see the power of the Spirit performed in you as it was that first Pentecost, all you have to do is ask. Jesus promised that the Spirit would be given to those who ask in faith.

But remember—you get what you pray for! Our lives are transformed by the acceptance of the indwelling Spirit into our hearts. The Spirit is the will of God in action. To embrace that will means to surrender our own in exchange. Life is not the same for those who consciously accept the power of the Spirit released into their lives. It is "kingdom come," as we pray in the Lord's Prayer: "Your kingdom come. Your will be done, on earth as it is in heaven." The kingdom is near, as Jesus proclaimed—as near as our embrace of it.

Gifts and fruits

The church traditionally teaches that there are seven *gifts* of the Holy Spirit, which enable believers to bring the work of the Spirit to fulfillment in their lives and in the world. The list of gifts is taken from Isaiah 11:2: wisdom, understanding, knowledge, counsel, fortitude, piety and fear of the Lord or reverence. (Only six of these gifts are listed in contemporary translations of Isaiah. In earlier translations, the repetition of "fear of the Lord" in Isaiah was interpreted to be a seventh gift, piety.)

Paul also speaks in detailed fashion about the gifts of the Spirit in his first letter to the Corinthians, most notably in chapter twelve. It is important to say that there is not a definitive number of gifts that the Holy Spirit has to offer. Seven is a number that is easy for the average child to memorize! But that does not mean there are exactly seven gifts, or six, or that Paul's list is better or worse than Isaiah's. A lot has been written, too, to distinguish precisely what one gains in the gift of wisdom as distinct from knowledge or understanding—and to draw a fine line between piety and reverence. More important than these distinctions, however, is recognizing that the ability to discern

God's will and do it is made available to us all through the Holy Spirit.

We also speak of nine *fruits* of the Spirit that witness to the action of grace in a person's life. Paul writes to the Galatians that a person's life will bear the fruit of what is sown and that a life sown with the Spirit will yield the nine fruits of "love, joy, peace, patience, kindness, generosity, faithfulness, gentleness and self-control" (Galatians 5:22).

Paul contrasts that list with the fruit of the world which he characterizes as "fornication, impurity, licentiousness, idolatry, sorcery, enmities, strife, jealousy, anger, quarrels, dissensions, factions, envy, drunkenness, carousing, and things like these" (Galatians 5:19–21). You get the picture. These two "orchards" are not to be mistaken for each other. You can often tell whether you are in the Spirit or in worldly territory by spending just a few minutes with a group of people—whether at church, in someone's home or at a concert. Don't be deceived. The location alone doesn't guarantee that the Spirit dwells within.

Fire and passion

The Holy Spirit, often depicted as the flame of Pentecost, can be thought of as the passion of the church. The Spirit is the "baptism of fire" that John prophesied would come with the arrival of Jesus. The Spirit burns at the heart of the church as the guiding light of our pilgrimage in faith. We are "temples of the Holy Spirit," carrying that fire within us like beacons for the sake of a world still enveloped in its own darkness.

How does passion find expression in the person captured by the Spirit? In what ways can the resulting fire and passion embody the activity of grace in the world? This passion can be seen in a very real way as the point where salvation history ceases to be only about what God has done or is doing in the world and becomes an invitation for the "enSpirited" person to do something as well. Whatever comes next on the road of salvation history is a result of the direction *you* choose to take. The witness of the Christian story is still being written. It is called the life of the church, and the book that has *your* name on it is wide open.

Questions to Explore

1. How would you describe the Trinity to a friend who asked you about it? What images would you use? What does the Holy Spirit mean in your life?

2. Whose spirit do you carry within yourself: your mother's or father's? A friend's or mentor's? How does the understanding of that presence within you help you to understand the indwelling of the Holy Spirit?

3. Consider Eastern traditions of spirituality such as yoga, in which breathing is part of the prayer or discipline. How does the image of breath relate to the life of God that has been communicated to you?

4. Which image is most useful in conveying an understanding of the Trinity: Father, Son and Spirit? Creator, Redeemer, Sanctifier? Lover, Beloved, Love Itself? Unity-within-community? Is there another image that makes this concept more concrete and meaningful for you?

5. Which image for the Holy Spirit is most meaningful to you: dove, advocate, fire? Why?

6. The sign of the cross is a common gesture in the life of a Catholic and central to the mystery of our faith. What does making the sign of the cross mean to you? What memories or insights does it evoke?

7. Pentecost sounds like a wild event in the history of the church. What is the wildest thing you've ever been part of in a church setting? How was it like or unlike the Pentecost event?

8. What might the gifts of the Spirit (wisdom, understanding, knowledge, counsel, fortitude, piety, fear of the Lord or reverence) mean for the church in the world today?

9. Imagine a "grace happens" bumper sticker. How might grace transform some of the uncomfortable realities in your family, parish or community?

10. Who among your family or acquaintances best exhibits the fruits of the Holy Spirit that Paul outlines—love, joy, peace, patience, kindness, generosity, faithfulness, gentleness and self-control? How does that person's example affect you?

Faith Response

1. Observe the form of a cross as it occurs around your city or neighborhood—on church towers, in cemeteries, or even in secular designs and the pattern of the streets. Meditate on the meaning of the cross and make the sign of the cross, mentally if not physically, each time you encounter it.

2. Pray often for the release of the Holy Spirit in your life. Use any words that come naturally to you, or pray the prayer the church uses on the feast of Pentecost:

   Come, Holy Spirit, fill the hearts of your faithful, and kindle in them the fire of your love. Send forth your Spirit, and they shall be created, and you will renew the face of the earth.

3. Create a Pentecost collage using powerful headlines or words you gather from magazines or newspapers or meaningful quotations from scripture. You may want to decorate it with images that remind you of the Spirit or use fire colors. Use the collage in your regular prayer or as brief meditation posted on your desk or refrigerator.

4. Consider which gifts of the Holy Spirit are already operating in your life or ways in which grace is offered to you in the context of your present relationships and circumstances. Resolve to cooperate from now on more fully with the indwelling Spirit as you feel its movement in your life.

Five

Finding Our Place in the Story: The Church

...We believe in one holy catholic and apostolic Church....
—Nicene Creed

What does the word *church* mean to you? Some of us come to this word with a certain amount of baggage. "It's a place they made me go when I was a kid." "It's a building where they sing and dance and whoop it up for God." "It's where they talk about sin all the time and what thou shalt not do." For some Catholics, practicing and former, it's a place "where they never stop talking about money!"

We all have our feelings and ideas about church. Some people recall church as a place where a fellow parishioner or even a priest or minister did some real unkindness to them. Some think of it as a shadowy building full of statutes and stained glass windows, where they talked about holy things in hushed tones, perhaps even in a foreign language. Some remember church as a mostly irrelevant experience: What you did there didn't seem to have much connection to who you were or what you did elsewhere. Probably the most common reaction people have to the idea of church is that it was a real drag. Services were boring, negative and too long.

Of course, there are remembrances of church that go the other way, too: It was a powerful experience of people working together for shared beliefs and values. It was a place where grateful people gathered to give thanks for what they have. It was a rallying point for the week, a chance to be reminded of what's real and what really counts. People with a good experience of church, though, are less likely to be talking about it in the past tense. For them, church remains a vital part of who they are and who they hope to become.

81

Holy See — conference (bishops)
diocese (local church)
parish

The church and its many parts

For the purposes of this conversation, let's consider the church not in terms of a place or building but as a living, organic community of believers. What we usually mean by church is only a single location of that community, called a parish if you're Catholic, and a congregation or assembly if you are Protestant. The parish, the smallest unit within the Catholic church, is normally led by a priest known as the pastor. Others, widely referred to as pastoral associates, may be assigned to serve the same parish. For Catholics, the "local church" is a technical term used to refer to a diocese. This is a gathering of parishes under the administration of a bishop, who has authority over all the pastors who act within the diocese. Sometimes a diocese is formed around a large city, such as Chicago. In other instances, it encompasses an entire state, such as Utah, where the small Catholic population is scattered over a wide area.

All bishops belong to a conference, defined by a nation or region, which meets periodically to address the issues affecting its members. Each bishops' conference is answerable to the Apostolic See. Sometimes called the Holy See, this is the governing body of the worldwide church, specifically the pope and the Roman Curia, residing at the Vatican. The Curia is composed of various councils and tribunals that administrate the Catholic church as a whole. Cardinals, appointed by the pope, form the College of Cardinals and elect the next pope.

The average Catholic will probably not deal directly with anyone other than his or her own pastor and his associates. An occasional glimpse of the bishop may round out your close-up view of the formal leadership of the Roman Catholic church, but "church" is not synonymous with the actions of these relatively few members that compose its clergy. Often we speak as though it is, as when we say, "The church teaches this to be true...." But the way we use language sometimes betrays our real intention—a lesson that emerged from the major council of the church held in the twentieth century.

An unexpected language lesson

Avery Dulles was a young priest of the Jesuit religious order at the time of Vatican Council II, held from 1962 to 1965. A council of the whole church is an uncommon event. The first church council was held in Jerusalem in the first century, at which Peter, James, Paul and others hammered out the missionary direction of the church. Other memorable church councils include the one at Nicea in the fourth century, which produced the Nicene Creed, and the Council of Trent in the sixteenth century, which responded to the issues raised by the Protestant Reformation. Vatican I, in the late nineteenth century, voted to affirm the infallibility of the papacy. But the council that Dulles attended was different from most of these councils in significant ways.

For one thing, it was a surprise that it was held at all. Pope John XXIII was old when he was elected pope in 1958, and no one expected him to be more than a "benchwarmer" or interim pope, a brief presence in the papacy until the next election. When he called for a church council, the Catholic world was stunned, even more so because of his reason. He wasn't going to condemn a heresy or mandate new laws. He wanted to till the soil for "a new Pentecost," a time of grace and mercy for the church.

"We are not born to be museum keepers but to cultivate a flourishing garden of life," Pope John told the council as it convened. It was time to open up some windows and let the Spirit blow through the church. It was time for *aggiornamento* (Italian for "updating") for the Catholic world. People were dismayed, and some Catholics felt threatened by the idea of change.

Avery Dulles sat in on these early meetings of the Second Vatican Council, listening intently to the discussions. The assembly was composed of the expected bishops and Curia staff, *periti* or "theological experts," plus observers from among Protestant leaders, including the premiere appearance of women at a church council. As each speaker offered a vision of the church, Dulles noticed that they used the word "church" to express different visions of church. He took notes and later published his observations using the term "models of the church."

Models for church

Which of the following statements sounds most nearly what you mean by using the word "church"? Try ranking them, 1–5, making 1 your most meaningful and 5 the one you least identify with:

(handwritten margin notes: "Institutional model ③", "mystical union ②", "herald ③", "community model ④", "service ⑤")

- The church is a religious organization, with a governing body, laws and moral principles, that directs the life of its members in accordance with God's plan for humanity.
- The church is the Body of Christ, to which I belong in a mystical sense, in which I participate through a life of prayer and holiness directed toward communion with God.
- The church is composed of those who are called by God and empowered by God's living word in the Bible to testify to the message of salvation through all the world.
- The church is a gathering of the faithful who celebrate the love of God and joy of salvation through acts of worship and real concern for one another as sisters and brothers in Christ.
- The church is a missionary body sent to minister to the poor, sick, grieving, victimized members of our society. The church exists wherever justice is done *(handwritten: "move to ②")* and love is made real in aid and sacrifice for the sake of the least powerful ones.

It may be hard for you to rank these, but don't worry: There is no correct order. In fact, there is no erroneous statement contained in the set of five. These were the broad categories church leaders used when speaking of the church at Vatican Council II. Dulles did not see these as rival definitions but as individual focuses within one definition of church.

Church as institution

When we speak of the church in terms of priests, bishops, cardinals and pope, as we did earlier in this chapter, we are talking about the *institutional model* of church. The institutional model is all about authority, a word that is highly respected by some people and sends chills through others. The institutional church refers to the organizing and governing body that decides what the orthodox or standard beliefs of the faithful should be. The institution of the church breaks things down into rules, guidelines and laws, as in the Code of Canon Law, for example, which defines the official teachings about marriage, the responsibilities of pastors, and the role of bishops, among many other subjects.

One clue as to whether something emanates from the institutional understanding of the church is to see if it's numbered. Seven sacraments, seven deadly sins, forty days of Lent, four weeks of Advent, five joyful mysteries of the rosary, three divine persons in the Trinity and two natures in Jesus all originate in the institutional church. The teaching authority of the church, known as the magisterium, defines, codifies and clarifies the beliefs of the faithful.

Another feature of institutions is that they determine the identity of their membership, the who's-in-and-who's-out feature of every group. Since an institution acts as its own gatekeeper, it has to set up a profile of who its members are. In the case of the Catholic church, membership is defined by receiving the sacrament of baptism. Complete initiation, however, involves three sacraments: baptism, confirmation and Eucharist. Membership can also be suspended, as in the event of excommunication, which is the loss of relationship to the church due to actions that are severe enough to separate a person from the community of the faithful. Excommunication is rare, however, and can be reversed.

In general, anything that has to do with structure, discipline, law, government, identity and definition represents the institutional model of church. The good news about the institutional model is that it offers the church stability, continuity and identity, which have allowed the church to carry on its mission for twenty centuries. Even a short-lived organization develops an institution to support its existence. How much more, then, has the church needed its structure to survive over the centuries?

The bad news about institutions, of course, is that they tend to collect baggage as they journey through the years. Institutions by nature resist change, promote passivity among unempowered members, attract power-mongers to their hierarchies (clericalism, the "priest-first" mentality that both clergy and members of the laity often unwittingly support, springs from this), and stifle prophetic voices that challenge the status quo. The institutional model of church, if left to itself, would run aground from its mission from time to time, needing wind in its sails from another source.

Consider your reaction to the term "the establishment" and you know how you stand in relationship to the institutional model. Did you ever have a bumper sticker that read "Question Authority"? Does somebody call you "boss" or do you answer somebody else's phone or do you work out of your home? Do you talk more about the "good old days" or dream about the days to come? Some of us naturally embrace institutions, while others tolerate them only reluctantly.

Church as mystical union

The *mystery model* of church is familiar to anyone who was a Catholic or knew a Catholic before Vatican Council II. If the hierarchy of the church was running largely on the institutional model back then, the laity was equally attached to the "otherworldly" aspects of the church. Revisit the scene: a Mass in an ancient language no longer spoken; holy rituals administered by people set apart from the rest by vows, clothes and a semi-cloistered life; popular devotions to the mysteries of Mary's life, the sufferings of Jesus, or the miracles of the saints, often recalled in highly evocative images; the sense of sacred times and sacred places marked off from the "profane" world we normally inhabit. This was the world that Catholics walked into— or knelt before—when they "went to church." This was the Catholic world that Protestants and others feared, felt suspicious of, or at least found very curious.

The veil of incense hung like a curtain over this world, emphasizing its separateness from the world outside. But what was inside this world was a real sense of union with the Divine that the church after Vatican II, for many, has failed to recapture. The mystery model of church is about the personal, even private, quest for holiness—the desire to communicate with and surrender to the God who loves me and calls me by name. Its deep sense of union with God and its respect for and emphasis on individual spirituality make this a very recognizably Catholic model.

These characteristics have not faded from the church, despite changes in its worship, language and "style." Certainly the personal prayer life of every Catholic continues to be a source of nourishment and strength. The communal rituals of the church are, now as ever, an encounter with the sacred that holds great significance for the believer. The good news about the mystery model is that it encourages the spiritual growth of the individual and supports the importance of the personal surrender to the heart of God.

The downside of an emphasis on mystery is that it can lead to an otherworldly approach to our life of faith. Is religion merely a system for the personal perfection of its members? Is it only about fostering a "God-and-me" relationship, or is there a responsibility to the world beyond the sanctuary? The mystery model of church, left unchecked, can lead to a split in a person's perception of the world: some things holy and sacred, most things secular and profane. But the world is not "bad," nor is the life of the spirit simply "good" in an undifferentiated way.

If prayer is one of your gifts, then you have a natural affinity for the mystical. If you meditate, love silence, revel in ritual and have a hunger for religious experience, the mystery model is a powerful component of your definition of church. If, on the other hand, you consider yourself a practical person who finds meaning in what you can build, fix or achieve with your time and effort, this model may be difficult for you to appreciate. If you hunger to see results and grow impatient with ceremony, the mystery model is not your native element.

In a sense, the models of institution and mystery are polar opposites; yet they came into being in tandem. They both support the intuitive need for many people to have their relationship with God reside both within a communal structure and in personal encounter with God. People who are comfortable with one of these models of the church are usually not uncomfortable with the other.

For those who are squirming at the thought of either of these models, however, there are three more for your consideration.

Church as herald

What do you think about the Bible? Is it the inerrant, inspired word of God? Is it the centerpiece of God's self-revelation, the last word on every subject, a companion, a champion, a guidebook, the Good Book? Or have you never read it? Do you not even own one? How you answer these questions may determine whether you think of the church as being ultimately the *herald of the good news*. Some have called this model of church distinctly "Protestant" in that it elevates scripture to center stage, much the way the mystery model is "Catholic" because it uses sacred symbol and ritual as the source of its strength. The herald model of church has in our time been championed by fundamentalist expressions of Christianity, which interpret the Bible in a literal way often foreign to its original writers' intentions. Because Protestant fundamentalism in particular has stressed the herald model of church, many Catholics have shrunk from identifying with it.

Many of us have heard the stereotypes of Protestants who can quote chapter and verse from scripture as opposed to Catholics who have on their coffee tables a beautifully decorated Bible that has never been opened. These stereotypes are misleading. Many mainstream denominations within the Protestant or Reformed tradition of Christianity do not emphasize familiarity with scripture in the automatic, memorized style of the stereotypical "Bible thumper." And many Catholics have a much better sense of scripture than they imagine because of their lifelong fidelity to the Mass, where both Testaments are proclaimed publicly on a weekly and daily basis.

From the time of the early church, the herald model has been in evidence. The writers and the evangelists who wrote gospels and letters to various communities frequently quoted *their* scripture, what we now call the Old Testament, to underline the authority of their own teachings. The church fathers who wrote in the first centuries after Christ used the books of the New Testament as the primary source of authority for their decisions. The documents issued by bishops' conferences and the Vatican today are underpinned with references to scripture. Certainly, scripture continues to be not only the authority behind the message but the message itself.

Jesus invited his followers to proclaim his gospel "to the ends of the earth." Being a herald of good news doesn't have to mean standing on an overturned milk crate in the park, shouting scripture verses at innocent passersby. Yes, the herald model includes the Bible shouter, and the televangelist and the person who slips a religious tract under your windshield wiper. It motivates the person who knocks on your door to have the salvation chat with you, the well-dressed and courteous young men who stop you on the street and even the people who wear saffron robes and play tambourines in the airport.

But the church as herald appeals to people who write books like this one, the pastor in the pulpit facing his community each Sunday morning, the woman who taught you Sunday school, religious educators of children and adults, missionaries, retreat leaders, parish enrichment speakers and just about anyone else who gets up publicly to proclaim the word of God. *You* are be a herald every time you take a stand because of what you believe and have the courage to own up to that motivation if someone asks you why.

The upside of the herald model of the church is that it provides a reason and method for outreach to the world. It does not keep the gift of faith to itself, as the mystery model might be tempted to do, or for its own membership, as the institutional model did for centuries. The church as herald fulfills Jesus' command to take the gospel "on the road." It provides testimony to those who might not hear the good news otherwise. It is a teacher, a guide, a lighthouse to those who are lost in the night. The herald model of church is quite fearless.

The herald model can also be simply preachy. The worst of

church can be the herald model gone awry. "Practice what you preach" most certainly emerged as a saying because of the many evangelists whose lives made their words mere hypocrisy. The herald model of church can also be stillborn: It tells everyone what to do, but it does nothing in itself to actually change the world for the better. "Words, words, words," Hamlet once wearily sighed. The herald who substitutes words for action is fooling no one.

Church as community

What if the best and most admirable people you knew were throwing a party and invited you to come? And what if the party never ended but went on and on for eternity? And what if this party had the best food and superb wines, the music was excellent and the company warm and wise? How could you say no?

For some people, this is what the church is: a remarkable invitation to *the* event of all time. The church is a vast assembly of friends—no, family—called together to share something so wonderful that it is worth everything we own to get in. The church is the pearl of great price that Jesus talks about in his parable (Matthew 13:45–46). The church is not to be missed. It's where the action is.

For those who have experienced communities of faith like this, you don't have to be persuaded that they are possible. For those who haven't, there probably isn't much that can be said to convince you that they exist. The church as sacramental community—the community that becomes the good news it bears—is a heady experience. It is a gathering of friends who know how to dance and want to sing. Worship really is a celebration. The news is not only good, it *feels* good! The church as community is a Christian utopia.

The *community model* of church places its emphasis on the assembly, just as the herald model highlights scripture. The community itself becomes a source of revelation. Often such communities will practice ecstatic speech or have prophets in regular attendance. Epiphanies, which are manifestations of God's presence and power, are not unusual in the community

90

model of church. People in such communities expect God to "perform a work" or to be involved in their daily lives.

To some, this may sound like heaven: Where do we sign up? For others, who like to keep a low profile in religious places, it all sounds too loud and chummy. Do we really need all that fellowship to find God? Do we really need to be everyone's friend?

The sacramental community model works if you love a party, enjoy people, make friends easily, like to share. But it will be a hindrance to authentic spirituality if you are shy, private, prefer sacred space to be silent and would rather be alone with God. Obviously, people attracted to the mystery model and those drawn to sacramental community are not the same people.

This model is valuable because it makes the necessary shift from "I" to "we" in the religious enterprise. Christianity is a faith where "two or three are gathered" by Jesus' own definition. And if the "more" can be the "merrier," so much the better. Also, a vibrant community illustrates a vital, living expression of faith that attracts outsiders and "playacts" the kingdom of God in microcosm.

Alas, the problem with any utopian community is the same: What about when it springs a leak? People are notoriously unwilling to forgive a paradise that does not live up to its advertising. Many parishes operating on a sacramental community model go ballistic when their pastor is transferred and the new pastor doesn't want to "party." Or perhaps there is a fracture into camps: those who see the Holy Spirit working in the pastor versus those who discern that the pastor is possessed by a demon. Since most authority resides within the community itself in this model, the community model of church can have mutually conflicting discernments about where this ship ought to be sailing.

People who have been in and out of utopian communities become realistic about them. They are great while they last, but don't throw away your suitcase.

Church as servant

Perhaps you've been patient through this list of church models, but still have burning questions that aren't being addressed. Who cares about worship style, you ask? It's not important to you how you pray or who you obey or what you say. The gospel challenges us to do what Jesus did, and the church is primarily concerned about how we serve others.

Maybe you are one of those people who is naturally inclined to act when you see injustice done or suffering gone uncomforted. You can't walk past a homeless person without feeling the desire to get involved. You can't look at those ghastly pictures in magazines about famine and war-torn countries without sending money or even volunteering to assist the Red Cross in some way. Perhaps you have spent time in the Peace Corps or do regular volunteer work at a soup kitchen or with a tutoring program. You have three pets you took in as strays and you can't even throw away a houseplant gone brown because, after all, it's still alive.

The most perplexing thing to you is that a lot of church-going folks don't share your view of the church. To tell the truth, you may not even have much passion for the Sunday worship experience. It seems empty to you, a waste of time when there is so much that needs to be done. You feel sure Jesus wouldn't have been praying in church (well, synagogue) while the sick needed healing and the poor needed food. You feel compassion, guilt and a need to personally address the suffering in the world. Being like Jesus, you reason, is more important than talking about him or even praying to him.

Welcome to the *servant model* of church. Many Christians—though perhaps not enough—share this drive to *be* an incarnate word of justice and not simply to *talk* like one. The herald and servant models, naturally, are in tension, just as the emphasis on ritual of both the mystery and the community models is lost on servant adherents. And the servant model frequently butts heads with the institutional church as well. You might call the servant model the maverick of the bunch.

The good news about the servant model is obvious. Who could argue that this viewpoint isn't dead-on gospel? Certainly

Christians must do as Christ did: "Just as you did it to one of the least of these who are members of my family, you did to me" (Matthew 25:40). Generosity toward the poor, compassion for the suffering, and tirelessness in fighting injustice are concerns strongly upheld in both Testaments. You can't ignore these responsibilities and expect to be recognized in the reign of God (see the judgment parable of Matthew 25).

Of the five models of church, this one is the hardest for me to fault. I tread lightly as I point out these few concerns, not wanting to have the memory of Mother Teresa, Cesar Chavez and Dorothy Day testifying against me at the last judgment. Servant model adherents can swerve into self-righteousness very easily, because they *are* doing what is truly righteous. They can also develop Messiah complexes because of the life and death struggles they witness up close and sometimes join in solidarity. Church-as-servant believers may neglect prayer, scripture and the church community in favor of their work: "My work is my prayer; the people I serve are my gospel." Lacking the support from fellow believers, they may become embittered, cynical and even lose their faith in church completely.

The servant model attracts lone rangers and rugged individualists with strong opinions, but it is best lived out in tandem with a vital life of prayer (Mother Teresa), an insistence upon community (Catherine McAuley, founder of the Sisters of Mercy), and even with a meaningful relationship to the institution it both serves and challenges (Archbishop Oscar Romero of El Salvador).

Five models, one faith

So which model of the church is right for you? Children of course want simple answers: no grays, only black and white. Adults, however, know from experience that often answers aren't so simple. The truth is that for Catholics all five models of church are vital components for a mature faith life. We may be naturally inclined to one or two of them, but we can't ignore the others. To some degree, the faith of a Christian requires efforts in all of these directions: respect for the institution and its usefulness, a prayer dimension, a public witness to our beliefs, a strong relationship to the community of faith and a bold active stance against injustice. The first four, one might say, are needed to support the last.

Spend some time considering your understanding of what church is supposed to be. Which models of church do you feel best meet your needs right now? Which ones are most challenging for you? Plant yourself firmly where you are and strive to grow in the direction where you feel weakest. The only "dangerous" expression of church is the one gone wildly monochromatic. Consider the following statements as warning signs:

Extra ecclesia, nulla salus. (There is no salvation outside of the church.) Once uttered by members of the Catholic hierarchy and expressed in papal documents, it was a cry from a rabid "institution" believer that the institution was synonymous with the kingdom of God. Narrowly understood, this is not a teaching of the Catholic church.

The more I pray, the holier I am. This is a comforting idea, but even Teresa of Avila, who prayed a lot more than most of us, would disagree. Prayer is crucial to the life of faith—Jesus prayed frequently throughout his ministry—but there is no direct correlation between the amount you pray and the jewels you will wear in your crown in heaven. This statement expresses the viewpoint of a "mystery" believer who's lost perspective.

Sola scriptura! (Only scripture!) I don't mean to pick on Martin Luther, who had many legitimate beefs with the institutional church of his time. But the idea that divine revelation and authority reside within the Bible *and nowhere else* is contrary to the experience of centuries of the faithful who have had visions, dreams and other manifestations that have brought new understanding to the church—not to mention the power of the eucharistic assembly, through which Christ is present in a very real way according to Catholic understanding. "Only scripture" is the motto of those who are too narrow in their search for truth, and carried to an extreme it can lead to fundamental-ism.

We can build a beautiful city, yes we can, yes we can. Hmmm. Perhaps. This line, lifted from the 1960s performance of *Godspell*, illustrates the sometimes naive expectations of "community" builders. The beautiful city is a worthwhile goal, but it can't exist for its own sake and it has to be willing to fail, to fall and to forgive. Often, the community model is too fragile, in the end, to survive a dose of reality, and this statement comes back to haunt those who utter it.

Don't talk to me about church. I'm too busy saving the world! A person devoted to the servant church model is a creature both admirable and fierce. But servants who lose perspective will begin to forget that the Lord is in those they serve and begin to mistake *themselves* for the Messiah. When you begin to think that the salvation of the world depends on you, you know you've gone too far.

The marks of the church

No matter where you find yourself within the models of church, you know you are a Catholic if you adhere to four basic elements or marks of the church. They are found in the Nicene Creed: "We believe in one holy catholic and apostolic Church."

The last lines of the creed were hammered out as direct responses to heresies being taught in the fourth century, so each word is deliberately chosen. The church is *one* because it cannot be divided by human powers. As Paul wrote in 1 Corinthians: *We are many parts, we are all one body* (1 Corinthians 12:12). As one Body in Christ, the church shares a unity that Jesus promised for all time. At the Last Supper, Jesus prays that his followers might be one, just as he and his Father are one (John 17:11).

Jesus' unity prayer is one compelling reason why many Christian denominations today are committed to ecumenism, which is the search for unity among all who put their faith in Christ. For of course the word *church*, often used by Catholics (and in this book) as shorthand for Roman Catholicism, means more than the local parish or even the Catholic community worldwide. The church refers to all members of the Body of Christ, whether Catholic, Orthodox, Anglican, Methodist, Baptist, Congregationalist or the many other expressions of Christianity. The church is one because of her source in the Trinity, as the *Catechism of the Catholic Church* says (n. 813). The catechism further calls ecumenism a "holy objective," the reconciliation of all Christians into "the one and only Church of Christ" (n. 822). This objective calls Christians into the pursuit of unity in good works, principles and fellowship.

Catholics also believe that the church is *holy.* We have an image of holiness that is decidedly unhelpful: pious people at prayer, eyes squeezed shut, hands clasped, a halo glowing above their heads. Real holiness, though, has to do with the presence of the indwelling Spirit of Holiness in our lives. If God dwells in us and acts through our lives, then we show evidence of genuine holiness, whether we are particularly pious or not.

The church is holy because grace—God in action—operates through the church and the love of Jesus is manifest within it. This doesn't mean there are no sinners in the church. There are nothing *but* sinners in the church! But sinners, those who chronically choose their own will above God's, are nonetheless called to be saints (from *sancta*, Latin for "holy").

How is the church *catholic*? In the first century, Ignatius of Antioch used the word *catholic,* meaning "universal," in reference to the church. Wherever this church leader went, the communities he established witnessed to the same "fullness of Christ," the same Spirit and gifts. As the church expanded to more distant lands, the same message was taught, the same Eucharist celebrated.

Paul never used "catholic" to describe the church, but he did speak of the need for all to think and live in harmony (Romans 15:5). Harmony, which is not the same as uniformity, embraces diversity and then strives for the perfect blending of voices, singing different notes within the same key, making beautiful music together. The catholicity of the church is not a mindless suspension of personal opinion for the sake of the

96

cause, but a thoughtful commitment to sharing ideas within a basic framework of values. These values will be discussed later in Chapter Eleven.

The Catholic church believes its authority is based on *apostolic succession*, the idea that the authority of the church comes from Jesus' commission to the apostles. That authority was passed from leader to leader, from generation to generation, through the laying on of hands, a gesture of conferring leadership performed during ordinations. (More on vocations is found in Chapter Eight.) Catholics speak of an unbroken line of apostolic authority traced from Peter, to whom Jesus gave the keys of the kingdom (Matthew 16:18), up to the modern papacy. The church's apostolic authority gives the magisterium the right to form new responses to the world as history adds new dimensions to the discernment of the faithful. Jesus didn't tell us precisely how to respond to the nuclear arms race, the present-day economy, or emerging issues in medical science. But the guidelines for moral living that he prescribed assist the magisterium to consider its teachings for the present age.

We are the church

Most of us still tend to lapse into discussing "the church" in an institutional sense, meaning the body of leaders out there on all levels who tell the rest of us what to believe and how to behave. But a central definition of church remains in Paul's metaphor of the Body of Christ. There is no church "out there" apart from you and me and many others like us who together comprise the Body of Christ. Like the story of the Israelites in the Old Testament and the story of the disciples around Jesus, the story of the church is now *our* story. If we are passive in our membership or absent altogether, then the whole church suffers—much as one failing organ makes the whole body malfunction. No part of the body is without its place, its value and its dignity. Your part in the enterprise of church is beyond price.

Questions to Explore

1. Describe your childhood experience of church. Was your family mostly positive or negative about church membership? How have your experiences of churches or church folk colored your understanding of church today?

2. "We are not born to be museum keepers, but to cultivate a flourishing garden of life." How does this statement by Pope John XXIII coincide with your vision of church?

3. Review the ranking you made at the beginning of this chapter of the five statements about or descriptions of church. Has your ordering of those five statements been altered by what you've read in this chapter? If it has, how and why has it changed? If it has not, how would you defend your initial ranking?

4. What is the best thing to you about the institutional model of the church? What is the most challenging thing about it? Outside of church, who or what has authority over your life at this time? How do you react to that authority?

5. Is prayer easy or difficult for you? Do you pray with your own words, use traditional prayers, meditate silently or employ some other method? Do you prefer to pray alone or in groups? Does public ritual help or hinder your ability to pray? Explain your answers.

6. Have you read or do you read the Bible regularly? Do you feel comfortable reading and meditating on the Bible by yourself, or do you benefit more from a Bible study group? How do you react to the preaching you hear in churches, on television or radio? How do you tell the difference between "good" and "bad" preaching?

7. Are you a "people person"? Do you get energy from being in groups? Do you like to sing, dance, make new friends? Do you think church should be a place to form meaningful relationships? Why or why not? Has a parish ever been your primary community of support or socializing?

8. How do you rate yourself as a social activist? Do you give money to charitable causes? Volunteer when it's for a cause you believe in? Vote primarily on the basis of your beliefs? Work full time for humanitarian purposes? Does your level of activism meet what you think is demanded by the gospel, or do you feel you should be doing more? Explain your answers.

9. Is your faith in conformity or in conflict with the idea of the church as "one holy catholic and apostolic"? If there is a part of that statement you don't accept, explain why.

10. Have you thought of the church as primarily a place, an organization or a community? How does the idea "We are the church" compare with what you've been taught to think about church?

Faith Response

1. Visit local churches and read their literature, especially their mission statement or creed, which is often at the back of the church on leaflets or in the church bulletin. Attend a worship service if you can. Try to identify the model(s) of church out of which they operate. Consider how their sense of church compares with yours.

2. Talk with friends who do not share your faith or faith tradition. Ask them what church means to them. Enter into respectful dialogue with people of differing faiths as well as Christians of different denominations. What common beliefs do you find in such conversations?

3. Make a commitment to strengthen the aspect of church that is hardest for you to accept. If you are not one who prays regularly, make a commitment to a prayer group or to regular, personal prayer. If the Bible is foreign to you, read a small passage daily or join a Bible study group. If social justice work frightens you, volunteer with a friend to participate in one time-limited project. If the idea of community does not appeal to you, attend a Charismatic Mass

or visit another high-spirited community of worshipers to test the waters. If institutions turn you off, read one of the U.S. Catholic bishops' best documents of instruction, such as *The Challenge of Peace: God's Call and Our Response* or *Economic Justice for All.* Or pick up a copy of the diocesan newspaper and see what good things the institutional church is doing.

4   Consider ways that religious prejudice may keep you from acknowledging how God is working in the lives of others. Observe how those who worship differently from you still honor the same God. Pray for the grace to withhold judgment on others and to seek the unity among his followers that Jesus wants.

Six

Welcome to the Feast: Sacraments of Initiation

...We acknowledge one baptism for the forgiveness of sins.
We look for the resurrection of the dead,
and the life of the world to come. Amen.
—*Nicene Creed*

Things are not always as they appear. A discarded napkin in a restaurant may contain the notations of the next scientific genius. A withered wildflower on a dashboard is the last memento of a lost love. A child at play views a junkyard as a kingdom. What one values may be worthless to another. It is the rule of every yard sale and antique store, and it is all bound up with our way of seeing value differently.

Common things, we know, can hold priceless realities. A lump of rock contains a gemstone in the rough. A tiny ring of gold represents fifty years of faithful love and sharing. An item's appearance doesn't always reveal its real value. A thing's value may depend on our understanding of it.

A central understanding of the Christian worldview is that of incarnation: the idea that God's life can be translated into our own, Spirit takes on flesh, creation is imbued with the stamp of its Maker, human beings are made in the likeness of the Divine. This means that even common things can hold sacred realities. In this incarnational understanding, flowing water means life, a simple table set with bread and wine is an encounter with God, a slather of oil signals a commissioning, words of forgiveness bring freedom, an exchange of vows opens onto a world of love.

The sacramental worldview, as a Catholic might call it, is a way of seeing that is attentive to the way God's presence takes on flesh all around us. It means looking for God in the ordinary encounter. The face of the least of our sisters and brothers is the face of Christ. The ordinary is the revelation of the extraordinary.

Sign, symbol, sacrament

What is a sacrament? There are many famous definitions we can use to unpack this word, but a warning goes with any of them: Explaining a sacrament is like explaining a kiss. Best to talk less and kiss more, if you want to arrive at a meaningful understanding. Having said this, the basic way to talk about sacrament is to compare it to what we mean by the words *sign* and *symbol*. Paul Tillich, a Protestant theologian, was the first in modern times to unpack these three ideas together. First of all, begin with a *sign*, which is an object we use to communicate meaning. Let's consider a stop sign, for example. We want people to stop at intersections, but it would be impractical to have someone posted at every intersection shouting "Stop!" So we invent stop signs. (Actually, we invent language and then writing, but let's not get too technical.) S-T-O-P means "halt," but you don't need to be able to read to know this, because the international community has agreed that red octagons mean stop, too. So a stop sign is a combination of signs, really: a language event and a mutually shared perception that red octagons mean stop.

Now, there is nothing about the word *stop* that makes it *mean* stop; we English speakers just decided that it does. And there is nothing about a red octagon that means stop; again, it's a shared perception based on mutual agreement. That's how signs work: They communicate what we all decide they mean. So an arrow pointing down means the elevator is moving in that direction, and a blue parking space is for disabled drivers or passengers only.

Then there are *symbols*. Symbols are also signs we use to communicate meaning, but they go further than that. Symbols *participate* in what they represent, so a symbol attains a higher level of meaning. Think about the flag of the United States, for instance. As a sign, it has certain components that communicate its meaning, like color and design. The number of stars and stripes represents the number of states and colonies, respectively, and the colors represent certain ideals. These aren't arbitrarily chosen, as the eight sides of a stop sign are, but the numbers and the colors have meaning related to our history and self-understanding.

Consider how people feel about their flag, how they react when it is captured, abused or destroyed. If it were a stop sign, nobody would feel personally insulted by its destruction. But the flag, as symbol of our country, represents the country in a direct way. When someone abuses the flag, we use a word like *desecration* to describe the act. *Desecrate* contains the root word "sacred" in it; it is the opposite of *consecrate*, to "make sacred." To desecrate a flag means to challenge its sacred character. So symbols carry much more significance than signs. We are getting closer, obviously, to the meaning of sacrament.

A sacrament is a sign in that it communicates meaning and also a symbol in that it participates in what it represents. But a sacrament dares to go one step further. For Catholics, a sacrament not only participates in what it represents, it *is* what it represents. A sacrament, to quote Saint Augustine (who is, after Paul, the next great architect of Christian theology), is efficacious; that is, it "effects transformation," it makes something happen. And, to be very clear, it makes something happen not through the "magic" of a ritual but because God chooses to make it happen. So a stop sign says stop all day but it can't force someone to stop. A flag, which is a symbol, represents its country all day but in no way protects it. But a sacrament of initiation literally brings someone into communion with the church. A sacrament of forgiveness truly makes forgiveness real. A sacrament of matrimony effectively joins two lives. A sacrament of Eucharist actually makes Christ present in a shared meal. For those who believe, these are not mere signs that communicate an idea or symbols that remind us of history and identity. Sacraments do what they say they do.

103

What are the Catholic sacraments?

The seven Catholic sacraments are baptism, confirmation, Eucharist, reconciliation, matrimony, anointing of the sick, and holy orders. That's the short answer, at least, to that question. The long answer requires a little history lesson, since there haven't always been seven official sacraments of the church. At times the church has recognized as few as three sacraments, and in certain parts of the world it has acknowledged as many as twenty-two. The Council of Trent, defining church practices in response to the Protestant Reformation, recognized the seven sacraments that are currently celebrated by Catholics, although other Christian denominations do not view all seven as sacraments.

Listing seven sacraments answers the question "What are the sacraments?" only in a technical sense. There seem to be as many approaches to defining the sacraments as there are theologians in church history. Augustine spoke of them as occasions that open up the possibility of falling in love with God. This poetic understanding is similar to the metaphor of a kiss: Falling in love is an experience that can be broken down chemically and psychologically, but it is not really absorbed until one has personally surrendered to it.

The traditional parochial school answer is that a sacrament is "an outward sign instituted by Christ to give grace." That is a concise answer, first offered by John Calvin. "A sign that gives grace" is another way of saying that a sacrament does what it says it does. The idea that sacraments are "instituted by Christ," however, can be misleading. In one sense each sacrament can be said to be derived from the ministry of Jesus, but it is not historically accurate to think of Jesus as having baptized, officiated at weddings, or ordained priests. Jesus did of course support marriage in his teachings, heal the sick and forgive sinners regularly, invite people to share in his kingdom, "confirm" faith wherever he found it, and call people to roles of leadership and service. The sacraments we celebrate today have their foundation in the example of Jesus, and in that sense he "instituted" them, but the number and structure of the sacraments has been determined through the long tradition of the church.

Sacraments as revelation

One of the most influential Catholic theologians of the last century, Karl Rahner, defined a sacrament as "that which reveals and conceals God." A sacrament *reveals* God because it communicates God's Spirit or grace in its ritual action and reception. It also *conceals* God because, like any symbol, a sacrament points to what is unseen. The God of Abraham revealed in a smoking brazier, the God of Moses met in a burning bush, the God of Mary encountered through an angel—each is the divine Presence mediated through a finite representative. As the evangelist says, no one has seen the face of God (John 4:12).

Perhaps the best way to illustrate what sacraments do is to say, as Rahner did, "Christ is the sacrament of God." Jesus is the face of God we can see. And in the same way, "The church is the sacrament of Christ." The church is the face of Christ that the world can still see through us. And then the church presents seven sacraments to make the divine encounter tangible for us. Jesus reveals God, the church reveals Jesus, and the sacraments concretize the revelation of the church. Each is a sacrament, or mediating sign, of the other.

The seven sacraments the church celebrates can be spoken of in three categories: sacraments of initiation, healing and vocation. The rest of this chapter concerns the initiating sacraments: baptism, confirmation and Eucharist.

The sacraments of initiation

The sacraments of initiation used to be one sacrament, or at least they were delivered in one encounter. If you've ever been to an Easter Vigil service where the Christian initiation of adults is celebrated, you've seen the restored rite similar to the way it was administered in the early church. Those who desire to join the church study for months or even years, praying and discerning in the process known as the Rite of Christian Initiation for Adults (RCIA). They arrive at Holy Saturday night as the elect, prepared to receive full initiation into the church. They have spent many Sundays attending the first part of Mass, called the Liturgy of the Word, and then leaving after the homily to continue their study of scripture and church teaching. At last their study and prayer and desire have brought them to Easter and the reception of the initiation sacraments. During the long and elaborate Vigil Mass, the elect sit with sponsoring members of the parish, participating in a ritual of light and scripture story. Finally they rise and approach the priest for baptism. The water is poured over of the head of each of the hopefuls—if the parish has a baptism pool, they may even experience full immersion as in the early church. Shortly after their baptism, they may be joined by others who have studied with them who also want to become members of the Catholic church. These others were baptized as Christians in other denominations, so they are not rebaptized. Instead, like the newly baptized, they stand and make a full profession of faith in the Catholic church

Next, the whole group—newly baptized and newly professed—approach for the sacrament of confirmation. They are anointed with the oil of chrism, which the church consecrates each year for this purpose. By this anointing, they are called to be witnesses to their faith in Christ. They are often given new names, which they have chosen to remind themselves of the new life they are called to live as disciples. And when the whole parish community rises to receive communion, these new Catholics lead the procession, receiving the body and blood of Christ for the first time as fully initiated members of the church.

Anyone who has become a Catholic as an adult in the recent past has likely been received into the church through the RCIA. This rite preserves the original sense of the three initiating sacraments being movements of a single symphony.

The order of the sacraments
It is possible to be confused by the sequence of the sacraments of initiation. Shouldn't it be baptism, Eucharist, and then confirmation? If this is your reaction, then you are acknowledging that you or someone you love is a "cradle Catholic," baptized as an infant. Cradle Catholics are generally baptized within the first year, receive First Eucharist (also called First Holy Communion) at age seven, and are often confirmed in their early teens.

They also receive the sacrament of reconciliation, also called penance or confession, before their First Communion. So they seem to get four initiating sacraments, and in a different order than those in the RCIA.

Historical accident has more to do with today's sequence of initiating sacraments than theology has. The sacrament scramble came about in this way. The early church certainly conferred the rites of initiation in the RCIA order: baptism, confirmation, Eucharist. Confession of sin would have been unnecessary, since baptism is the sacrament that frees one from all past sin. The elect were baptized by their local leaders, confirmed in their faith by the bishop and then, as full members, received the Eucharist, the holy food of the community.

And that was it, as sacraments go. The first century didn't have official rituals for other sacramental moments; that came later—in some cases, much later—in the church's history. (See Chapters Seven and Eight for more on the history of individual sacraments.) The twisting and separating of the sacraments of initiation came about gradually—and not without theological mayhem.

The first separation was the result of the availability of ministers. The normal minister of baptism was the local leader, who was available yearly for the Easter Vigil. But by the third century, the church had grown so much that the bishop could not be present yearly with every community under his care. So, in the Western church the confirmation of the faithful became a separate "moment," celebrated whenever the bishop was in town.

The fourth century saw more changes. Until then, baptism was seen as an adult decision, following years of discernment and preparation. Babies were baptized, but only as members of households where the adults were likewise embracing the faith. We can see how entire households were brought to faith in the story of Cornelius in Acts 10. But in the fourth century, controversy arose around the issue of original sin. A teacher named Pelagius believed that human nature was essentially good and that people could live lives free of sin if only they worked at it hard enough. Pelagius may have been an optimist, but he was also considered a heretic. Augustine condemned his teaching, insisting that human nature was essentially distorted by original sin and could not resist sin without the gift of divine grace. With a certain amount of passion, Augustine preached that all humans were condemned to eternal damnation but for the grace available in baptism. When parents heard that, they began to get their babies baptized immediately, rather than waiting for their children to become adults. With infant baptism becoming more and more the standard, confirmation gradually drifted later and later into a person's life, since the church couldn't exactly "confirm" the faith of someone who was pre-verbal.

In the mid-1500s, the Council of Trent tried to create a formal order for the reception of the early sacraments. It recommended baptism for infants, followed later by confession (well established as a sacrament by the Middle Ages), confirmation, and finally First Eucharist. That worked well until the twentieth century, when Pope Pius X had other ideas. In 1910 he lowered the age for the acceptance of Eucharist to "the age of reason," judged to be the age of seven. If seven-year-olds, the pope reasoned, could discern right from wrong and had a sense of personal sin, they should also share in the full reception of grace available to the adult.

Well, that sounds like a fair and good plan, except no such provision was made for earlier reception of confirmation. Eucharist now came *before* confirmation as a matter of course. And once the order of the sacraments got switched, their meaning was altered. Of what use was confirmation when a person was "in full communion" with the church already at age seven? Confirmation no longer seemed like a sacrament of initiation, since full initiation was gained as soon as one came to the Lord's Table. It became "a sacrament in search of a theology," according to some theologians, and some have considered it to be a sacrament of "coming of age," much like a Jewish *bar mitzvah*. Although the RCIA has restored the order of the sacraments of initiation for those who receive them as adults and some parishes are experimenting with confirming children at an earlier age, at this time the order remains for most cradle

Catholics as Pope Pius X rearranged it: baptism, Eucharist, confirmation.

Baptism: An invitation

Imagine that you have received an invitation in the mail, penned by the hand of some remarkable dignitary (the president, the pope, the world leader you most admire, or a celebrity you would love to meet). The invitation is not simply to a dinner but to join a very exclusive club. You are invited to rub shoulders with the giants of your generation. You will have personal access to the greatest minds, the creative talent, the cutting edge leadership that will shape the future of our world. You will not only make their acquaintance but be counted as one of their number. You will be among the movers and shakers!

The cost of this membership, as you anxiously scan the rest of the letter, turns out to be nothing. It's free! Well, wait a minute. It's not free. It costs nothing in dollars, but there are certain commitments that members must make. Anything, anything, you say. Then you read the fine print: "All members must die in order to gain full benefits within this organization." You throw the letter away. Another time, perhaps.

This may seem a poor ad for the sacrament of baptism, but it is only half the story. If you had not thrown the letter away so hastily, you would have read this part:

> The initial death of members will be immediately reimbursed with new life, free from all former debts and obligations, accompanied by strength and vigor not previously experienced, for the purpose of assisting the membership in its task of transforming the world and preparing a future of hope and promise for all.

Some of us would still decline the invitation, unwilling to face that "initial death." But a full appreciation of baptism includes understanding the full power of the symbol of water. What, after all, does water do?

Our sacrament of water

"How happy is our sacrament of water," church father Tertullian wrote in the second century. Water *is* a reason to celebrate. Water quenches thirst, refreshes the spirit, cleanses the body. It is synonymous with life because it provides rain for crops and replenishes our oceans. Water is the largest component of the human body. Without water, there is no life.

Water is also one of the most terrifying and destructive forces in nature. Water causes flooding, drowning, incredible destruction. And it doesn't take much water to kill; a person can drown on little more than a cup of it.

Finally, water is creative. Wending through its gradual courses, water carved out the majesty of the Grand Canyon and countless other remarkable landscapes with a gentle power that is observable only over millennia.

These aspects of water come into play when we speak of the sacrament of baptism: Water brings life, but it also brings death. Water is above all a gradual, creative force, transforming our lives in time, though we may not be aware of its power.

Baptism in its primary sense is about membership in the community of Christians. It is an invitation to new life within the Body of Christ, the church, but that new life is achieved at the cost of the old life. A New Testament letter quotes a Christian hymn: "If we have died with him, we will also live with him" (2 Timothy 2:11). The new life in Christ is available only to those who are willing to die. But die in what sense?

We have to die, fundamentally, to ourselves. "You must consider yourselves as dead to sin and alive to God in Christ Jesus," Paul teaches (Romans 6:11). We can't hang onto our false selves, that part of us drawn to concupiscence—the sin of wanting more and more, also called original sin. We have to let go of our (let's be honest) defective wills and surrender to God's perfect will. Surrender isn't easy, and it can feel exactly like a death. But paradoxically, for Christians it is the one sure way out of death and into authentic life.

Baptism is, then, the powerful sacrament of death and life. Through it, we are cleansed and purified of sin, free from its bonds and ultimately delivered from its bottom-line effect, which is death. Physically speaking, our bodies will still face death and decay. But the life that never ends, in the world that is to come, is open to us.

The cross, the white robe, the candle, the oil

All Catholic baptisms are performed using the trinitarian formula: "I baptize you in the name of the Father, and of the Son, and of the Holy Spirit." The Catholic church also recognizes any Christian baptism in which the trinitarian formula is used. The threefold sign of the cross during the rite accompanies a Christian from the moment of baptism and acceptance into the church.

The person baptized, whether infant or full-grown adult, wears a white gown at baptism to signify his or her newness in Christ. White is for purity, of course. It also represents membership in the assembly spoken of in the book of Revelation, those who "have washed their robes and made them white in the blood of the Lamb" (Revelation 7:14).

The baptism candle is a sign of "the light of Christ" that burns in the heart of every believer. At infant baptisms, the godparents, who speak in proxy for the child, hold the candle. At the Easter Vigil, the godparents or parish sponsors light the baptism candles from the flame of the Paschal Candle, the towering candle of Easter from which the entire assembly receives its fire during the ritual of light that begins the service. The burning candle is a reminder of the Pentecost fire and the gift of the Spirit.

In the case of adult baptism, oil is not administered, since it will be used shortly in the ritual of confirmation. Baptized infants, however, receive an anointing with oil to seal their faith, affirming the presence of the Holy Spirit who is present to them through their initiation. Oil was the mark used to sign kings, prophets and other leaders of the community. The word *Christ*, after all, is really a title signifying "anointed one." The signing with the oil implies that *we* are Christ—members of his Body, the church, and have become sacrament for a world hungry for the revelation of God.

111

But what if...?

People often wonder what happens to a baby who dies without baptism or an adult who dies before receiving the sacrament. Are such people excluded from the heavenly feast because of a technicality? But remember, God *chooses* to work through the sacraments but isn't *bound* by them. Exceptions to the rule are the providence of God. For example, take the case of the minister of the sacrament. Although a priest or ordained deacon is considered the ordinary minister of baptism, the church recognizes a valid baptism, in case of emergency or danger of death, when it's performed by a layperson. The person who does the baptism doesn't even have to be a Catholic or a Christian...or even a believer in God! So long as the baptism is performed in fulfillment of the wishes of the person in danger—or, in the case of an infant, according to the wish of the parent—that baptism is valid. The church, it is said, "supplies" the required faith.

But what if there's no water available? The church recognizes the pouring of any liquid that is available.

But what if no one's available, and the person is dying alone? What if the person wanted to be baptized, but was killed suddenly before he or she was able to communicate that intention to anyone? What if a morally good person who never heard of Jesus or set foot inside a church dies unevangelized by the gospel? The Council of Trent offered the concept of the "baptism of desire." This is a beautiful theological basket woven to defend God's power to supply whatever is needed in any emergency. According to the baptism of desire, any baptism that is desired is accomplished in the sight of God. Thus people who sought to live a good life and who die ignorant of the gospel are not condemned for what they did not know.

So don't worry about the what-ifs.

Somebody is going to bring up limbo, so we might as well deal with that, too. Augustine was very hot-headed about the necessity of baptism *or else,* and he frightened many a parent about the eternal loss of an unbaptized child's soul. He went so far as to say that an unbaptized child would certainly be consigned to the fires of hell. What this says about God's justice and mercy, of course, makes us cringe today. So medieval theologians softened the blow by proposing the existence of a state called limbo. Limbo was defined as a condition of being caught between earth and heaven (*not* between heaven and hell), in which an unbaptized person continued in a state of "natural happiness," though not enjoying the full presence of God.

Modern theology questions the underpinnings of this idea. The official teaching of the church today about limbo is...well, it's in limbo. It has not been officially revoked, but neither is it promoted. It is fair to say, as American theologian Richard McBrien does, that limbo "plays no role in contemporary Catholic theology."

Confirmation: Called to testify

Say you've been watching a trial on television for weeks. The prosecution has been hard on the defendant, and it looks like the accused doesn't have a chance. All along, the defense has been murmuring about the surprise witness that could upset the case and set this person free. At this point, everything rests on that one witness. Whatever he or she reveals or withholds will spell life or death for the accused. And then the day arrives at last. The surprise witness is called.

And that witness is *you.*

Surprise, indeed. What a responsibility! Well, that is the essential position of the Christian in the world. Humanity stands accused of sin—hard to contest—condemned to death for the gamut of injustices we perform. You, however, know something that could set people free: the freedom of the children of God revealed through the forgiveness of Jesus Christ. If only you will dare to speak out, the world would be saved.

The Advocate of the church is the Holy Spirit, and the Spirit is alive in every person of faith. We allow the Spirit to act when we surrender our will and allow the Spirit to act in us. But human freedom is a thing so sacred that even God will not trespass on it. If we choose to cling to our will and not permit the Spirit access to our lives, then the Spirit is stifled. It is as if we hold God's breath.

Confirmation is the sacrament by which we claim our responsibility to testify to the life of the Spirit in the world. We embrace the Spirit who dwells in us through our baptism and agree to be *apostles* for the truth, literally "those who are sent."

Shifting symbols

As we have noted, confirmation has gone through several theological and ritual mutations in its history. Originally, it was one sign within an overall sacramental ritual of initiation performed at the Easter Vigil. The event of baptism was not really distinguishable from the anointing—confirmation—that followed. Even in the signing with oil, both the local leader of the church, the pastor, and the bishop marked the newly baptized with the same chrism. There was a real unity of symbol and meaning in these two rituals of initiation.

By the ninth century, the custom of separating the event of confirmation from baptism led to further reflection on the meaning of the sacrament. Theologians began identifying the release of the Holy Spirit with the laying on of hands and the anointing with chrism, both conferred by the bishop. By the thirteenth century, Thomas Aquinas, the great Dominican theologian whose writings have defined much of the church's teachings well into the present time, was speaking of baptism as "Christian birth" and confirmation as the sacrament of "Christian growth." Still, confirmation was understood as a ritual of confirming the baptism of the believer in preparation for full reception into the sacramental life of the church through the Eucharist.

The Council of Trent listed the signs of confirmation in greater detail. First came the laying on of hands by the bishop, accompanied by a prayer for the gifts of the Holy Spirit. Next, the individuals were anointed with the chrism oil. Finally, the bishop struck a light blow to the cheek, along with saying the words "Peace be with you."

The blow to the cheek, which has since been dropped from the ritual, has been explained to many generations of Catholics as a reminder of the hardships that may befall a person who is faithful to the truth. The elimination of this gesture does, however, point to a shift in perception about the sacrament. Separated from the ritual of initiation, confirmation came to function as a sacrament of Christian maturity, preparing the confirmed to be a "soldier" in Christ's "army." Rather than a sacrament of initiation, it had become a sacrament of graduation and commissioning.

Confirmation today

Since the Second Vatican Council of the 1960s, the rite of confirmation has suffered from multiple personality disorder. The documents of the council called for a restored order for the sacraments of initiation for adults, and so the RCIA has gradually worked its way back into practice on the local level. In 1971, also as a result of the council, a revised Rite of Confirmation for children was published. (Actually, it was promulgated, which means it became official teaching the moment it was published.) The revised rite reaffirms the initial order of sacraments for children as well, preserving the practice of infant baptism while urging the preparation of children for "the fruitful preparation of the sacraments of Confirmation and Eucharist" (Apostolic Constitution on the Sacrament of Confirmation, n. 3). The document is explicit about the preferred order of baptism, confirmation and Eucharist, but it does not explain practically how this should be achieved. In the end, it gives permission for individual bishops' conferences to confirm children at a later time "for pastoral reasons." Standard practice has become the most compelling pastoral reason of all.

In most cases, then, confirmation remains a sacrament of Christian maturity for older children and a sacrament of initiation for adults. In the children's rite, the ordinary minister of confirmation is the bishop. In the case of adults, the power to administer the sacrament is delegated to the pastor when it is conferred as part of the RCIA.

Called by a new name

It has been the practice of those to be confirmed (called confirmands) to choose a new name at the time of their confirmation. The confirmation name has no civil status and is not meant to replace the person's current name. It is a Christian name that draws upon the patronage of a particular saint or biblical figure to accompany a person's journey in faith. (For more on patron saints, see the discussion of saints in Chapter Twelve.) Confirmation names are not an official element of the rite, but they capture the imagination of many who take seriously their commitment to testify to their faith. Those to be confirmed are urged to read the lives of the saints whose names they are considering and to meditate on the virtues of that person's life as inspiration for this new step in faith.

Eucharist: A celebration of thanks

The importance of food is something about which none of us needs to be convinced. Apart from being nourishment for our bodies, food is one of the primary elements of human celebration. A birthday cake, a wedding reception, a party "just because it's Friday," a special dinner for two—all highlight the way a shared meal has become the premiere human expression of our joy. When we gather to celebrate, there's almost always food on the table.

The gospels are full of stories about meals. It seems that Jesus was invited to a lot of parties: a wedding feast, dinners with the Pharisees, receptions at the homes of sinners, and of course there was the Passover meal he would share with his friends the night before he died. In fact, Jesus was so popular at parties that the elders of his day grumbled that he was "a glutton and a drunkard" (Matthew 11:19; Luke 7:34). Jesus also told a lot of stories about parties. He compared the reign of God to a banquet.

When Jesus sought a way to have his friends remember him, he didn't have to look far. Paul tells the story in his first letter to the Corinthians:

> The Lord Jesus on the night when he was betrayed took a loaf of bread, and when he had given thanks, he broke it and said, "This is my body that is for you. Do this in remembrance of me." In the same way he took the cup also, after supper, saying, "This cup is the new covenant in my blood. Do this, as often as you drink it, in remembrance of me." For as often as you eat this bread and drink the cup, you proclaim the

116

Lord's death until he comes.

The church calls this shared meal by the name of Eucharist, which means "to give thanks." We give thanks for the life of Jesus and also "proclaim his death," because through that death and subsequent resurrection we come to experience the love and compassion of God.

Bread and wine

The two elements of our Eucharist are bread, "which earth has given and human hands have made," and wine, "fruit of the vine and work of human hands," as the priest speaks of them during the Mass. These ordinary components—bread, wine, and the humble human labor that transformed them from wheat and grapes—are swept into the drama of salvation history and become the most vital way by which God is made known in the Christian world. God is as accessible to us as a shared meal set with the most common foods. Like the travelers going to Emmaus, we recognize Christ in the breaking of the bread (Luke 24:13–32).

Bread and wine were ordinary foods in the ancient Middle East. They are also miracle foods in the stories of the Bible. God sends manna or "bread from heaven," for the Israelites to gather each morning during their years in the desert (Exodus 16:4). The prophet Elisha multiplies loaves to feed the people during famine (2 Kings 4:42–44). Jesus multiplies loaves in all four gospel accounts. Bread may be common, but for many people, its abundant availability is an event quite uncommon.

In the same way, the story of the wedding at Cana reveals a new abundance to be found in wine. Water is turned to wine at Jesus' word and there is more than enough for all—and it is a far better "vintage" than can be appreciated by those already drunk on more worldly wine (John 2:1–11).

Real Presence

A pragmatic boy in religious education once raised his hand and asked, "So what do you *get* with Holy Communion? You said we get membership with baptism and the Holy Spirit with confirmation. But I don't see what we get with communion." One of his classmates looked at him with dismay. In a hushed voice, she replied, "You get Jesus!"

Yes, we get Jesus. The girl was correct. But just how we "get Jesus" has become one of the divisive issues of Christian history. It is sad that the sign of our great unity has become one of the most obvious examples of our disunity. In a nutshell, Catholics believe in the Real Presence, namely, that the bread and wine actually "become for us the body and blood of Jesus Christ." During the era of the Reformation, Protestant leaders were divided about this teaching. Some, such as Martin Luther and John Calvin, adhered to the idea of Real Presence, but others preferred an understanding of Eucharist as a memorial meal. John Zwingli, for instance, spoke of the Lord being truly present in the assembly but not in the elements of the meal.

The Catholic teaching has remained grounded in the idea of Real Presence. The official word, *transubstantiation*, is from Thomas Aquinas and means that the bread and wine themselves take on the *substance* of Christ's body and blood. This is where the difference between a sign and sacrament is significant. The bread and wine don't simply *remind* us of Christ. Christ is actually *present* in this food. As we incorporate this meal (in-corporate; literally, "take into our bodies"), we are also incorporated into the Body of Christ. In the most meaningful sense, we are what we eat: bread for the hungry, light of the world, word made flesh, sacrament for others. We "reveal and conceal" God within the testimony of our lives.

Catholic belief in the Real Presence is why all the consecrated wine is drunk at communion time and any leftover consecrated hosts, the unleavened bread wafers commonly used, are stored in the tabernacle. The tabernacle is the secured place of honor where the body of Christ is reserved until needed at another Mass or to bring to the sick. It is a reminder that Christ is perpetually present in his church, that is to say, among his disciples, as he promised.

Hunger

Karl Rahner observed that some things are understood not by grasping but by being grasped. This brings us back to the idea of a kiss, an act known best only in the experience. We've said so much about history and theology and ritual that we might forget what sacraments primarily are: more than words, more than signs, more than symbols. Talking about sacraments explains only the external realities. To go further, we have to let the sacraments reveal themselves.

One thing Eucharist reveals is the reality of our hunger. Monika Hellwig, an important lay theologian of our time, has made this observation by looking not only at the sacrament but also at the world. Hunger is the basic driving force of humanity. World history has been shaped by it; most people who have ever lived on this planet were consumed by the need to assuage it. In our fairly affluent society, we forget that most people of most generations didn't live as we do. Even most people alive right now are driven by the need to find enough food to eat, and their lives will revolve around that quest until they die. Hunger is one of the deepest realities of what it means to be human.

This is why it makes sense that God would choose to come to us, in every generation until the end of time, as food. God encounters us at the weakest and most vulnerable level of our lives. Our lives can be severed like a thread, and one vital thread that ties us to life is food. We are all people who hunger, and so our God comes to us as food.

A seat at the table

Baptism and confirmation are one-time-only initiating sacraments. Eucharist, however, is not only an initiating sacrament but available to us on a daily basis. Any Catholic who has received First Eucharist and is not bound by a state of serious sin can approach the communion table. (More in the next chapter about sin and healing.) Because we believe in the Real Presence of Christ in the Eucharist, the church asks that those who do not share that belief refrain from participating in this meal. The thinking is that unity cannot be achieved by imitating the ges-

119

tures of togetherness. In the Middle Eastern understanding of meal kinship, if you eat with us you become one with our family. Eucharist cannot be a fast-food option; it is a lifelong commitment to share with the community of faith all that you are.

Questions to Consider

1. Name a common or seemingly worthless thing that you value highly. What makes it valuable to you?

2. Give an example of destruction that you would consider to be "desecration." What kind of moments seem "consecrated," or imbued with holiness, to you?

3. Which definition of "sacrament" makes the most sense to you? Review the previous sections and highlight the terms or images that are most meaningful to you.

4. Think of an event in your life that may have "revealed and concealed God." Would you call that event a sacrament? Why or why not?

5. Describe the rites of the Easter Vigil, if you have seen them. Describe a baptism you may have observed—Catholic or Protestant, infant or adult. What made these events meaningful to the people who participated in them?

6. The invitation of baptism is to new life through death. In what concrete ways might you be asked to "die" to your present way of life?

7. How might confirmation call you to testify to your faith amidst your family, community or workplace?

8. If you have a confirmation name, explain its significance and why you chose it. If you don't have a confirmation name, consider which name you would choose today and why.

9. Name some people with whom you celebrate the good times of your life. How are these celebrations like and unlike the eucharistic meal?

10. In what places, events or people do you experience God as really present in your life? Describe the experience to the best of your ability.

Faith Response

1. Celebrate water! Go for a swim, take a long bath, drink deeply from a spring. Meditate on how water revives you, body and spirit.

2. Testimony is hard work. List the values you care most about and how you testify to your belief in them. (For example, taking care of the earth is a priority. Therefore you recycle, conserve energy, buy rainforest-friendly products.) Measure how well your testimony meets your values.

3. Share a special meal with people you care about. Reflect how, in the preparation of the food, the selection of the guests and the setting of the table, you create an event where celebration is fostered. Consider how your preparations make unity among your guests more likely.

4. Reflect on Monika Hellwig's idea that the Eucharist is related to the hunger of the world. How concretely might you feed that hunger? How might you involve some friends in your response?

Seven

Keeping Heart and Soul Together: Sacraments of Healing

We live in a remarkable world, full of beauty and promise. We enjoy wonderful relationships that bring love and happiness into our lives. Being alive is a miracle in itself, as we celebrate the wonder of what it means to be gifted with time and breath. Some days, we wake up to a room full of sunlight and can't help feeling grateful for the simple goodness of another day of living.

Sometimes.

At other times, human life is fraught with sadness, brokenness and pain. Things go wrong: with our world, with our relationships, with our bodies. Being human means taking life on its own fragile and changeable terms, "in sickness and in health, for richer, for poorer, until death...," as a kind of private pledge between body and spirit. Some days, it's hard to live, to be conscious, to deal with reality as it comes to us.

Two kinds of losses

Life is subject to two categories of losses: the kind we cause and the kind we cannot control. Certainly we are responsible for some of the trials in life. Our jealousies, for example, can lead to unpleasant scenes and awful silences. Our anger can ravage the peace in our homes. Our bitterness can crush the capacity for love in our relationships. Selfish decisions can result in lonely nights, and being unwilling to forgive can make our hearts like stone. Our sin, we can say in spiritual terms, generates much of the loss we suffer through the years.

But other losses come into our lives unbidden. Who looks for illness, accident, injury? Who cultivates aging, with its grad-

123

ual weakening and surrender of vigor? Who would not prevent the suffering or death of a loved one, if only it were possible?

Add to these the natural catastrophes that destroy whole populations with one blow—unfortunately referred to as "acts of God"—or the major movements of institutional evil, such as wars, terrorism and economic injustice. Then we realize there is a lot of hurt in our world that one individual cannot control.

The reality of loss and pain precipitates a crisis in every person, sooner or later. Religion was invented partly as a means of understanding what suffering and evil are all about—admittedly with an eye to controlling these fearful forces as much as possible. As we explored in Chapter One, early writers of the Hebrew story perceived that the original harmony intended by God was broken by the human desire for more. "Original greed," as we might call it, corrupts the human will so that sin has become the norm and not the exception in our lives.

But not everything that goes wrong in our lives can be directly attributed to our sin. Is cancer a divine response to a person's sinfulness? Does a person who dies young "deserve" it any more than a person who dies after ninety years? Does an earthquake in San Francisco spell out God's wrath for Californians? What about floods in the heartland of America, hurricanes in the southern states, wars in Europe, famine in Africa? Is God so very mad at all of us?

Job raises his hand
The leading authority on human loss is a fellow named Job. The biblical character Job is not an historical person. He is the hero of a folk tale that questions the idea that all human misfortune is the direct result of personal responsibility. The original folk tale of Job, found roughly at the beginning and end of the biblical book by that name, has been sliced open by later authors to insert several theological arguments about the meaning of suffering and the presence of evil in a person's life.

We have a metaphor for long-suffering people: "patient as Job." But in fact Job was not patient at all. He was, by God's own admission in the story, just about the most virtuous person who ever lived, guilty of nothing in particular. And when God allows the Accuser to "test" him with tragedy after tragedy, Job protests loudly, curses the day of his birth and demands an audience with God. In other words, his response is not pious resignation but a natural human reaction to injustice familiar to anyone who has ever suffered.

When Job's very religious friends come by to console him, they encourage him to confess the sin that—to their minds—has made God so intensely angry with him. Job refuses to admit to a sin he has not committed. When the sin-suffering connection is presented to him, he is like the over-bright child in the back of the class. He raises his hand in protest: "This answer is not true!"

Suffering, sin and the need for healing

The book of Job raises some serious questions about traditional religious answers to the gritty problems of sin and suffering. And if you sit down and read the book of Job, one of the longest books of the Bible, you will not find a direct answer to the questions it raises. It is "protest" literature that reminds religious-minded people that we do not have all the answers sewn up in our theology. Theology is, after all, our humble attempt to understand and explain God. God, on the other hand, reserves all divine explanations until the end of time.

In the meantime, the story of Job underlines the pervasive connection between suffering and sin. Both are "evil" to us, occasions of terrible harm. Though a disease or devastating storm may bear us no ill will in a personal sense, the harm that comes to us is not lessened by the fact that there is no malevolent force behind it.

Because suffering and sin are both dark forces in our lives, we can speak of a need to be healed of both of them. We have all experienced the need for bodily healing in times of sickness or injury. We also know the power of psychological healing, when our hearts are heavy and the comfort of a friend's presence helps to dispel the pain. In the same way, we can carry a burden of soul-sickness when we fail to love God, others or ourselves the way we should. That occasion of sin, too, can be lifted, and spiritual healing can awaken our love again.

125

Sacraments of healing: The touch of love

The church responds to the human need for healing in two sacramental moments. One is the sacrament of reconciliation, which is also called penance or confession. This is our sacrament of healing for the occasion of sin in our lives. The other is called the anointing of the sick and focuses on weaknesses of the body.

Of the seven sacraments, no two are as misunderstood and underused as these. Perhaps because we find it so hard to think of ourselves in terms of failure and weakness, many of us avoid both sacraments. Yet of all the sacraments, they can be the most personally enriching experiences of a Catholic's life. They are, relatively speaking, private sacraments. Though all rituals of the church are public acts involving the community of faith, healing sacraments are usually sought out because of a personal need of an individual and are celebrated in a lower key, often in smaller gatherings of family or even between the individual and a priest.

With so much need in our world for healing and liberation from pain, a new appreciation for these special sacraments is something to be hoped for. Have you ever felt cool hands on your face when you were burning with fever? That gentle touch of love is what the church intends to offer in these moments of healing.

Reconciliation: Restoring friendship

So you've done it again: You've argued with your spouse (parent, sibling, child or friend) and the silence now yawns between the two of you. The hot words or the cold season has gone on too long and the pain is becoming unbearable. You wish you could take back what you said, what you did, the whole thing. You wish you could unbreak a heart.

You know you were wrong. Okay, maybe there's some fault on the other side too, but that does not change the fact that *you* know that *you* were way out of line. Pride has kept you from making amends until now. Playing lawyer in your own defense is making things worse. You have to accept your own guilt in this. You wronged someone you love, and it wasn't pretty. You

126

are really and truly sorry.

But fear holds you back from saying the words you long to say. You're afraid, first of all, that it's too late. There may be no love left after all this silence. You are afraid, also, that the pain goes too deep. How will either side ever forget what has been said? You're afraid nothing will change. You were, after all, a rotten spouse (friend, sibling, child or friend) and you haven't changed. What's the point of saying you're sorry when you know in your heart that you're still the same person inside as the one who was wrong in the first place? You're afraid your loved one will reject your apology, hurl bitter words that will stab like knives. You are afraid, in the end, that the one you wronged will simply say "No" and close the door on your relationship. And where will hope be after that?

You summon up the nerve, go to the person you have hurt and clear your throat. "I'm so sorry " you begin, but already the arms are around you, tears of joy dampening your cheek.

"Thank you for coming" is all you hear, over and over. "I'm so glad you've come. I forgive you. I love you so much."

A sacrament of relationship

Human beings were created for relationship. One earlier catechism defined human existence this way: "God made me to know, love and serve him in this world and to be happy with him forever in the next." Using John's gospel definition that "God is love," we can say that Love needed a beloved in order to fulfill its purpose. God created us in order to share divine love and friendship. What could be more wonderful?

God knew right away that we needed others in order to be happy. "It is not good that the man should be alone" (Genesis 2:18). So male and female we were created, and in couples, families and communities, we continue to thrive. We need relationships for our happiness and well-being, but they are also fertile territory for anguish because of sin. Our selfish decisions will always tear the fabric that binds us to God and others. In the context of our selfish decisions, we also become alienated from our truest selves, which is as people made for love.

So it is possible to talk about sin as "the act or omission

127

that alienates us from God, from one another or from ourselves." The Greek word for *sin* that Paul uses means "missing the mark" or "deviating from the way." We can think of sin as what happens when an archer sends his arrow out in search of the bulls-eye but aims at the wrong object. There is no hope that he will hit the target. We miss the mark when we send out our love in search of assets instead of people, when we try to possess people with our love instead of supporting them, when we reject God's love in favor of becoming little tin gods in our own lives.

Reconciliation is a "sacrament of opportunity" in that it provides us with the occasion and the means to retrace the steps of our alienation and to take aim once again with corrected vision. This "repositioning" of ourselves suggests another Greek word: *metanoia* or conversion, which literally means "turning." The prophets repeat over and over in the Old Testament that all we have to do is turn to God and we will discover that God is waiting for us. Jesus makes this clear in the story of the Prodigal Son (Luke 15:11–32). It isn't necessary that we make the long journey home to God, only that we turn and stretch out our arms to the One who loves us and reaches out to us always.

The naming of the sacrament
This sacrament has undergone many name changes in its history. Jesus might have named it the "sacrament of forgiveness," because forgiveness was the business Jesus was in. In the gospels, Jesus goes about forgiving the sins of people who do not even ask for it. He forgives people in the act of healing their bodies, as if one thing led naturally to the other. On the cross Jesus forgives those who are killing him: "Father, forgive them for they do not know what they are doing" (Luke 23:34). He also reconciles a criminal on a neighboring cross as both of them are dying (Luke 23:39–43).

Early Christians considered the example of Jesus and employed the advice of James, who recommended, "Confess your sins to one another and pray for one another, that you may be healed" (James 5:16). From the time of the early church, those who fell into serious and public sin were required to make a public acknowledgment of contrition and perform an act of penance to make retribution for the sin. A thief, for example, had to admit his theft, restore what he had taken, and accept his penance from the bishop. It is no wonder that this ritual would have been known by the name penance, since the stress was on the public act of retribution.

It wasn't until the sixth century that private confession of sins to a priest, along with privately assigned acts of penance, entered into the rite of what became popularly known as confession. The emphasis shifted to the actual recitation of the litany of one's acts of uncharity. The theology of the sacrament shifted too, becoming a ritual of recognizing oneself as a sinner before God.

Since the Second Vatican Council, the sacrament has been known as reconciliation and the new name means a new emphasis in the rite. It is once again perceived as a sacrament with the accent on forgiveness (what God does) and not on sin (what we, regrettably, do.) This is not your grandmother's sacrament of confession, not the closed-curtain affair that television and Hollywood delight in parodying. The sacrament of reconciliation is a return to the spirit of what Jesus offered to those who cried out for his help along the streets of Galilee and Judea: an assurance that our sins are forgiven and healing is here.

The form of the rite

Reconciliation follows the four main steps that were a part of the earlier celebration of the rite: confession, contrition, satisfaction and absolution. Confession means an acknowledgment of wrongdoing. Contrition is showing "a lively sorrow for sin," as many were taught in parochial school—in other words, really meaning it when you say you're sorry. Satisfaction, or penance, is agreeing to perform some sign of "restoring what was lost" by sin, as in forgiving someone who has waited for your compassion or committing oneself to a more regular routine of prayer. And absolution is the priest's action, on behalf of the church, of accepting your contrition and formally assuring you of God's forgiveness.

129

Be clear on this: The *priest* does not forgive your sins, nor has God withheld forgiveness until you show up for the rite. When he accepts your apology, the priest represents the whole church, not just the "institutional" church but the entire Body of Christ. Since sin is the severing or injuring of a relationship, the priest, in accepting your contrition, stands in for the community you have wronged. He reminds you that Jesus is the Lamb of God who takes away the sin of the world. This moment is not unlike when you stand on the doorstep of one you have wronged and come to speak your words of sorrow for the pain you've caused. That person has long ago forgiven you the trespass—see how quickly those arms are around you? But still it was necessary for *you* to say those words, for *you* to come and receive the assurance of forgiveness and love. Sin is a crime against relationship, and only in relationship can it be healed.

What's new about reconciliation?

The changes in the ritual are more than cosmetic. For one thing, the box with the heavy curtain and all the rituals of anonymity are rapidly vanishing. You will still see confessional boxes in older churches because architectural furniture is hard to put out on the curb. Most churches, however, now have reconciliation rooms in which you can sit with the priest, face to face, and speak honestly about the circumstances of your life. (Some churches still retain the option of anonymity for people who find this change daunting.)

Older Catholics are accustomed to a rite that began with a formula of blessing ("Bless me, Father, for I have sinned...") followed by a rapid-fire list of personal offenses. In the new rite, Catholics are invited to begin by listening to a reading from scripture about the joy God takes in one returning sinner (Luke 15:7) or another suitable passage. Although many who experienced the old rite of confession might have a hard time thinking of it as a celebration, the accent now is on joy and homecoming.

After the scripture reading, the penitent is encouraged to consider ways in which he or she may have failed to love or to act with justice. Sometimes we may have a clear-cut sense of sin on our hearts ("I verbally abused my child because I was stressed out about money"; "I've been cheating on my spouse"). Often we will find ourselves involved in a pattern of injustice or lack of love that is harder to define by a particular act or two. It may be we've come to a place in life where we are ready to grow deeper in our relationships with God and with others. ("I realize my prayer life is only half-hearted. I want to learn to pray better." "I've never really forgiven my parents for the way they raised me, and I am ready now to let that anger go and free up the space in my heart for love.")

It is not recommended that you try to confess every injustice you've ever committed, unless this is your first confession and all of your sins are pretty serious. In general, people concentrate on one or two areas of their life in which they feel called to grow in love.

Then comes the time for that "lively sorrow for sin" known as contrition. After the confession of sin, Catholics used to recite a formal act of contrition, which is a memorized prayer that every generation has recited somewhat differently. If you know a version of that prayer, feel free to use it. If you don't, you may borrow the words of the Jesus Prayer, "Lord, have mercy on me, a sinner," or you can ask for forgiveness any way you know how. Some people are easily moved to tears, and such tears during confession *are* a lively sorrow for sin. Others will make do with words in a variety of ways, saying, "I'm sorry I have done wrong, and I ask for the grace to do better."

Following the expression of contrition, the priest may offer moral guidance or spiritual direction, such as asking you to reflect on a passage of scripture or to sit in quiet for a while and pray for a virtue you have admitted to lack. This may, in fact, be the penance he offers you. The penance is intended to be a support and encouragement to "go and sin no more;" it is not meant to be a punishment for "being bad." If you have admitted to treating your children harshly, for example, the penance will likely be to ask their forgiveness and to be especially gentle with them in the future.

At the end of the guidance and administration of penance, the priest will "absolve you of sin," using the familiar sign of the cross. The words of absolution are the only set formula for the ritual, and only the priest has to know them. All you have to do is say "Amen!" (*Amen* is Hebrew for "Let it be as you say.")

Communal celebrations of reconciliation

All sacraments of the church are intended to be celebrations by the whole community—public acts of worship of God and of witness to the faith we share. In the sacrament of reconciliation, we celebrate the gift of God's forgiveness and of our joyous restoration of friendship with God, with one another, and with our truest selves.

That is why the church encourages the communal celebration of reconciliation as well as the more private confession of sin we have just described. Many parishes celebrate reconciliation services during Advent and Lent. During these services, the selections of music and scripture readings remind us of the great loving mercy of God. We express a spirit of confidence in God's forgiveness and gratitude for the generous gift of divine love. There may be time for general intercessions, which are brief prayers of petition from among the community, or perhaps a time of shared silent prayer. An examination of conscience may be read aloud or available for individual use. This usually consists of a series of questions to ask yourself about the state of your relationship with God and others.

Usually toward the end of a reconciliation service, there will be an opportunity for individual confession of sins. Several priests will be available in private areas within the church and you may go to speak with one if you wish. Music is often played to ensure the privacy of these confessions. Some people prefer to sit and meditate during this time or to leave at the end of the communal aspect of the celebration.

How often should you receive this sacrament?

Older generations of Catholics were taught they had to receive the sacrament of reconciliation before receiving the Eucharist. This might mean, for someone who went to daily Mass, that he or she would go to confession every day! This understanding of the sacrament came from a deep reverence for the Eucharist and a strong sense of personal sin. While it is good to feel reverence for the Eucharist and to awaken to the realities of sin in our lives, it isn't necessary to receive the one sacrament in order to prepare for the other, unless you are conscious of serious sin.

Serious sin, it should be noted, is not measured by how bad you feel about it. Arguing with a friend may make you feel terrible, but that should not keep you from the Eucharist, which is in itself a sacrament that "makes our peace with God," as we say at Mass (Eucharistic Prayer III). The grace of the sacrament of the Eucharist is sufficient for the minor states of sin in which we always find ourselves. Serious sin, as the church defines it, is a departure from the will of God in a matter of gravity, deliberated over in advance, and freely chosen with full understanding that this action would separate you from the will of God. This type of sin is hardly something you do every day. It would be in the category of deliberating over the murder of a neighbor, in full knowledge that it would be a very serious violation of God's command not to kill, and then going out and committing the act.

For the most part, we spend our lives entangled in situations of lesser sins that become grave in our lives when they become part of a pattern. While not "serious" enough to separate us entirely from relationship with God, they are serious enough not to be taken lightly or considered irrelevant. Whenever you become aware of these patterns in your life, especially in a situation or relationship where sin emerges completely unmasked, it is certainly time to approach the sacrament of reconciliation.

Otherwise, as a general rule, a frank examination of conscience and reflection on your life should be a regular part of your spiritual health care. Receiving the sacrament of reconciliation once a year during the Lenten season, which is naturally geared toward personal scrutiny, or semi-annually—perhaps at Christmas and at Easter—is a good idea for anyone not currently struggling with a critical situation of sin.

Anointing: Facing human limits

A community is disrupted by an earthquake that devastates the city and destroys homes and lives. Fear and desolation set in as the people survey the rubble and mourn their losses. Can there ever be peace or security after this hour?

A woman waits in a hospital room before surgery. She knows a hip replacement is routine for people of her age, but still she is worried about how her life may change after the operation. Will she be able to walk all right? Will there be pain? Will she lose her independence?

A father has watched his child fighting a chronic illness for years, and even though the doctors do not think this current bout of fever is life-threatening the father wants to marshal some force against what is harming this young life.

A young woman is huddled in her apartment, alone. Last month a co-worker raped her, and her sense of herself has been violated, along with her body. Gradually she has been losing contact with her feelings, her friends, her family. Though she has made an appointment to see a therapist to talk about the trauma, still as a Catholic she longs to talk to someone who shares her faith about her shame, horror and rage. Does God understand her anguish?

Which of these people should seek the sacrament of anointing? All of them!

Healing in the gospels

The anointing of the sick is a "body sacrament," as personal and visceral as any encounter can be. It has its roots in the healing ministry of Jesus, who addressed the whole person: body, mind and spirit. Jesus wasn't out there giving just spiritual direction in the towns between Galilee and Jerusalem. He saw the suffering of human beings in various states of distress: "Heal my daughter!" "My son is possessed by a demon!" "Lord, that I might see!" A woman who had been bleeding for twelve years didn't even ask; she just grabbed him by the cloak as he passed, hoping for a miracle (Mark 5:25–29; Matthew 9:20–22; Luke 8:43–48). Lepers came at him in groups, begging to be restored to health and to return to the community. The mentally ill followed after him, screaming their recognition of his power. People brought their sick and injured friends to Jesus and lay them at his feet. In all these instances Jesus responded with a touch, a word and the power to heal and restore. He never said no. No matter how sick or injured or disabled the people were, Jesus touched them, spoke with them and healed them. Three times in the gospels Jesus even restored the dead to life (Mark 5:38–42; Luke 7:11–15; John 11:1–44).

The sacrament of the sick

The early church readily took up the ministry of healing. Even during the time of Jesus, the disciples went out in pairs to accomplish marvels in his name. Peter in particular goes on to become a renowned healer; people lay their sick on the streets so that his shadow might fall on them as he passes by (Acts 5:15). Healing was one of the gifts of the Spirit that Paul catalogues. The letter of James speaks about how the community should respond to an occasion of illness:

> Are any among you sick? They should call for the elders of the church and have them pray over them, anointing them with oil in the name of the Lord. The prayer of faith will save the sick, and the Lord will raise them up; and anyone who has committed sins will be forgiven.
>
> —James 5:14–15

From the first century, then, the practice of anointing the sick seems to have been celebrated very much as it is today.

The sacraments administered in emergency or terminal situations have been referred to as "last rites." They include reconciliation, anointing of the sick and Eucharist. In the case of a death that has been long-awaited, the last rites would normally involve only the Eucharist, in this case called Viaticum, which means "with you on the way," a spiritual food for the journey. Prayers that accompany these rites provide comfort and encouragement to the person who is about to take the last great journey of faith, as well as to those who are present at the time.

Older Catholics may use the term *extreme unction,* which

135

means "last anointing," when referring to the sacrament of the sick. Both the terms "last rights" and "last anointing" reflect an understanding of the sacrament as intended only for those who are close to death. Because of this, the sacrament of anointing of the sick fell into rare use over time, becoming identified with approaching death. Many older Catholics today are still reluctant to ask for an anointing because they were taught that it is reserved for those in the last hours of life. But the church now emphasizes that the sacrament is for anyone who is hurting, not just for those facing imminent death.

What happens in an anointing?
Because of the use of the oil of the sick, one of the oils consecrated by the church for sacramental use, we are reminded in this sacrament of the use of oil in baptism, confirmation and holy orders (for more on holy orders, see Chapter Eight). In these sacraments, oil is used to commission a person to testify to his or her faith in Christ. In a very real way, the person who seeks an anointing in sickness is also receiving a commission. The person in need of healing testifies in the midst of family and friends that faith in Christ is the center of his or her life and that nothing can change that. As Paul wrote:

> Who will separate us from the love of Christ? Will hardship, or distress, or persecution, or famine, or nakedness, or peril, or sword? ...No, in all these things we are more than conquerors through him who loved us. For I am convinced that neither death, nor life, nor angels, nor rulers, nor things present, nor things to come, nor powers, nor height, nor depth, nor anything else in all creation, will be able to separate us from the love of God in Christ Jesus our Lord.
> —Romans 8:35, 37–39

When the community gathers, the priest greets and welcomes them, much as he does at the beginning of Mass. He offers prayers and shares a scripture passage or two. He may give a brief reflection and lead the community in prayer of intercession, if circumstances permit.

Then comes the rite of anointing. The priest lays hands on the head of the one to be blessed and prays for the gift of healing. He offers a prayer of thanks for the holy oils of blessing. Then he anoints the person's head with oil and possibly the hands as well. The laying on of hands, the blessing and the signing with the oil comprise the rite of anointing. Depending on the circumstances, the gathered faithful may continue with the celebration of the Mass, including the reception of the Eucharist, or the rite may end with the anointing.

There is no limit to the number of times you may request this sacrament. You do not have to be facing death in order to approach a priest for an anointing. If you have a desire for the prayer of the church on behalf of your health, the sacrament of the anointing of the sick is available for you.

Communal celebrations of healing

Let's go back to the situation of the city that has been devastated by an earthquake. Certainly, any community can have its confidence shaken and spirit crushed by a natural disaster. Just as bodies can suffer harm, so too a community can suffer the physical, psychological and spiritual effects of disaster and be in need of healing.

Healing services can go a long way to bring a community together to find peace and consolation. Like reconciliation services, a healing service is a community form of the more private sacrament, and it may include the opportunity for individual members to come forward for a personal anointing if they so choose. A city that has suffered a terrorist attack, an epidemic of illness, or other tragedy may find this opportunity to gather and pray with the victims and their families a powerful experience of healing and hope.

Of course, not all instances of human suffering are appropriate for a communal service of healing. As in the circumstance of the woman who was violated, she may want the consolation of the sacrament with only a close friend or family member to support her.

Healing and wholeness

Both sin and sickness can be occasions of crisis and alienation. We may become alienated from God, from one another, or from ourselves and long for a remedy to help us rejoin the human family. The sacraments of healing can be part of our movement toward regaining that unity and give us courage to go forward in hope toward what God has prepared for us.

Questions to Consider

1. Describe an occasion in your life when you felt a need for healing. To whom did you go for that healing? What happened?

2. What losses have you experienced that were within your control or came as a direct result of your decisions? Name some losses you have suffered that were beyond your control.

3. Consider Job's rejection of the religious answers of his day about the meaning of human suffering. When have you felt that your experience did not match the religious answers you had been taught? How do you bridge the gap between your experience of suffering and the sometimes inadequate religious responses you hear?

4. What do you think is the connection, if any, between the presence of suffering and sin in the world? How would you describe the relationship between those two factors?

5. Recall an experience of physical healing you have had. Also recall an experience of psychological healing you may have had, as when a friend has lifted the burden on your heart. How are these events the same? What makes them different?

6. Think of a person who has forgiven you a great offense. How did it make you feel? To whom have you offered similar forgiveness? What have these occasions taught you about the nature of forgiveness and its ability to heal?

7. Which of your relationships are most frequently in need of mending? What are the "relational tools" you use to mend them?

8. What factor makes you most reluctant to approach the sacrament of reconciliation? What makes you most eager to do so?

9. Looking back, when could you have benefited from a sacrament of healing and anointing? Who among your family and friends is presently in need of healing?

10. Describe how can you be a healer and reconciler within your community.

Faith Response

1. Is there someone you haven't forgiven, living or deceased, who may still be waiting for your forgiveness? Is there someone, living or deceased, you have wronged, from whom you need to seek forgiveness? Create your own ritual of forgiveness and seek the reconciliation that is needed. Break some chains and free some prisoners.

2. Name a circumstance in your life that needs healing. Prayerfully consider what real healing would entail. Seek the companionship of a friend or spiritual director and explore together a route toward healing.

3. Reflect upon the agenda for healing in our world: the ravaging of our planet, the hostility between nations or classes of people, misunderstandings between women and men, or other concerns important to you. How can you make a difference regarding these or other issues? Commit yourself to be a healer and reconciler within your family or community.

4. Pray regularly for the communities you see in the news that suffer from the effects of human or natural disaster. Pray for individuals you know who suffer from bodily or spiritual need. Pray for the release of the gift of healing upon those who cry out for it every day.

Eight

People of Love and Commitment: Sacraments of Vocation

Ask any child: "What do you want to be when you grow up?" The answers are enthusiastic and not at all conservative: "I want to be a singer!" "I'm going to be a space traveler!" "I'm going to be a famous writer and be read all over the world!" Ask students at a university what they dream about and the results often come down to a disheartening monotone: "I'm going to make a lot of money." Ask adults in our society what they hope to accomplish in life and the response may sound even more faint-hearted: "I just want to meet my obligations" or "I want to avoid failure and get through each day."

We start out in life with big dreams, but our window on the world and its possibilities often grows smaller as we grow older. Some would say we become realistic; others say we simply grow disillusioned. The world, our relationships and our potential don't live up to our ideals, and we may lose sight of the vision we once held so brightly. Much of the time, we let arbitrary or mundane factors shape the direction of our lives: "The economy looked good for business, so I studied accounting." "My heart was in teaching, but the money was in computer science." "I wanted to marry someone who shared my values, but in the end I married the one who was available at the time I was ready." "I wanted to have children, but it never seemed like a good time to start a family."

Called to freedom, created for love

We often find ourselves feeling not in control of the course our lives take. We may feel pressured to surrender the gift of our free will in order to meet the expectations of parents, mentors or the culture in which we live. "Keeping up with the Joneses" is a consciousness that creeps in when we aren't looking. "What will the neighbors think?" is more than just a joke in the background of our decision making. We find ourselves concerned about appearances and meeting certain standards, even when we don't entirely agree with them. How many people sigh and quote favorable statistics or make excuses based on cliches they've heard: "Well, I didn't want to take on the extra work, but we owe it to our kids to send them to the best schools." "I wanted to go to the Peace Corps for a year, but given the job market it was more realistic to get in on the ground floor of my career right away." "I'm not comfortable with the way this company makes its money, but I have bills to pay."

An old prophecy, however, reminds us that God's call is always away from slavery and toward freedom: "Out of Egypt I called my son" (Hosea 11:1). The God who once saved the chosen people from Pharaoh's slavery also redeems us from our debt to sin and its bondage. To somehow take on that yoke again is, to say the least, not a grateful response to the call of discipleship. We are invited to experience "the freedom of the children of God" (Romans 8:21) and not to take up the chains of the world and its servitude again.

We were created not to meet the world's obligations but to respond freely and fully to the call of love that the One who called us into being expresses in our lives. God calls out from the heart of prophecy, "I have loved you with an everlasting love" (Jeremiah 31:3). Though born of love and called God's "beloved," we sacrifice our identity when we choose a vocation that does not permit us to express that love with all our heart.

Discerning your vocation

"Vocation" means a summons or call. For some people, that call has been explicit all life long in an early inclination toward science and discovery, for example, or a natural ability to paint. For others, the call may be implicit; they may feel a great capacity toward caring for others but not a clear sense of how to translate that into a life's work. If you are entirely at sea concerning your vocation, you might want to consider spiritual direction. Many priests and religious serve as spiritual directors, and many lay people are also trained or naturally gifted to assist others in the quest for self-knowledge. A parish or diocesan office may be able to provide you with a list of people to contact.

Whether you seek spiritual direction or pursue a clarification of your vocation in a less formal way, you will find that prayer is an indispensable part of the process. Placing yourself trustingly in God's care, you pray for divine guidance. You might not be knocked off your feet, as Paul was, as a sign of your calling. Rather, like most of us, you will find God's will for you in reflection and prayer, in seeking advice, and in the courage that comes with practicing your faith.

During the process of discernment, discuss your vocation ideas with a friend who shares your faith and values. Discerning the movement of the Spirit in our lives has always been a task of the community of faith. Faith sharing, one-on-one or in a small group that meets regularly for the task of "spiritual conversation," is a valuable way to see the road down which God may be leading you.

Some of us like to pray for clear signs to aid in our discernment. Others pray simply for clarity, a feeling of peace, or the courage to do what has already been made known to them.

Our common vocation

Through our baptism, all of us share one vocation: to follow Christ. In that sense, we can call baptism the first and ultimate sacrament of vocation. The common call of all God's people is "to do justice, to love kindness, and to walk humbly with your God" (Micah 6:8).

Some of us who went to parochial school a generation ago can recall when "having a vocation" was defined narrowly as a divine call to be a priest or a religious sister or brother in the service of the church. Marriage was also acknowledged as a call from God, but it did not receive the kind of preparation and discernment that a vocation to church ministry enjoyed.

The fact is that the two official sacraments of vocation, matrimony and holy orders, do not cover the full range of pos-

143

sibilities for God's call in our lives. Like the other sacraments, they are particular moments in the life of grace that the church has lifted up to testify to the work of God's Spirit among us. But these moments do not limit where God is at work in our hearts, and they do not encompass the boundaries of God's presence in our world.

We might dream a little about other moments in our lives that outline our purpose in a clear and particular way. What about a sacrament of parenthood at the birth of a child? What about a sacramental enrollment into the status of widowhood? In times past, the church did recognize new states in life as a deepening and defining of our primary allegiance to Christ. As we noted in Chapter Six, the church *at this time* recognizes seven official sacramental moments. But these are intended to direct us to the many, many moments in our lives when the Spirit of God is ordaining us in a particular circumstance to surrender to God's loving purpose.

If any sacrament can be said to consecrate each one of us to God's holy will, that sacrament is baptism. It is the only "vocational" sacrament that one needs in order to participate in God's call and desire for our lives.

Matrimony: Called to faithful love

Most people in our culture get married sooner or later. Marriage is the norm and has become for many a rite of passage into adulthood. Some marriages last a long time. Other marriages see a couple through a particular stage of life, but the couple fails to make the transitions necessary as they grow and change and the marriage fails. Still, most couples believe when they get married that their relationship has what it takes to survive and will last a lifetime.

The church offers its members the opportunity to consider marriage in the same way we consider all of life's actions and decisions: as a testimony to our faith in Christ. The call to matrimony is a commission to witness, through a life of fidelity, love and service, to the enduring love of Christ. Christian marriage is not an act to be undertaken lightly. Seen through the lens of vocation, it is not simply a pledge to take on a partner

144

and companion for life. It is much more than being in love and wanting to live together legally. Since Catholics believe that common things hold sacred realities, we believe that marriage is a call to the couple to reveal God's love to each other and to the world.

Better together

In the book of Genesis, the first couple was joined together to become "one flesh." The man declares upon encountering the woman, "This at last is bone of my bones, and flesh of my flesh" (2:23). Each married partner takes on a new identity in the reality of the other. The couple can no longer live only for themselves but exist now in loving, faithful companionship with each other. Their sexual union incarnates the reality of the spiritual union that is manifest between them. They are united: body, heart, spirit and life.

The marriage bond is a holy matter for Catholics. The church takes the union of two people so seriously that it considers the official ministers of the sacrament of matrimony to be the couple themselves. The priest is present as the church's witness and also offers a blessing in the name of the church. And though the ritual of marriage, or nuptial rite, that ratifies the union usually takes place in a church, the physical consummation of the marriage is a critical element of the union, according to the law of the church.

In the mutual surrender of two lives, sexual desire finds its fulfillment. The tenderness of human passion nurtures the marriage bond. The couple's willingness to share their love with children and to nurture and protect them is a sign of the couple's openness to God's good gifts.

Two people who choose to consecrate their love in matrimony should agree that their commitment to each other makes them better people than before. Less inclined toward selfishness and more willing to sacrifice for the sake of the other, married people find within the natural rhythms of shared living an antidote to the often narcissistic individualism of our society. They learn to give and not only to acquire. They create, through the refining lessons of love, what we call the domestic church; that is, their home becomes the primary faith center of their lives.

For those who enter into it with a sense of vocation, marriage can become the way of discipleship. Fidelity, hope and love blossom between spouses and among families. The fruits of the Holy Spirit—love, joy, peace, patience, kindness, generosity, faithfulness, gentleness and self-control—flourish as testimony to the presence of Christ in their home.

Paul has in 1 Corinthians the preeminent words on the subject of love. Those who have spent their lives in the shared struggle to grow in love know exactly what he's talking about:

> Love is patient; love is kind; love is not envious or boastful or arrogant or rude. It does not insist on its own way; it is not irritable or resentful; it does not rejoice in wrongdoing, but rejoices in the truth. It bears all things, believes all things, hopes all things, endures all things. Love never ends.
>
> —1 Corinthians 13:4–8

The testimony of marriage

The marriage ceremony employs many symbols that witness to the faith of the couple. Local custom and aesthetic sensibility will shape certain outward aspects of the wedding, but the nuptial rite itself contains the kernel of all Catholic worship: the reading of scripture, the conferral of the sacrament, general intercessions and a final blessing.

The rite of marriage begins when the priest calls upon the couple to publicly express their intentions. Both persons must agree that they are present by free choice, that they intend fidelity to their spouse and that they accept the sacrament as a lifelong commitment. They will also be asked if they are open to the gift of children and the responsibility of their formation in the faith. (For older couples past the time of childbearing, this question is omitted.) Following these questions, the bride and groom make their promises to each other and exchange rings. The rite ends with the church's blessing.

Although it's easy to focus on the wedding ceremony itself as the sacrament, the real sacramental quality of a marriage is achieved and known only through time. Couples who are faith-

146

ful to their vocation not only grow closer in tenderness and concern for one another but become an inspiration and consolation to those who share in their lives. Together the couple attains the courage to become people of justice and hope within their communities. They open their homes and share their resources with others. The love they create together spills over into their wider families, workplaces, neighborhood and community. Their children mirror the values they observe and are taught. The atmosphere of goodness permeating such homes becomes an overwhelming testimony and source of encouragement for others who seek to live by gospel standards.

Together, a couple joined in a sacramental bond grow stronger in their faith and more effective in their Christian life than they could have become alone. Their vocation to love and be at the service of the other is apparent to all who are blessed by their friendship.

Marriage and church law

The marriage between two Catholics is a straightforward matter, canonically speaking. Such a marriage contracted between two faithful members of the church is understood to be a lifelong commitment. There is no natural impediment to such a marriage, which means that no condition exists to prevent or challenge its validity. The sacramental bond between two Catholics with no extenuating impediment, such as a prior marriage or kinship, cannot be dissolved. After a period of waiting and preparation, and under the guidance of a priest, deacon or pastoral team, many couples choose to be married within a nuptial Mass, a marriage rite celebrated within the context of the Eucharist.

In the last century, though, the trend has moved in the direction of many Catholics marrying someone who is not a member of the Catholic church. Since Vatican II and the success of the ecumenical and interfaith movements (the attempt to dialogue with and understand Christians of other denominations or people of other religions), the Catholic church has seen that interdenominational and interfaith marriages can lead to faith-filled and holy unions.

147

Still, according to canon law, an impediment to marriage exists when a Catholic intends to marry someone who is not Catholic. If the intended spouse is baptized but not Catholic, the canonical impediment to the marriage is known as the prohibition against "mixed marriages." The prohibition is commonly dispensed or waived so long as the Catholic member promises to raise any children of the union within the faith. The choice then remains to celebrate the sacrament within a nuptial Mass or to celebrate the nuptial rite by itself. Since non-Catholics are not invited to share in the sacrament of Eucharist (see Chapter Six), it is a courtesy to the non-Catholic spouse and his or her family not to place them in a worship environment that may be alien or awkward for them. Many couples in this situation therefore choose to celebrate their marriage as an independent nuptial rite.

When a Catholic chooses to enter into a union with someone who is not of the Christian faith, an unbaptized person, the canonical impediment is known as the prohibition of "disparity of cult." This law is also commonly dispensed after the same assurances mentioned above are given, and a special rite for celebrating marriage between a Catholic and an unbaptized person is used. If you have a question about a particular situation, you may contact a priest or call the chancery office of your diocese.

Annulment

Catholic teaching makes clear that a valid sacramental marriage cannot be dissolved. Therefore a Catholic may not remarry except in the event of a spouse's death. Some Catholics may find it necessary to separate from a spouse for critical, valid and extenuating reasons, but separation from a spouse does not affect a Catholic's status within the church. Even a civil divorce does not undo the sacramental marriage bond or affect a Catholic's standing within the church.

Some divorced Catholics, however, may want to remarry. If it is determined that a valid sacramental marriage has already taken place, a second marriage within the church is not possible. However, under certain circumstances, it may be possible to receive an annulment, which is a formal judgment rendered by the church that the original marriage was invalid according to the terms of sacramental marriage. The process of annulment consists of a review of the circumstances of the first marriage to determine its validity. Some factors that can lead to an annulment are lack of free consent on the part of one of the parties who contracted the marriage, the intent of one party to engage in a trial marriage rather than a lifelong bond, or the psychological inability of one or both partners to commit to a sacramental marriage.

A person who is granted an annulment is then free to marry within the church. The church offers no judgment on the fruitfulness of the first union for the couple involved nor does an annulment affect in any way the legitimacy of children. An annulment is a judgment by the church only about the sacramental validity of the marriage.

A vocation to the church

We have talked about baptism as the purest sacrament of vocation, since it expresses our common call to follow Christ. There are two vocational sacraments that define the primary relationship through which to answer that call. Matrimony, as we have just seen, is one of them, whereby people find that a relationship to spouse and family is the best way to respond to Christian discipleship. For others, the call to serve others may be answered through a commitment to the church at large through religious life or priesthood.

Priesthood is the only vocation to the service of the church that is celebrated as a sacramental moment, called holy orders. The call to live in a religious community as a sister or brother is expressed through a profession of vows (traditionally poverty, chastity and obedience) but is not considered a formal sacrament. The role of the priest has seen great evolution over history, and the dust of change has certainly not settled in our own times. The reforms of Vatican II—in theology, liturgy and the church's self-understanding in the modern world—have left their mark on the role of its ordained leadership.

So what does it mean to be a priest? In a historical sense, the priest of ancient times was a mediator between God and humanity. It was the priest who led the cultic rituals and sacrifices that bound a people to their gods and kept the cosmic peace. In the Letter to the Hebrews in the New Testament, Jesus Christ is described as the perfect and final high priest for those who follow him, rendering the multiple ritual sacrifices of old unnecessary. Since Christ alone mediates the reconciliation of heaven and earth, the main role of the ancient cultic priesthood has essentially been retired.

As the church teaches, we all share in the priesthood of Christ through our baptism. Those who believe in Christ are a nation of priests, a holy people consecrated to God's service. But the *ordained* priest is at the service of the common priesthood of all believers. He is, we can say, "a priest to the priests." Paul writes about how the many parts of the body help each other. Certain parts of the body have a special relationship, such as the eye and the hand, for example. Hand-eye coordination allows us to accomplish extraordinary things. The relationship of the priest to the other members of the church, known as the laity, is like that.

The primary responsibility of the priest is to proclaim the good news of Jesus Christ, and the Sunday homily during Mass is when that proclamation is made most directly to the assembly as a whole. The administration of the sacraments is reserved to the priest, with the exceptions we have indicated earlier (baptism, confirmation, matrimony—all under prescribed conditions). Service at the Table of the Lord in the Eucharist is the most evident and central aspect of the priest's vocation. In the Eucharist, the good news of Jesus is offered to God's holy people in word and in sacrament.

Serving God's people

Much of what we have said about the vocation to marriage could also be said about the call to holy orders. Orders, too, is an invitation to love, to testify to the presence of Christ in the world. Holy orders is a vocation directed toward fidelity, hope and love within a shared life—though in holy orders the life is shared between the ordained person and the community of God's people. The call to orders should make a better person of the one who answers the summons—freer to grow, serve and share the blessings and talents that God has given him. As with marriage, a vocation to the priesthood cannot be forced but must be entered into freely and with joy.

People generally equate holy orders with the call to priesthood. Though that is most often the form the call takes, there are actually three stations to which one can be ordained: as a deacon, a priest or a bishop. (One is *appointed* to become a cardinal and *elected* as pope.) Deacons serve the diocese in the task of preaching and in works of charity. They may also baptize, officiate at marriages and lead funeral services. A deacon may be married or celibate.

Since the eleventh century, the Roman Catholic priesthood has been reserved to celibate men. Diocesan priests are ordained for a particular diocese and serve at the appointment of and in cooperation with the local bishop. Priests may also belong to religious orders (see the section on consecrated life) and serve at the discretion of the superior of their communities with the permission of the local bishop.

Bishops are ordained by other bishops from among ordained priests. A bishop's role is to serve the church as a teacher and shepherd of his diocese. He works in communion with his fellow bishops in a conference, such as the United States Conference of Catholic Bishops (USCCB), headquartered in Washington, D.C. The conferences of bishops worldwide exercise the teaching authority of the church, the magisterium, together with the pope, who is the bishop of Rome.

Symbols of service

During the rite of holy orders, the bishop confers authority on a candidate for deaconate or priesthood through the laying on of hands. A deacon receives the book of the gospels as a symbol of his ministry to preach the good news. This will become the central work of his vocation. Some deacons, however, are transitional, or temporary, deacons, who will later be ordained as priests. At the ordination of a priest, the newly ordained receives the paten and chalice as signs of his role as the one who presides at the eucharistic celebration. The paten is a plate upon which the bread to be consecrated is placed; the chalice is the cup that holds the wine.

A priest is also anointed with the oil of chrism. This is a sign of the outpouring of the gifts of the Holy Spirit needed to fulfill his vocation of service to the whole church.

A bishop will likewise be anointed with chrism at his ordination. During the prayer of consecration of a bishop, the book of the gospels is held open above the candidate's head, signifying the authority of God's word over his life. He is given a ring as a sign of his fidelity to the church. A hat and staff, called a miter and a crosier, are bestowed on him—signs that he is called to be both leader and shepherd to God's people.

Consecrated life

Not everyone who has a desire to serve the church is called to ordination. Some feel a summons to religious, or consecrated, life. They join together in new "families" as sisters or brothers, living a shared life of celibacy in community. Religious communities of women and men each have a charism, or gift, that marks their congregation or order for special service. The Franciscan community, for example, has a charism for poverty, choosing to live humbly and in direct service to the poor. The Paulists feel a particular call to preach the gospel using the modes of contemporary culture: film, radio, publishing and the Internet. Sisters of Mercy have a charism to show compassion for those who are suffering, and so their order has come to be identified with hospitals and the care of the destitute. Other religious communities have a charism to teach or work in foreign missions. Some live a life of cloistered contemplation and prayer in monasteries as monks or nuns.

Some religious may not feel called to community life but rather to dedicated solitude. Hermits devote their lives to praising God and praying for others in strict separation from the world.

Deeper religious commitments that do not require public vows within the church are also possible. Tertiaries, or Third Orders, are formed by those women and men who want to share the charism of a religious community in addition to their commitments to marriage or the single life. They associate with the religious community through promises and meet regularly for instruction and prayer.

Answering another call

If you don't feel a yearning to be ordained, get married, join a religious community or congregation or live in desert solitude and pray, that's perfectly all right. You are no less the object of God's love and can be a Catholic in good standing. The fact that there are only two sacraments of vocation sometimes makes those of us who aren't drawn to either of them feel like the parade of grace has marched by and left us behind. Some people feel concern that there is a sacrament for priests and not for women and men in religious life or that ordination is not available to women. Those who do not or cannot marry also may feel like they remain sacramentally undefined or unnoticed by the church.

In his book *Community and Growth: Our Pilgrimage Together,* Christian writer Jean Vanier includes a prayer written by a woman named Therese that sums up the full desire of those who don't find a place within the sacraments of vocation as they are currently practiced by the church.

We who are not committed to you, Jesus, in either a consecrated celibacy or marriage, we who are not committed to our brothers and sisters in a community, are coming to renew our covenant with you.

We are still on the road to which you have called us, but whose name you haven't given us; we are carrying the poverty of not knowing where you are leading us. On this road, there is the wound of not being chosen, not being loved, not being waited for, not being touched. There is the wound of not choosing, not loving, not waiting, not touching. We don't belong. Our house is not a home; we have nowhere to lay our head.

Even though we become impatient and depressed when faced with the choice of others, unhappy when faced with their efficiency, we still say "yes" to our

153

road. We believe it is the road of our fertility, the road we must take to grow in you.

Because our hearts are poor and empty, they are available. We make them a place of welcome for our brothers and sisters. Because our hearts are poor and empty, they are wounded. We let the cry of our thirst rise to you.

And we thank you, Lord, for the road of fertility you have chosen for us.

—Community and Growth

Pursuing our vocation

No one is without a vocation; that is, no one is left behind when God calls. Each person has been uniquely created to share in the work of salvation history. No matter what form your particular vocation takes, the call is basically the same: to follow Christ through the heart of the world by sharing your love with others. Every vocation is therefore a call to relationship with God and others. Even the hermit in the woods shares his or her love, because the hermit is praying for us. The love Christians bear cannot be spared and must not be wasted. The sacraments of vocation are touchstones for the great service of love to which we are all summoned and needed. It is of great importance, therefore, that we weigh thoughtfully the life we have, the gifts we are given, and the time and opportunity that is ours to use. Our vocation, in the end, is not about our career. It's about how we choose to spend our love.

Questions to Consider

1. What dreams or wishes did you have as a child about how you would spend your life? Which of them have been realized? Which do you still hope to pursue?

2. How would you rate the important decisions you have made for your life: perfectly free, mostly free, partly free, or not free at all? What factors have made you less free? How has your faith made you more free?

3. When is your love being spent to its fullest? Do you feel dissatisfied with some of the ways you have spent your love? Why?

4. Describe your vocation. Are there any deep-seated doubts about it? What are they? Have you always known what you wanted to do, or are you still searching? What factors help you in defining the call that you hear or are listening for?

5. When you try to make life decisions, are you more inclined to pray, talk with a friend, seek spiritual direction, reason it out by yourself, or use some other method to discern what you should do? Explain your inclination.

6. Name one or two marriages you have observed that match up with the ideals of sacramental marriage. In what ways are those marriages different from some of the others you have witnessed?

7. In which of your relationships—with a spouse, family member or friend—do you feel like a "better" person than when you are alone? How does that relationship draw out the better person in you?

8. Reread Paul's love poem, "Love is patient, love is kind," in 1 Corinthians 13:4–8. Describe the circumstances under which you have experienced the virtues of love as Paul describes them. What other characteristics would you add to his list?

9. Have you ever thought about a vocation to religious life? To the priesthood? What appeals to you about the idea? What are the least attractive features to you? Why?

10. What ways of life or vocations besides marriage and religious life have you seen that are a blessing for the world? Describe what makes those ways of living holy for you.

Faith Response

1. Dream about new sacraments you'd like to see practiced in the church. What would they be like? Who would be eligible to receive them? What symbols would be used to represent their meaning? Who would confer them? The things you would consecrate, or make sacramental, are already holy in the eyes of God. Bring them to God in prayer and ask for the guidance of the Holy Spirit on how to celebrate them.

2. Consider the tools of discernment: prayer, spiritual direction, faith sharing. Try to practice those that seem appropriate for you. Reflect regularly on the direction of your life and on the decision-making process you use.

3. Think about the commitments you have made in your present life: to family, friends, job or other obligations. Are they rooted in your faith or in other, more worldly, values? How might you deepen your commitments or widen their Christian dimension? You may want to talk with other people who share your faith or situation about how they bring their faith and responsibilities together.

4. Now might be a good time to look into booking a weekend or one day at a retreat center. If such a full getaway is not possible, make arrangements to spend part of a day or a few hours in a quiet, beautiful place that has special meaning for you. Surround yourself with the symbols of your commitments: photographs, trophies, a cross. Reflect on the relationships of all of your obligations and especially how they relate to your faith in Christ.

Nine

Me, Talk to God?
The Practice of Prayer

I freely admit that prayer is an intimidating prospect. For those who have never attempted it or haven't made it a regular practice in their lives, prayer can be a gargantuan effort. The idea of talking to God, who cannot be seen and who does not talk back—at least not in the way we normally carry on a conversation—seems a little scary, perhaps a little silly, and makes many people feel rather inadequate.

I found three main impediments to prayer in my life and the lives of those brave souls who venture hesitantly into the arena of prayer. They can be expressed as follows:

1. I don't know why I'm doing this.
2. I don't know what to expect from this.
3. I don't know what to do.

If the answers were as simple as these questions, no one would have a problem with praying to begin with.

A brief and personal history of prayer
In the beginning, there was talking. Adam and Eve spoke to God and God spoke back. But when sin got into the picture, Adam and Eve started hiding from God. This mythological story seeks to explain the rift between humanity and our Maker. It suggests that once we start hiding in a relationship, talking gets more difficult and less clear. Pretty soon, even when we're talking, we're not saying much—and never the truth. The conversation lags, as does the relationship.

Lying, cheating and murdering make up a good share of the first stories of the Bible. It's really difficult to carry on a conversation with other humans with that kind of behavior going on, much less with the Source of all goodness and love. I dare say there wasn't much vital praying going on among the

157

human race until Abraham's arrival on the scene. And the God who showed up in the quiet of his thoughts was a God Abraham had never heard of before, though he was already a hundred years old. This God promptly made a couple of strange deals with Abraham: Leave your homeland and your relatives; take your old, childless wife and begin a new nation with her.

Abraham never develops a really pious relationship with his God. He doesn't do much of the kneeling-down variety of prayer we are used to. Abraham continues to dicker with God every chance he gets. He rescues the life of his nephew Lot, for example, by asking God to spare any good people who live in Sodom and Gomorrah on the eve of the planned destruction. Dickering is a very popular, if primitive, way of praying. Even today, we sometimes confuse God with the host of *Let's Make a Deal*.

Isaac, Abraham's son, is not documented as having a noteworthy prayer life. Perhaps that incident of being nearly sacrificed as a child to his father's God left Isaac queasy about getting close to God. The only prayers Isaac is known to have prayed are the blessings for his sons. It doesn't take a therapist to figure out why this was important to him.

Jacob, of the next generation, was a trickster who ironically gets tricked himself. For him, prayer was a struggle, literally. Once he had a remarkable dream of communicating with heaven as angels travel up and down a ladder between heaven and earth. Jacob wrestles with an angel at night and is left a little lame. But the struggle gives him a new identity: He is Israel, the one who "tussled with God."

Jacob has twelve sons, but Joseph is the only son who is mystically minded. Joseph prays, and, like his father, he dreams. The dreams he has and those he interprets for others become powerful forces in his life and in the destiny of the people of Israel.

Moses is the person who draws closest to the original relationship of humanity with God. He and God talk regularly after their first encounter at the burning bush. At the top of Mount Sinai, in fact, Moses sees God "face to face"—a vision that leaves Moses physically altered. His face takes on such a radiance that

158

no one can look at him, and he has to veil himself.

Deal-makers, wrestlers, dreamers, seers. This litany might discourage you if you've never returned from prayer glowing as Moses did. But it does give us a sense of the wide range of experiences some of the great participants in salvation history had in communicating with God. And this is by no means an exhaustive list. There is Moses' sister, Miriam, who praises God in dance and song at the Red Sea. Hannah, mother of the prophet Samuel, prays in canticles or songs, as did Mary, mother of Jesus. Brave Judith, in the book by the same name, prays and fasts in solitude before beheading the general who threatens her nation. The prophet Jeremiah, a rather depressive soul, prays most often in laments, and Isaiah just as often breaks into praise. Ezekiel fasts for forty days and then has wild and fantastic visions. Jesus retreats into the desert for a similar period and meets the devil. You never know what you're going to encounter when you enter the territory of prayer.

Still, prayer is the natural habitat of the believer. In the gospels Jesus goes aside often to pray, and if Jesus needed to pray often, we do even more. Paul suggests that we pray "unceasingly." That's quite a lot.

What is prayer? Why do we pray?

Looking at the various ways people relate to God in the Bible gives us at least this much information: There is no one right way to pray. If some sing and dance and others fast and weep, we can believe that God is willing to work with us a little on the matter of style. King David, who is reputed to have been a musician and singer, wrote at least some of the psalms gathered under his name, and they fall into categories familiar to anyone who has ever been moved to pray: praise, thanksgiving, intercession and lament. Basically we are expressing our love, gratitude, need or pain when we pray. Any honest emotion is a good place to start.

But why start at all? What is prayer all about? Edward Farrell wrote a book called *Prayer Is a Hunger,* and the title gives us the best reason to pray I've ever heard: We pray for the same reason we eat. We pray because we are drawn to it, because the need is planted in us and we respond to it. Just try praying out of a sense of obligation and you see how empty it is. Then consider a time when you were driven to pray because of a compelling need. When you are hungry for prayer, it's as automatic as breathing.

When we fall in love, the hunger we feel for the beloved is intense and overwhelming. Just being together is everything; being apart is unbearable. When there is any distance between us, we strive to fill it with words: phone calls, letters, e-mail. We may also use symbols to make our love present and tangible: flowers, gifts, a song requested on the radio. People in love are never out of touch, even with vast miles between them. As our relationship with God deepens, prayer can become a near constant state of expressing our love and experiencing God's nearness.

But many of us are not at the passionate state about God, yet. We're still at the timid, getting-to-know-you stage, and that's the time when prayer seems most unlikely. What do you say to a near stranger? How do you carry on this conversation authentically? Catholic novelist Flannery O'Connor was concerned about the issue of being genuine in prayer. She shrank from some forms of prayer that did not match her reserved, intellectual nature. The devotional prayer popular in her generation was charged with emotion and fervor, and praying that way made her feel like she was "wearing someone else's finery." In the end, she concluded, "I can never describe my heart as *burning* to the Lord (who knows better) without snickering."

The moral of the story is, don't try to pray someone else's words unless they are comfortable for you. There are shelves and shelves of prayer books out there, but for some people (or for all of us at certain stages of our lives) the best prayer is the one that comes spontaneously from the heart.

More than words

A Jesuit professor of mine used to say, "Learning to pray does not mean yammering at God but learning how to listen." Often we put so much emphasis on our side of the conversation that we begin to think prayer is all about *us*. We might instead want to consider prayer as clearing a space in our lives for *God*. In every relationship, we create a place in which to invite the other. This space may be literal, as in setting a place for someone at our table. Or it may be interior, as in making room in our heart to care for another. We also make time for others if we seek to know them better. Time and space are two important elements in welcoming another into our lives.

When we want to pray, then, it makes sense to pay attention to time and space. What kind of time do we intend to allot to this relationship? If the time is rare, grudging and divided between prayer and some other task, prayer can be like listening to a friend on the cell phone while driving to a meeting. We shouldn't be surprised if the quality of both the conversation and the driving suffers. As we have learned well in our extra-busy contemporary world, quality time is better than sheer multiplication of minutes. If fifteen minutes a day is what you've got for prayer, choose your tithe from the "first fruits" of your day. Just as the people of Israel gave their best lamb or the finest fruits of their harvest to God, find a quarter hour when you are still and attentive inside. Your prayer time may be at either end of the day, or it can be a wonderful break between busy events. Choose a place you really would want to share with someone you love: your favorite chair, a porch swing, a park near the office, a quiet downtown church. Relax. Before you leap into the conversation with God, just be together for a while and acknowledge the presence of the One you have come to be with.

This may sound completely unworkable to you if you've got a spouse, kids, a job or can't remember when "spare time" was last on your agenda. I'm suggesting that we all have to make time for the relationships that count or risk losing their vitality. And our relationship with God may be one of those relationships.

Start small with your attempts to pray. Start with five minutes. If place is an issue, become good at creating your own "sacred space" by lighting a candle at your desk, transforming it for a few minutes as you concentrate on the Light of the World. If your five minutes for prayer is on the subway, carry something in your pocket that you can touch to keep you mindful: a rosary, a cross or some other object with special significance. Or you may want to consider an article of clothing that orients you to the activity of prayer. Just as people of many religions use a special rug or shawl or cap to create a "chapel within," you can wrap yourself up in an old comforter and *become* the sacred space you're looking for. This is not an outlandish idea; scripture calls our bodies the temples of the Holy Spirit. If God dwells within us, we don't have to look far to have our prayer encounter. All the exterior arrangements we make for prayer are simply to support our easily distracted humanity.

My old Jesuit professor said one thing more that stayed with me: In the end, we become what we worship. If we make our relationship with God a priority, our union with the Divine is inevitable. If we spend all our efforts in ensuring a place for ourselves in this world, we can't be too surprised if we become worldly people.

Prayer and ritual: What to expect

The *communal* prayer of Catholics is *ritual* prayer. More specifically, it is *liturgy*, which means a "public act of service." Our liturgy is not simply for ourselves but also for the sake of others. It serves the community in its formal witness and inspires us to greater service. Ritual prayer involves many of the same elements as personal prayer: time, space and people. But it also involves symbolic action, entered into communally. For people who find community naturally appealing, ritual prayer is easy to enter into. For loners and rugged individualists, it's an acquired taste.

Some things to note about ritual prayer, according to well-known liturgist Aidan Kavanagh: It is not magic; it is not entertainment; it is not an end in itself; it is not about how you feel. And most important, no matter what anyone tells you, the communal prayer of the church is not set in stone. Nothing the church does has "always been done this way." Just as we do not exist for the Sabbath but the day exists for our sake, so too rituals exist for our sake and not we for them. Or as Kavanagh puts it so nicely: Jesus told us to go, teach and baptize, but he did not tell us how to do this *liturgically*.

Knowing what ritual *isn't* puts an end to the superstitious approach to liturgy, but it's also useful to know what ritual *is*. Much has been written in support of the idea that ritual is a way of "wasting time" with God. As startling as that sounds, the idea borrows from the concept of ritual sacrifice. When ancient peoples made burnt offerings to God, they took those things most valuable to them and surrendered them to the flames. They offered their best animals and best fruits to God. After the destruction of the Jerusalem Temple by the Romans in A.D. 70, however, the Jewish community no longer had a sacred place to sacrifice their offerings to God. So the rabbis came up with the idea of offering prayer time. They offered "a sacrifice of praise" in place of the sacrifice of goods.

What is more valuable to us today than our time? Giving a few minutes from our day or week can be like consigning a bit of our lives to the flames. Unlike other things we give our time to, religious ritual produces nothing tangible. There is nothing to take home, nothing to look at when it's over. It is a perfect "burnt offering" of our time: We take an hour of our lives and give it back to God. Since we desire to be with those we love, we relinquish time simply to be together with our community of faith.

But ritual is more than a gift of time; it also reminds us who we are. Our rituals are part of our identity. Think of the rituals that define membership in your family: the week at the lake in the summer, eating kielbasa or Jello salad at every family gathering. We also have national rituals, like fireworks on the Fourth of July or the long weekend in September in celebration of labor. Most important, we tell stories at our ritual gatherings, often the same stories each time. These stories become as deeply a part of us as any scripture. Altogether, these generations of stories over time become part of our personal story.

A rabbi once said, "It is not so much that the Jews have kept the Sabbath as that the Sabbath has kept the Jews." Our rituals remind us not only who we are but who we want to be. The first step to achieving something is to dare to dream it. Are we really the body and blood of Christ for the world? The sacra-

163

ment of the Eucharist tells us that we are, but often it doesn't seem that way. So while we wait for our feelings and our actions to catch up to this reality, we remind ourselves of its truth by sharing that eucharistic meal over and over and over.

Along with sanctifying our time and defining our identity, rituals make the past come to life again. The Jewish community, and later the Christian church, have held to the idea that what *has been* becomes *true again* in our ritual. This idea is known as *anamnesis* in Greek: The past becomes present, and what was, is now. If you've been to a Jewish passover meal, or *Seder*, you may have noticed that the leader tells the story of the exodus from Egypt in the present tense, as though it is happening right then to those gathered around the table. Likewise, Catholics understand that the Eucharist is not simply memorial supper of Jesus' last meal with his disciples. Recognizing ourselves as the present-day disciples around the eucharistic table, we are not remembering the past so much as participating in the present reality of Jesus among us.

Liturgy and time

How do we recall and celebrate the past? And why do we do it? Most of us find meaning and a sense of identity in remembering where we're from and what has gone before. In good times and in bad, past events and relationships have shaped who we are now and where we're headed. That's why we return to the old hometown, locate childhood friends on the Internet or keep ties with our families. Who we are, for better and for worse, is at least partly a response to the journey we've taken so far.

Birthdays, anniversaries, reunions and other special days dot our calendars from year to year. It is no wonder, then, that the church adopts a similar method for recalling and honoring the events and people of salvation history. The church year, also known as the liturgical year, begins in late November or early December with the season of Advent. This season marks the four Sundays before Christmas and is a time of "waiting in joyful hope" for the coming of Christ into our world. Although the past event we are commemorating is the birth of Christ 2000-

plus years ago, we are also preparing for the return of Christ at the end of time, known as the Second Coming. The stories of Advent are about the darkness of the world giving way to the light of Christ.

Advent is followed by Christmas, which is celebrated as an octave, or eight-day feast. The next great season of the church is called Lent, which lasts roughly forty days. Lent is a time to meditate on our need for ongoing conversion of our lives and repentance for what is wrong with us and our world. The season ends with a three-day feast known as the Triduum: Holy Thursday (Mass of the Lord's Supper), Good Friday (recalling the crucifixion of Jesus), and Holy Saturday (the vigil of Easter.) The Triduum celebrates—with all the liturgical skill at our command: music, decoration, fire, story, ritual, symbol—the high holy days of the church, for we commemorate Jesus' dying and rising. At this special time we also receive adults as new members of the church with their reception of the sacraments of initiation: baptism, confirmation and Eucharist.

The feast of Easter, celebrating the resurrection and glorification of Jesus and lasting about fifty days, is joyful in character. It ends at the feast of Pentecost, when we recall the descent of the Holy Spirit upon the church and celebrate the gifts of the Spirit present in our midst. The rest of the liturgical year used to be called the season of Pentecost, since we continue to live as the church inspired by the Spirit. But it is currently known as Ordinary Time, a greening time for growth in discipleship. Lasting about thirty-four weeks, it ends at the Feast of Christ the King, just before the new liturgical year begins anew with Advent.

The scripture readings proclaimed on Sundays throughout the church year follow a three-year cycle, to cover as much of the Bible as possible in the daily readings at Mass. During the first year, Year A, the gospel of Matthew is read. In Year B, we concentrate on Mark. In Year C, we listen to Luke. The gospel of John is proclaimed here and there throughout the three years, especially in Cycle B, since Mark's is the shortest of the gospels.

Each of the feasts and seasons of the liturgical year are

characterized by colors, reflected in the priest's vestments and often in the cloths or other decorations used in the church. Advent is about emerging from the dark, so purple is the prescribed color, though some parishes use midnight blue to distinguish Advent from Lent. The octave of Christmas is white, as are all feasts of Christ. Lent is purple, for repentance and majesty. Easter is white, and Pentecost, because it is a feast of fire, is red. Ordinary Time, we are not surprised to learn, is marked by the color green.

But the liturgical calendar is not the only calendar the church follows. We also acknowledge the sanctoral cycle, in which the heroes of the church, the saints, are honored. The feasts of saints are scattered throughout the calendar, normally celebrated on the day of their death or some other day associated with them. There are more feasts honoring Mary than anyone else, except Jesus. Some more notable saints' feasts are Patrick (March 17), Francis of Assisi (October 4), Nicholas (December 6) and All Saints Day (November 1). Feasts of Mary include the Solemnity of Mary, Mother of God (January 1), the Assumption of Mary (August 15), the Immaculate Conception (December 8), and Our Lady of Guadalupe (December 12).

The Eucharist

The Eucharist is often called the "great prayer of the church." More commonly known as the Mass, it is celebrated every day of the year except Good Friday, when another liturgy in commemoration of Jesus' crucifixion and death is substituted. Each Sunday is known as a "little Easter" in the church, because the assembly of believers comes together to share in the Paschal, or Easter, Mystery of Christ.

The Paschal Mystery is simply expressed in these words from the liturgy: "Christ has died, Christ is risen, Christ will come again." This is the core of our faith in the central Christian message. Jesus surrendered his life for the reconciliation of the world, took on our death so that we can share in his life right now and in the world to come. He was raised from the dead on Easter Sunday and will return to be "all in all," to make all creation united and whole in the unending reign of God.

The Paschal Mystery may be three short statements, but it basically covers everything from here to eternity.

For lifelong believers, the Paschal Mystery is a familiar idea and easily acceptable. For others, it is a thorny issue that must be resolved for faith to be at all possible. Why should the death and resurrection of Jesus have meaning for me? How can I know that he has risen? Why should I believe that this man who died was the Son of God and that he will come again?

It is important at once to distinguish two words: *faith* and *knowledge*. The truth is that no one can *know* that the Paschal Mystery is for real, because it's a matter of faith. The nature of mystery is that it is not completely revealed, only glimpsed and experienced and trusted. When we try to turn faith into knowledge, we find ourselves applying scientific principles to a realm that cannot be laboratory tested. But perhaps a more familiar example will help to express this idea.

How do you know that someone loves you? Words of love are used, but words can be false. Deeds of love are performed, but it could be an elaborate plot to deceive you. People report to you that they too have seen and can verify that you are loved, but witnesses sometimes lie. In the end, the only sure reason we believe we are loved is because we *experience* love. We can wait forever for the evidence to mount and can test our lover for the rest of our life, but we will never find peace until we simply trust in the love and rest in it.

Because faith is a gift, we cannot force ourselves to believe. But neither do we have to wait until all our doubts have been answered. We can take a tip from the man whose boy had epilepsy and who approached Jesus for a cure. Jesus asked him if he believed. The man, shaken to his soul by the suffering of his son and his desire to save him, answered honestly, "Lord, I believe. Help my unbelief!" And that was enough for Jesus, who said a mustard seed of faith—the meager potential of faith—was plenty (Mark 9:17–29, Luke 17:5–6). In most of the critical decisions we make in life, we don't wait to have all the answers, to settle all the loose ends, to make certain all the variables. We learn as much as we can, weigh the consequences of each side, and then act. Thus it is with our faith in God. At some point, we have to make a leap. Whom will we serve—God or material wealth? Jesus warned us that we can't serve both.

Those who choose Christ, then, approach the Eucharist as celebration and communion. *Eucharist* means "giving thanks," and there is much to be grateful for in the Paschal Mystery. Forgiveness of sin, reconciliation with God and life everlasting are also mysteries in the sense that they are beyond our ability to fully grasp; we can always understand more about them. Our Eucharist celebrates these wonders and also nourishes us in the very life of God we have been promised.

The Mass has two main parts, the Liturgy of the Word and the Liturgy of the Eucharist. The Liturgy of the Word begins with the sign of the cross and a Penitential Rite, in which we acknowledge the brokenness of our hearts and our world due to sin. The liturgy normally includes a reading from the Old Testament, the epistles, or letters, and then one of the gospels. The readings are followed by a homily, which is an opportunity for the preacher to "open up" the word of God that the assembly has just heard. The Liturgy of the Word concludes with the Prayer of the Faithful, also called General Intercessions.

The Liturgy of the Eucharist moves the action of the ritual from the pulpit, also called the ambo or lectern, to the Table of the Lord, most commonly called the altar. After a short preface, the presiding priest offers the Eucharistic Prayer on behalf of the assembly, during which he consecrates the bread and wine as the body and blood of Christ. The faithful are asked to proclaim "the mystery of faith," which is generally one of four summary statements of the Paschal Mystery. At the conclusion of the prayer, we offer the Great Amen, our assent of faith to the Eucharist. The Communion Rite follows, during which the assembly prays the Lord's Prayer and calls upon the Lamb of God to be merciful. Communion is then distributed, and shortly after that the Mass is ended.

A word should be added about the Concluding Rite, or Dismissal. It may seem like just a utilitarian way to get everyone back out to the parking lot, but its intention is much greater than that. In the concluding dialogue, the presider says, "The Mass is ended; go in peace to love and serve the Lord." This is our commissioning, to go and live as disciples of Jesus. For this commissioning, we give thanks. The liturgy of the Mass concludes on this note.

Liturgy is like literature, with a beginning, middle and end; plot, characters and situation; and a story to tell. It can seem daunting to a newcomer, but if you stay with it the Mass carries you through the years and sings its love song over and over, reminding you who you truly are and who *we together* truly are: the free children of God. Some may worry that a lifetime of religious ritual is brainwashing us. I reply that the world is brainwashing us all the time—through media, advertisement and the deluge of our consumer culture. You get to choose which forces form and inform your soul. Choose thoughtfully!

Other ways Catholics pray

I regret this can be only a brief survey of some ways that we Catholics carry on our dialogue with God. The Mass is central and universal; the rest of the methods of prayer are optional and varied and their appeal depends on your personality as much as anything. If prayer is new to you, try as many kinds as you can and find what is most helpful. If you are really out at sea on this, finding a good spiritual director to guide you can be very fruitful.

Praying the Psalms. The psalms are the prayer book of the Bible. They were written as sung prayers and they are broken up into convenient pieces, 150 in all, and praying them daily is as old as the church (actually, as old as the synagogue!). The psalms cover a wide range of human experiences, and some will seem archaic, some radically contemporary. Though at times one is amazed at the emotions expressed in these prayers—people can really say that to God?—praying a psalm every day offers this comfort: Nothing we think and feel is off limits in our relationship with the One who knows us better than we know ourselves. Shop around and find a translation of the psalms that sounds good to you. Some people like the King's English. Others prefer a modern sounding or "inclusive language" version.

Praying with the Bible. This is an expanded version of praying the psalms, often called *lectio divina,* or divine reading. You read a verse of scripture aloud, then meditate on it silently for a while and let it speak to your heart. Some people like to select a book of the Bible and follow along, verse by verse, over a period of months until they complete it. Some prefer the scatter-shot method, picking a verse or two at random. Many appreciate the various page-a-day meditation booklets that do the choosing for you. You may want to memorize a Bible verse each day, or copy down those that speak most powerfully to you and reflect on them regularly. Those who are community minded may prefer praying in a Bible study setting—meeting in homes or church once a week or month, taking a longer passage or an entire book of the Bible and spending more time praying over it and discussing it.

The Liturgy of the Hours, or Breviary. This prayer is for people who love liturgy, tradition and psalms. The breviary is the official prayer of the church, mandated for priests and required as well in monasteries and many religious communities. It can be hard to pick up by yourself if you haven't prayed it with others first, learning how to place the ribbons that mark the sections and getting the general hang of it. The breviary employs psalms, scripture, music (if it is chanted in community) and prayers for the "sanctification of the hours" to remind us of the holiness of all hours. Some modified versions of the Liturgy of the Hours exist for individual use, but the Hours is designed to be a communal prayer and you can generally find a religious house of prayer nearby that would welcome you to join them.

Adoration of the Blessed Sacrament. If your world is chock full of words already, you may be looking for some silence. Contemplation in the presence of the Blessed Sacrament, reserved in the tabernacle in every Catholic church, may be what you're looking for. Some people use booklets of devotional prayer even here, but sitting and meditating in the Real Presence of God does not require any extraneous equipment. If you've "yammered at God" enough and want to listen for a change, here's your chance. Some parishes hold regular times for adoration when groups gather, but you can do this alone any time the church is open.

Contemplative Prayer. Teresa of Avila called contemplative prayer "nothing less than a close sharing between friends." Like Adoration of the Blessed Sacrament, it is prayer that finds its source in silence, but its focus is always unity with God. The time of day for this form of prayer and the amount of time spent in it vary. The beginner may find himself or herself mainly fighting off distracting or even discouraging thoughts. In time, however, the practice of meditation leads to a deeper surrender of mind, heart and spirit to the presence and will of God. Visiting a monastery or reading the spiritual classics of mystics like John of the Cross, Teresa of Avila and Thomas Merton will give you a taste of the fruits of contemplation.

The Stations of the Cross. Also known as the Way of the Cross, but popularly called "The Stations," this walking meditation is designed to be a mini-pilgrimage for those unable to go on actual pilgrimage to the Holy Land. With its roots in the Middle Ages, this devotion was started by the Franciscans as a meditative walk through designated moments in the passion of Jesus. It is presently composed of fourteen (sometimes fifteen) stations along the journey, ranging from Pontius Pilate's sentencing Jesus to death to the placing of Jesus' body in the tomb. The optional fifteenth station depicts the resurrection. Stations are installed along the walls of practically every Catholic church, and booklets that offer reflections are available to stimulate your own prayer. Mother Teresa and Brother Roger of Taize have written two of the better contemporary reflections. (See the Appendix for a list of the traditional stations and of scriptural stations.)

The Rosary. So many devotional practices in honor of Mary exist that I include only this one as an example. (But see Chapter Ten for more on the mother of Jesus.) The rosary began as the "poor person's" book of psalms. Wanting to pray the psalter as the monks did but unable to read or afford a book, the peasants surrounding the monasteries of Europe were encouraged by the monks to pray the Hail Mary over and over. The Hail Mary is a simple prayer based on some verses from Luke's annunciation story, followed by a request for Mary's intercession for us. If one prays 150 different psalms or one prayer 150 times, so the rationale went, it is all the same to God. Fingering knots on a string to keep count, the peasants participated in the prayer of the church with great zeal, and the praying of the rosary gradually took shape until its present, stylized form. Now including standardized prayers at the beginning and end and framing each decade (ten Hail Marys) with an Our Father and Glory Be, the rosary has developed an entire ritual around its original simple repetition.

Fifteen meditations called mysteries are divided into three categories: joyful, sorrowful and glorious. These mysteries focus on significant moments in the lives of Mary and Jesus. The average rosary string has five sets of decades, so to pray all the mysteries, one must go around the body of the rosary three times. Most people pray only one set of mysteries each time they pray the rosary. The rosary can be prayed alone or in groups. Societies exist in some communities to gather before daily Mass to pray it. (See the Appendix for the texts of the Our Father, Hail Mary and Glory Be, as well as the lists of the mysteries of the rosary.)

Charismatic Prayer. For some people, most rituals are too stiff and formal. If you are not afraid of a little passion with your religion, check out the Charismatic renewal. Since the 1960s—but one might argue, since the early church—folks have received the gift of the Holy Spirit in the form of ecstatic speech called tongues, or glossolalia. They gather to pray for a further release of God's Spirit in their lives and in the church as a whole. Often a gift of healing is also manifest in such communities, as well as prophecy and other gifts of the Spirit spelled out by Paul in 1 Corinthians 12. Charismatic prayer is hard on those who are shy, but for folks who find other forms of prayer dull and unexciting, a Charismatic prayer meeting may be what you're looking for. The diocesan chancery office should know where the meetings are held.

Retreats and days of recollection

However we choose to make prayer a regular part of our faith life, all of us need a little jumpstart now and then to renew our spirits. Weekend retreats are available all over the Catholic world in monasteries and retreat centers, usually within driving or public transportation distance of wherever you are. There is generally a suggested fee, though I've never known a retreat location not to offer a reduced rate for someone in need. Retreats may be "directed," with a person renowned for holiness or wisdom guiding a group meditation through the weekend. Or they may be "undirected," which is best for those seeking the quiet to wrestle with their own demons or discernment. Even on an undirected retreat, however, you can ask to see a director for individual direction once or several times during your stay. Beautiful scenery, simple meals and space to sort out your life are what most retreat experiences offer.

Sometimes, a weekend away is not manageable but an evening or afternoon of reflection is possible. Many parishes offer times of recollection during the Advent and Lenten seasons or more regularly if there is interest. If your parish doesn't have a reflection time scheduled when you need one, you can gather with friends or plan one yourself. Be creative! The elements of scripture, music, sacred space and a chance to reflect and pray can be adapted for nearly any situation.

Fasting, prayer and almsgiving

This is the classic spiritual combination, practiced by Jews before Christianity began. Jesus also taught these spiritual disciplines in his Sermon on the Mount (see Matthew 6). Fasting prepares us to acknowledge our limits and hunger for God. It is also a form of penance for sin. Prayer undertaken while fasting engenders a greater sense of urgency and purpose, since we are predisposed to the spiritual through denying the flesh. Almsgiving is a work of mercy and justice that puts us in a right relationship with God and others. During Lent, in particular, the whole church is urged to perform these three practices together.

The habit of prayer

The best way to pray is to pray, Dom Chapman wrote in his *Spiritual Letters*. He added: And the less one prays, the worse it goes. My own experience proves this out. When I have been faithful to prayer, it comes effortlessly, and when I fall out of the habit of prayer, it becomes harder to regain my footing. This is as true of prayer as it is of exercise, diet or any other discipline, including working on a relationship: Fidelity is typically the most direct path to success.

When I grow lax, I revive my desire for prayer by reminding myself why I do it. Reading the spiritual masters of any age—Augustine, Hildegard of Bingen, Teresa of Avila, Thomas Merton, Henri Nouwen—helps me to recover the hunger for prayer in my own life, just as a picture of Lance Armstrong, who won the Tour de France after battling cancer, reminds me why I get back on my bike. In the fourth century, Augustine said our hearts are restless until they rest in God. The desert fathers, spiritual masters of the early church, saw society as a shipwreck that each individual needed to swim away from to save their lives. Nouwen reminds us that in our world "the temptation is to go mad with those who are mad." Prayer helps us to regain the center of our life and not to forget that as Christians we have taken the name of Christ for our own.

Questions to Explore

1. Explain why you do or don't pray regularly. How do you pray? What are the biggest obstacles to prayer in your life? How do you overcome them?

2. Which description fits you best as a person of prayer: a deal-maker, a wrestler, a dreamer, or a seer? Why? Which ways of praying appeal to you most?

3. Consider the four categories of prayer in the psalms: praise, thanksgiving, intercession and lament. Which of those terms characterize your prayer? What other kinds of prayer do you use?

4. Under what circumstances do you experience prayer as a "hunger" in your life? Are you more apt to turn to prayer when you hear good news or bad? Why is that, do you think?

5. Do you spend more time speaking or listening in prayer? Why? How does this shape the experience you have of God in your prayer life?

6. Which kinds of prayer appeal to you more? Personal or communal? Spontaneous or ritual? Why? How do your feelings about ritual prayer affect your experience of the Mass?

7. What does the ritual prayer of the church, especially the Mass, teach you about your identity?

8. Describe rituals that your family celebrates and looks forward to each year. What do they tell you about yourself and your family? What is your favorite feast or season of the church year? Why?

9. How many of the "Catholic ways to pray" in this chapter have you participated in? How do you feel about each of them? What do you like or dislike about them? If you have ever been on a retreat, describe your experiences of it. Is making a retreat something you might do or do again? Why?

10. To you, what are the most compelling reasons to pray? How might those reasons affect the way you approach prayer in the future?

Faith Response

1. Evaluate your present habit of prayer: satisfying/unsatisfying, adequate/inadequate, challenging/not challenging, changing all the time/unchanged in years. Based on your evaluation and given the information in this chapter, consider what you might do differently. You may want to talk over your concerns with a spiritual director, friend, spouse or pastor.

2. Consider how you feel about praying alone, with a partner, in a small group, or ritually in the eucharistic assembly. Make a special or renewed commitment to one of these

avenues of prayer and make it a more regular part of your life.

3. Visit a Catholic bookstore or website and look for a spiritual classic or modern spiritual master that you have been wanting to read. You may want to ask a friend to suggest a favorite book for you to read. If you cannot bring yourself to read nonfiction, try the short stories or novels of Flannery O'Connor or Walker Percy, or read anything by Frederick Buechner or C. S. Lewis, both Protestants who have written inspiring fiction and nonfiction.

4. Learn more about the practice of prayer by attending talks on spirituality or by participating in Bible studies or faith-sharing groups in your parish. Get a copy of a nearby retreat house schedule and see if any of the topics or themes may interest you. Best of all, if you know really holy people, ask them to share with you their wisdom about prayer.

Ten

Mary: Daughter of Zion, Mother of Us All

If the cross is the most enduring symbol of Christianity, Mary is perhaps the most widely recognized icon of Catholicism. Along with the papacy and the sacraments, Mary is among the most easily identified elements of the Catholic church for outsiders. In the history of art, she has been represented more than any other woman since the goddesses of the ancient world. Celebrated in prayers and images, in song and theology, she may be the best known woman in human history. Hers is a unique partnership with God in the story of salvation, and we all share a crucial relationship with her. Amazingly enough, along with this young Jewish woman, we too are called to bring the Body of Christ to birth in our world.

Yet what do we really know about Mary of Nazareth? Who was she? What did she say and do? What do the names and titles by which we know her tell us about her role in time and eternity? When we look beyond the serene face in the many portraits, all of which come from artists' imaginations, we find that there are many Marys. Yet the woman herself remains largely a mystery.

Mary's story

Let's start by making a list of the things we know—and think we know— about the mother of Jesus. Her story begins with a visitation by an angel who tells her that a special child will be given to her, in a way quite out of the ordinary. According to the prophet Isaiah, this child will be Emmanuel, "God with us" (Matthew 1:23). Mary consents to this extraordinary event, calling herself a servant of God (Luke 1:38). It is important to realize that Mary could have said no to this invitation, just we are free to say yes or no to the incarnation in our lives.

177

Then Mary goes to her elderly cousin Elizabeth, who has also been found with child under unusual circumstances. The two women comfort and support each other in their remarkable pregnancies. When Mary returns to Nazareth, she marries her betrothed, a man named Joseph, who marries her despite her pregnancy because of a vision he receives in a dream. The child is born among animals in a stable in Bethlehem, his birth attended by shepherds and angels and later by Magi, or wise men, bearing gifts.

When their child is only a few weeks old, Mary and Joseph present Jesus at the Temple in Jerusalem, which was the custom. A prophet named Simeon calls him the child who will save the world, a light to the nations. A second prophet, Anna, continues to proclaim this good news to all who will listen.

Twelve years later, during another visit to the Temple, Jesus is separated from his parents, who think he is with relatives. When they find him days later in the Temple, his mother scolds him, telling him that she and his father have been very anxious about him in his absence. Jesus corrects her, noting that they should have known that he would be in his "Father's house." Then he returns with them to Nazareth and continues to advance in "wisdom, age and favor" before all. Mary ponders all these astonishing events in her heart.

Mary's role in the adult life of Jesus is sparsely indicated. She was with him at the wedding feast in Cana and urged him to act, launching his public ministry. Although Jesus' relatives are mentioned a few more times in the gospels, they are usually offstage. There is no evidence that Mary traveled with Jesus during his years of active ministry, although one gospel account mentions that Mary was present at the crucifixion. At that time, Jesus consigns her to the care of his disciple John. In the Acts of the Apostles, Mary is included among those who remained together in the upper room after the resurrection.

That's it! That is all we know of Mary from the Bible. The rest comes from legend, tradition and dogmatic statements the church has formulated through the centuries. Each of these faces of Mary helps us to understand not simply who Mary is but who she is *for us.*

Mary in scripture

Mary's role in the gospel accounts evolved over time and varied with who was doing the telling. In Mark's gospel, the first to be written, Mary does not appear directly in the story at all. Mark's account contains no birth narrative, beginning, as it does, with the ministry of John the Baptist. The only two references to Jesus' mother in Mark are brief. In chapter 3, the scribes declare Jesus possessed, and his concerned mother and family appear outside the place where he is preaching to take him home, because people are saying that he is "out of his mind." Later, when Jesus preaches in Nazareth and is rejected by his home-town, they sneer at him by calling him "the son of Mary." In those times, referring to one's lineage by using the mother's name was the same as calling someone illegitimate (6:1–3). We can imagine that Mary's pregnancy before marriage was part of the rumor mill around Nazareth, a fact of their life together as a family.

Since Matthew's gospel tends to clean up any of the elements of potential scandal found in Mark, these references do not appear. Though the story of the rejection at Nazareth is told, Matthew changes the reference "son of Mary" to "the carpenter's son" and lets sleeping dogs lie (13:54–55). In general, Matthew shows little interest in the mother of Jesus, telling the story of the announcement of Jesus' birth through the dreams and actions of Joseph.

Most of the stories of Mary that we know are contained in Luke's writings. The annunciation by the angel Gabriel, Mary's acceptance (called her *fiat*, meaning "so be it"), her visit to Elizabeth's house, the details of the birth that appear in the Christmas stories, the presentation in the Temple, and the later finding of Jesus in the Temple are all unique to Luke. When Luke tells the story of rejection in Nazareth, he reports the crowd as simply asking, "Is not this Joseph's son?" (4:22) He also retells the story of Mary and her kin coming to find Jesus while he's teaching, but it's a softer version. Nothing indicates that they have come to take him home (8:19–21).

By the time John's gospel was written, Mary has taken on a symbolic role. John never calls Mary by name; she is always simply "the mother of Jesus." And to Jesus, she is "Woman," an image often used in the Bible for the whole people of Israel. John does not recount the birth of Jesus, but there is a kind of birthing story in the tale of the wedding feast at Cana in chapter 2. Here, Mary gives birth to the ministry of Jesus by first suggesting he act on behalf of the couple and then quietly arranging the details behind the scenes. Her confidence in God's will is as strongly expressed in this story as it is in her *fiat* in Luke.

Mary appears again near the end of John's gospel, when she stands beneath the cross of her son. Here again she assists at a birth, only this time it is the church that is being brought into being. Jesus surrenders her to the care of his disciple and he to hers (19:26–27). The Woman belongs to the disciple, and he to her. So did Mary come to be understood as both the pre-eminent daughter of Zion and the mother of us all.

The evolution of Mary's role in the gospels enables us to consider how Mary's role in our own story can "grow" on us. At different stages of our lives, we may approach Mary first as mother, then as perfect disciple, and finally as guide and wisdom figure. In each stage of her own story, she shows us how to bring God to birth in our world.

Mary's importance to us

The significance of Mary lies in her relationship to Jesus and his message. Nothing the church teaches about Mary can be understood apart from her son. Many of the titles we commonly use for Mary demonstrate that, such as Mother of God or Blessed Mother. Even the church's dogmatic statements about Mary, which we will look at later, relate to how God prepared her to become the woman who bore Christ and are meant to honor her for her role in salvation history.

With all the attention Mary has received from artists through the centuries, it would be easy to assume that Mary was a celebrity: a great teacher, a do-er of remarkable deeds, a particularly heroic individual. Our gospels don't record that. We actually know very little of what she said or did, and legends arose to fill in the gaps of our knowledge. Stories were told about her mother Anne's conception of her by smelling a rose, her life at home with Anne and Joachim in Nazareth, her early piety and vow of virginity, the extraordinary betrothal to Joseph, and a midwife's testimony to Mary's virginity after Jesus' birth, among others. These stories were written down as early as the second century, showing that interest in Mariology, or church teachings pertaining to Mary, has been around for a long time.

Certainly much is hidden about the life of Mary. But two powerful images have been given to us in great art, images that reveal her role most clearly: the Madonna with Child and the Pieta. These images confound reason and lift the veil on mystery. In the first image, the mother cradles her infant son, a new life that confronts the world with its utter fragility and at the same time announces its primacy as Lord of Life. In the second image, the same woman holds her son's lifeless body, her arms sturdy like the branches of an oak in winter. The baby is the source of all life and hope; this man's death epitomizes the darkest despair the world has known. Mary holds the baby and the crucified man with the same sure and gentle arms, holding life and death together with unbounded tenderness. In both images, Mary is the Christ-bearer, and this is what it means for us to bear Christ into the world. to bring forth life and to be strong and faithful in death. This is our task as Christians, and Mary's example, quiet in its authority, compels us to reflection and action.

As Christ-bearers, we recognize the call to hold our lives and deaths together with integrity. The church celebrates the optimism of every birth, as well as the personally difficult but spiritually profound celebration of each death, as an opportunity for new and greater life. In Mary's arms, we see our vocation vividly demonstrated. We are called to be that church, the church of the suffering *and* rejoicing, the church that answers with our own *fiat* to whatever God asks of us.

Mary's virginity

If the church asks us to consider Mary primarily in relationship to Jesus, we are still challenged to consider this woman who stands peculiarly alone in history as the Virgin Mother. People who are uncomfortable with the Catholic idea of mystery, those who cannot approach Mary except through the eyes of science, find their theological Waterloo here. It's important to remember that what we say about Mary is intended to illuminate her son, not her own story. The virginity of Mary, then, is not a statement about Mary. The doctrine of the Virgin Birth is not saying anything about the nature of sex or natural motherhood. It is not intended to suggest that virginity is a holier state than maternity. The virginity of Mary is essentially a statement affirming the *divine origin* of Jesus, a sign of the absolute newness that burst forth in human history with the arrival of God-made-flesh in a remote town in the backwaters of the Roman Empire over two thousand years ago.

This is not to say that the teaching about the virginity of Mary has not been used negatively toward married women or as an indictment against human sexuality in general, for history shows that it has. It is also in the record that theologians have spent inordinate amounts of time trying to figure out the biological implications of this extra-biological event. But when the evangelists were writing these stories, the understanding we now have of human reproduction was many centuries away. The story they related took its shape not from history nor from their primitive knowledge of biology but from the miracle birth stories of the ancient world, a few examples of which appear in the Bible.

The basic miracle birth story goes like this: A woman cannot conceive a child because she's too old, or is barren, or is alone. Then an angel appears to manifest God's interest in the situation. Someone delivers the revelation of an approaching birth. The name of the child is given, as well as his destiny—for it was almost always a male child. Next follows an expression of astonishment, and then a sign is promised. The stories of the birth of heroes were often told in this way. It's an ancient way of saying, "Put a marker on this name. The child born here will be significant later, for he has first been marked by God." The story of the birth of Isaac to Sarah, Samuel to Hannah, and John to Elizabeth are all told with these conventions in mind. What makes Mary's story unique, of course, is that the child is conceived without the intervention of a human father.

The miraculous birth does not imply that these women have transcended the natural order nor that they have accomplished something in themselves. God is always the progenitor of the miracle. These women are chosen to participate, but they are not responsible for the event. Sarah laughs at God's plan when she hears of it. Hannah weeps in supplication for a child, but she hardly forces God's hand. Elizabeth, as far as we know, is not even consulted; the deal is made through her husband Zechariah. In every case, it is God who chooses and God who acts.

Of all the biblical miracle-birth mothers, Mary alone is approached directly and is offered the opportunity to give her consent. Through her *fiat*, we recognize that a life of holiness means that we hear God, that we are *obedient*, a word that has "listening" as its root meaning. Mary listened when God spoke and turned her entire life in the direction of God's will, like a boat on the river current. Obedient living is not something one does spontaneously. It takes practice, attending first in small ways and preparing for the more challenging call. Though a young girl, Mary must have had enough experience listening for God that she could recognize the word of God, even when it came spoken in this wondrous new language of exceptional birth. And because she was listening, God chose her.

This may be why Jesus later refused to accept the praise of his mother that a woman in the crowd uttered: "Blessed is the womb that bore you and the breasts that nursed you." Those words attempt to honor Mary for the wrong reason: being biologically responsible for her son. Jesus knew she was exceptional for her obedient attention to God, so he replied, "Blessed rather are those who hear the word of God and obey it" (Luke 11:27–28).

Immaculate Conception

The Virgin Birth and the Immaculate Conception are two doctrines about Mary that are often confused, even by lifelong Catholics. The Virgin Birth really concerns the birth and origins of *Jesus.* The Immaculate Conception refers to the unique circumstances surrounding the conception of *Mary* by her parents, traditionally known as Joachim and Anne. This second doctrine, more abstract than the first and a little more theological, is easy to misunderstand. It holds that Mary was free from original sin, which afflicts the rest of humanity, from the moment she was conceived in her mother's womb, that the one who would give birth to the Messiah was always free from sin, original and actual. The Immaculate Conception concerns the preparation of Mary for her unique role in salvation history as the Mother of God.

Why would the church speak of Mary as being conceived without original sin, "without stain"? The idea is found nowhere in the gospels. They say nothing about Mary before the annunciation. The teaching of the Immaculate Conception was issued as a dogma, or definitive teaching, of the church by Pope Pius IX in 1854, though it was taught as early as the eleventh century. It originates in the reasoning that the woman who heard God speak so clearly at the annunciation must have been accustomed to being attentive to the divine voice. And if she made a habit of listening to God and could so perfectly attend to God's word, then it could be said that she was free of all the barriers that impede the attention we humans pay to the will of God. Sin blocks our ability to hear and follow the word that God speaks to us in our lives. Though Mary was born a human being like the rest of us and thus was therefore free *to* sin, yet she remained free *from* sin. Why is this so?

"*Potuit, decuit, fecit.*" This Latin phrase is the short way by which theologians have explained the event: "God could have done it, God saw that it was fitting, and therefore God did it." It basically means that God *could* have preserved Mary from the human disposition to sin, and it *would* have been appropriate or fitting to do so. So God *did* it.

The Immaculate Conception is not intended to be a magical statement about Mary's uniqueness but a doctrine about the nature of *Jesus*. For Jesus to be born, there had to be a Mary; for God to become one of us, human cooperation was necessary. If God were to choose a woman to participate in this radical plan, a woman like Mary would be most fitting: a woman perfectly

184

attuned to God's will. The Immaculate Conception of Mary is a theological way of explaining how God enabled Mary to be that person.

This may sound like cheating, but God breaks a lot of rules of the created order to attain divine ends—in this case, our salvation. Are we likely to argue, especially as we are all the primary beneficiaries of that decision? I, for one, am not going to quibble.

When coming to grips with the teaching of the Immaculate Conception, the point is not to get the details of the process straight—Did Anne smell a rose and conceive?—but to acknowledge that God takes care of everything. Obviously, as with the teaching of the Virgin Birth, we are not supposed to try to follow Mary's example literally. We learn from the Virgin Birth that, like Mary, we are asked to spend our lives intent on the voice of God spoken into our world at all times, in unique ways to our unique selves. The teaching on the Immaculate Conception advises us to relax: God's in charge; every last iota of our needs has already been provided for; whatever God may ask us to do, we will be given the grace and the fortitude to do it.

The Assumption

This is the third of the church teachings about Mary that are intimately related. It follows naturally from the first two: If Mary was preserved from sin, she should also have been preserved from the effects of sin. As we know from Paul, "the wages of sin is death" (Romans 6:23). But what happens to one whose life went untouched by sin? Can we imagine that God, who saw it fitting to prepare Mary from the moment of her conception for the role she was to play, would not acknowledge this at the end? Can we imagine that the sinless woman whose body was the very vessel of our salvation would be left to death and corruption as all others are?

As with the conception of Mary, scripture is silent on the matter of Mary's life after her presence in the upper room with the disciples at Pentecost (see Acts 1:13–14). Mary's end is not recorded. Tradition tells us that Mary grew old and then fell asleep, an event delicately called her dormition, or sleeping, and frequently treated in art. The dormition suggests that death never claimed the woman whose body was "the ark of the new covenant," the human tabernacle of the God made flesh. The church teaches, then, that rather than experience the wages of sin Mary was taken up to heaven at once to receive the reward of the just. In Catholic terms, Mary was taken up "body and soul into the glory of heaven."

What meaning could this event of Mary's assumption have for us? Certainly, it is an assurance of the destiny that awaits all who "fall asleep in the Lord," our own bodily resurrection at the end of time. But the timing of this teaching in church history is also instructive. Although the tradition of Mary's assumption is traceable to at least the sixth century, it did not become dogma in the church until 1950. Pope Pius XII had witnessed with the rest of the world the catastrophic events of the Second World War and had seen the pictures emerging from that era— images of human life cheaply and shockingly discarded. The harvest of hatred had been unimaginable; the pictures made it all too real, the endless piles of bodies treated like refuse. Part of the rationale for elevating the tradition of the Assumption to a dogmatic pronouncement was to respond before the world to the carnage with an affirmation of the sanctity of the human body. Human beings had abused human life and human flesh, but God cherished every life and would rescue us—soul *and* body—for eternity. The images of the war that paralyzed the world with the cheapness of human flesh were *not* the truth about humanity, said the church. The truth is that our flesh too will one day be lifted up in glory.

Our relationship to Mary

The role of Mary in the church is often misunderstood, especially by people outside the Catholic church. People ask if we worship Mary as a goddess. The correct answer is that we do not worship Mary at all. Worship and adoration belong to God alone. *Worship* is the activity of giving praise and thanks to God. *Adoration* is the highest attitude of prayer, engaging the body, mind and soul of the worshipper in acknowledging that

186

God is the source of all that is. What we offer to the saints, Mary above all, is *veneration*, which means reverence and respect for them because of their example of how to live a holy life in accordance with God's will.

Because of the story in John's gospel about Mary being given to the care of the disciple at the cross and he to her, we have come to embrace Mary as the Mother of the Church. A passage in the book of Revelation tells the story of a woman about to give birth while being pursued by a dragon. The child is snatched to heaven, while God preserves and protects the woman's life (Revelation 12). In this story, read during the celebration of the Eucharist on the Feast of the Assumption, August 15, we know that the woman is not intended to be Mary but an image of the church. Still, the images are interchangeable for Catholics, because the church is so intimately under Mary's patronage. Mary is often represented with a crown of stars and with the moon at her feet, as the woman in Revelation is described. Just as she bore Jesus in Bethlehem, the church bears Christ into the world until the end of time. The church's identification with Mary is very intimate because we understand that we share a common vocation with her.

Like Mary, we are called by God to give birth to good news. We too are asked to hold in our hearts the mysteries of faith in which we participate, to remember and to tell the story of Mary and her relationship to God. Like Mary at the cross, we must endure the suffering that comes the way of every faithful disciple. And like Mary at Cana, we ask her to intercede for God's action in our world wherever people thirst for the abundance only God can supply. Through Mary, we come to understand our vocation as church. She, most of all, teaches us that bearing Christ into our world is not a human work but can take place only through the power of the Holy Spirit.

Questions to Explore

1. Name some images of Mary that you have seen in art: in painting, sculpture, stained glass or other forms. What did each image teach you about Mary?

187

2. Which part of Mary's story in the New Testament is most meaningful to you? How does it affect your personal relationship to Mary?

3. Compare Luke's stories of Mary with those found in the gospel of John. Which Mary seems more accessible to you? Which story helps you to understand your own vocation more clearly?

4. What names or titles do you most often use for Mary: Blessed Mother, Virgin, Mother of God, Madonna or others? How does each help you to better understand her?

5. How does Mary's way of bearing Jesus in her arms (as an infant or after the crucifixion) illuminate the way you feel called to bear Christ? Give an example of how you see yourself as a Christ-bearer.

6. How do you listen for the voice of God in your life as Mary did? How does the story of the Virgin Birth help you to reevaluate how you listen to God? In what ways might you listen to God differently?

7. How has God uniquely prepared you for the work of your life? In what ways has your understanding of the Immaculate Conception changed after reading this chapter? How does this new understanding influence your thinking about vocation?

8. Does the doctrine of the Assumption of Mary alter your thinking about the sanctity of the human body? How? Where in our society do you see a need for implementing the teaching that human life and human flesh are holy?

9. How have you shown or might you express veneration for Mary? In what ways does your parish exhibit special reverence for the Mother of God?

10. Mary is called the Mother of the Church. Which do you think is the most important example that Mary offers to you in living the life of discipleship?

Faith Response

1. Choose an image of Mary that is especially important to you and provide for it a place of honor in your home. You may want to keep fresh flowers or a candle nearby as an expression of reverence.

2. Look for images of Mary in churches, museums or art books at the library. Learn more about the many faces of Mary and artists' interpretation of her throughout the centuries as she has come alive in the imagination of the faithful.

3. Pray the Hail Mary, the rosary, the Angelus or other prayers that honor the special relationship Mary had with her son, Jesus. See the Appendix for these and other prayers. If you do not know these prayers, ask your pastor, catechist or another Catholic to help you learn how to pray them. You may also obtain instruction booklets at any Catholic bookstore.

4. Contemplate the unique role Mary played in salvation history as the Christ-bearer. Consider one way that you can bear the good news of Jesus to your family, friends and community. Pray for Mary's intercession as you follow her example.

Eleven

Believing and Behaving: Elements of Catholic Morality

Moral living is like putting a jigsaw puzzle together: Right out of the box, all these pieces seem unrelated to one another, signifying nothing in themselves. But as you spread them out and turn them over, you begin to see connections that didn't seem to be there before: color, theme, shape, order. Some pieces are obviously part of the framework, setting the boundaries for the rest. As you start to link them together here and there, things start to make sense. With some time and effort (and maybe with help from friends) you begin to see what was unrecognizable before. And once all the pieces are in place, the big picture emerges. The fragments have become part of a much greater, coherent and meaningful wholeness.

For many people, the big picture of morality emerges over a lifetime, and some of the pieces are harder to put in place than others. The puzzling part of moral living comes in thinking that all the decisions we make are separate and unrelated. Actually they are part of the big picture of our personal integrity. Finding the relationship of each piece to others is sometimes very challenging and frustrating, and if a crucial piece is missing, then nothing around it can be linked with it. As in all of life's puzzles, "the devil is in the details."

One critical element in Catholic moral thinking is the process we call discernment. This is more than listing pros and cons on a sheet of paper and then deciding what to do based on the results. Obviously, many things we can decide on would be personally beneficial to us but in some ways are harmful to others or to the planet. Discerning what to do is not merely making decisions based on the immediate facts. It requires that we make wise decisions that respect the relationship *every* decision we make has to the big picture as a whole.

Christian discernment

People of faith believe that God sees the world in terms of the big picture all the time. God wants us to see the world in the same way in so far as we can, but sin distorts our vision and so we see, as Paul says, "in a mirror, dimly" (1 Corinthians 13:12). God created the world as a coherent, beautiful whole, but all we see is a box full of pieces and a puzzle to solve. The process of discernment is to help us to see beyond the effects of sin to what the world was supposed to look like...and still does in the everlasting vision of God. We can move in the direction of God's will for the world if we take the time to try to see what God sees. Sometimes this requires a great deal of religious imagination, because the more we are caught in the habits of sin, the harder it is to see beyond them.

If we believe that all the pieces in the puzzle box came from God, then we look to God for assistance in reconstructing the world as it should be. Where do you go for the tools you need to make life decisions, both large and small? Most of us, frankly, look to our culture. Without even thinking about it, we are hugely affected by the input of media, politics, art and the buzz of conversation of our peers. We make decisions about how to spend money, whom to vote for, how to act in our relationships, what our responsibilities are to each other and to the natural world—all based on the information and impressions we receive from the stir of words and images surrounding us. In the twenty-first century, we are surrounded by images of how to behave, what to want, what to say, what's okay and not okay to think and feel. This blanket of images around us is very comforting and often subtly restricts our freedom by telling us who we are and how to act—as men or women, as grownups or children, as Republicans or Democrats, as one race or another. Brainwashed daily with these images, we often react and make decisions in knee-jerk fashion, thinking we are being morally thoughtful, while in reality we are just doing what we've been told. Remember the old subliminal flashes of advertising used in movie houses? One minute, you're fine; the next minute, you really want popcorn or a soda.

When we employ Christian discernment in making up our minds about what to choose, we begin by deciding which criteria we will use to arrive at our conclusions. Mass culture cannot be allowed to play a role in this. Peer pressure and consumer want can have no place in the moral conversation. We cannot make decisions based on what we think we can get away with, what is legal in our society, or what everybody else is doing. We can't embrace an idea simply because it doesn't seem to hurt anyone in particular.

The tools we Catholics have at our disposal in discernment are plentiful: scripture, tradition, church teaching, our community of faith, prayer and the interaction of all these elements with our conscience. For Catholics, the informed conscience is the highest moral authority. That most certainly does not imply that we can do anything that we, personally, can "live with." It does mean that we have an obligation to inform our conscience with all the tools of discernment mentioned above, so that our conscience can function as a reliable compass to guide us in moral living.

The Ten Commandments

Ask people what are some good rules to live by, and most will point to the Ten Commandments, or Decalogue. Even people who do not consider themselves religious have no argument with most of the commandments as ethical teachings. There are several versions of the Decalogue in the Old Testament, but basically they go as follows:

1. I am the Lord your God. You shall not bow down before other gods.
2. You shall not take the name of the Lord your God in vain.
3. Remember the Sabbath day and keep it holy.
4. Honor your father and your mother.
5. You shall not murder.
6. You shall not commit adultery.
7. You shall not steal.

193

8. You shall not bear false witness against your neighbor.
9. You shall not covet your neighbor's wife.
10. You shall not covet your neighbor's goods.

Because these commandments of God are so familiar to most of us from our childhood, we presume we know them and keep them, even though we really don't. Here are a few ways we break the basic ten all the time:

- We choose to follow money, success, approval, celebrity, glamour or power over the will of God. (First Commandment)
- We use God's name as an expression of irritation. We use religious reasons as an excuse for getting our way, as when we judge others and assign the judgment to "God's will." (Second Commandment)
- We work on Sunday, even when it's not necessary. We obsess over our work, thinking it all depends on our efforts, never resting to honor God for what God has done for us. We refuse to participate in the Sunday liturgy because we "don't get anything out of it" or we're too tired. (Third Commandment)
- We ignore our parents. We neglect the elderly. We forget what we owe to the past. (Fourth Commandment)
- We kill in the name of the state in unjustifiable military actions, in abortion clinics, in business decisions that harm natural resources or break the body or spirit of workers. We also kill one another with prejudice. We crush the spirit of children by destroying their self-esteem and hope. (Fifth Commandment)
- We, men and women together, objectify each other sexually. Even when we don't actively violate the marriage bond, we are not faithful in our love. We do not support our married friends but often assist them in losing heart. (Sixth Commandment)
- We steal from the poor, as Basil the Great pointed

194

out, by not sharing our abundance with them. We steal the dignity of those who are disadvantaged. (Seventh Commandment)

- We gossip about others and enhance the details. We violate oaths we have sworn. We say what we cannot substantiate. We deliver one fact about a person as if it were the whole truth. (Eighth Commandment)
- As citizens of a consumer culture, we are the most covetous people on the planet. We are addicted to the pursuit of possessing, whether it's that car we can't afford or that person we can't—or shouldn't—have. (Ninth and Tenth Commandments).

Moral living, as Jesus pointed out, is not simply about following laws. It means understanding what the laws intend. Laws are like traffic lights. If you obey the absolute letter of the law and betray its spirit, for example, by running the yellow lights right up to the last instant, sooner or later you'll be in a wreck all the same. Traffic lights can't help you if you are intent on beating the system.

The Ten Commandments are great rules to live by, and if we followed them perfectly in their fullest expression, we'd do all right. But keep in mind, moral living is never the *way* to God but a *response* to God. And since God is love, as John tells us, the most natural response to Love is love. In this light, we see that sin is not some kind of moral accident, merely breaking a law, but rather the betrayal of love and friendship. The decision to love, on the other hand, is the fullest response to God's love for us that we can make.

In the end, the goal of moral living is not to win God's approval or to "get to heaven." God loves us unconditionally, just as much now as when we become a "better person." We cannot be more loved by God than we are right now, but we can certainly experience God's love better when we are in union with the divine will. In the realm of "Which came first, the chicken or the egg?" God's love comes first, and the desire to live morally follows that love. We are not moral because

195

moral laws exist to compel us. We *want* to be moral because divine love draws us into the heart of just and compassionate living. Morality is our response to God, who has loved us first.

The Sermon on the Mount

The Sermon on the Mount, with the Beatitudes as its capstone, is the flagship of Christian moral teaching. Sometimes the Beatitudes are regarded as the Thou Shalts, in contrast with the Thou Shalt Nots of the Decalogue. But these statements of blessing and joy do not really tell us what to do. They are promises of the happiness that is ours for living righteously. The Beatitudes contain blessings, such as the following:

Happy are the poor in spirit.
Happy are they who mourn.
Happy are the meek.
Happy are they who hunger and thirst for
    righteousness.
Happy are the merciful.
Happy are the clean of heart.
Happy are the peacemakers.
Happy are those persecuted for the sake of
    righteousness.

When we examine this list closely, we realize that a lot of these people who live this way aren't "happy" at all, in a worldly sense. Jesus is saying something very peculiar here. His words break like a surprise across the crowds of people who are suffering, hoping for justice, struggling against the power of sin in their lives. Congratulations, he is saying: You may have thought you were a loser, but in God's eyes the victory belongs to you.

We are the recipients of these blessings and promises when we do things like the following:

- We stand with the poor through our generous giving. We simplify our lives so that we do not live merely within our means but within our real needs. (First Beatitude)
- We look to God for comfort in the time of loss. And

196

we extend a comforting presence to others who are sad, lonely or suffering from depression. (Second Beatitude)

- We don't demand the limelight in every relationship. We don't expect applause for the good things we do. It isn't "all about me." (Third Beatitude)
- We not only want justice but are willing to work for justice, even if it means we stand to lose something that benefits us. We give up racist and sexist behavior, even if it's meant in humor. We reject the bottom line when the means for getting there are hurtful to others. (Fourth Beatitude)
- We forgive others, especially when it's hard and even if they don't say they're sorry or ask for our forgiveness. We forgive simply because it's what Jesus asks us to do and because God forgave us first. (Fifth Beatitude)
- We keep our hearts pure. We keep selfish impulses out of our love. We stop using people for what we can get. We are faithful to our relationships with God, our families, our friends and the community, especially the poorest among us. (Sixth Beatitude)
- We choose to be peacemakers. We reject violence in our words and in our actions. We promote nonviolent resistance to injustice. We adopt a spirit of gentleness, even with our enemies. We seek to reconcile divisions in our families and in our world. (Seventh Beatitude)
- We are willing to pay the price of discipleship, recognizing that Jesus, who followed God's will perfectly, was crucified for it. We should not expect not to suffer for doing what is right. (Eighth Beatitude)

Once I heard a preacher say, "God plays a game with us in which the losers win." So if you and I are "losers" in the world's bottom-line game of power and profit, we have reason to rejoice. But if you and I are "winners" today, we'd better make good friends among today's losers! That's what it means to be in solidarity with the disadvantaged or to exercise what Pope John Paul II called "the preferential option for the poor." We who have power and privilege are to put it at the service of those who do not. When choosing between decisions that will benefit the privileged or the underprivileged, our decision should "prefer" the latter. In this way, we further the common good and demonstrate that God does "hear the cry of the poor."

Sins of commission: The fatal seven

We have examined some of the key scriptures that Christians use to inform their conscience for moral living. The tradition of the church offers many other categories and criteria to consider in our process of discernment in addition to the Decalogue and the Beatitudes. In the Penitential Rite of the Mass, each of us asks forgiveness for "what I have done, and what I have failed to do." We recognize sins of *commission*, actions we perform that lead to evil, and of *omission*, inaction that permits or encourages the evil that others do. As much as we are expected not to harm others, we are likewise charged to take steps, when we can, to confront or denounce what we perceive as evil. Moral living impels us to consider both sides of the equation.

In the matter of sins of commission, avoiding the *capital sins* is a good place to begin. The capital sins, often called the seven deadly sins, are listed as pride, envy, sloth (laziness), lust, greed, gluttony and anger. Lists of attitudes that are a danger to moral living were compiled as early as Paul's household codes in the epistles (see, for example, Colossians 3:5–11). Evagrius Ponticus, a fourth-century Egyptian monk, first listed eight particularly malicious attitudes. Pope Gregory the Great in the sixth century coined the term "capital" to describe serious sins, and Thomas Aquinas refined the capital list to spotlight the seven sins we today call deadly. He noted that they are the fountainhead of all other occasions of human sinfulness.

Obviously, distinctions need to be drawn between being angry in a given circumstance and living an angry existence, between enjoying a good meal and establishing an insatiable appetite for creature comfort, between natural sexual desire versus a life of using others for personal gratification. If jealousy, for instance, exists at the center of our lives and haunts us in every situation, that should concern us deeply. And if we refrain from offering love, comfort, witness and assistance in lieu of a lifestyle centered on a couch in front of the television, we ought to beware.

Acts not to omit: The works of mercy

Having spelled out what we are *not* to do, church teaching readily supplies positive suggestions on what we are obliged to do, how we are to fulfill the obligation to *do* something. The *corporal works of mercy* remind us of basic material ways we can assist those in need. This list derives from the teachings in Matthew 25:34–40 and Isaiah 58:6–10. The seven corporal works are:

To feed the hungry
To give drink to the thirsty
To clothe the naked
To shelter the homeless
To visit the sick
To visit the imprisoned
To bury the dead.

These seven activities incorporate our belief in the value of the human person, the dignity of the human body and the worthiness of human beings, regardless of our judgment of them. As with the Decalogue, we find in their broadest expression the call not only to care for the needs of others with our charity but also to strive to bring about changes in the system that treats people unjustly and without compassion.

In the same way, the *spiritual works of mercy* offer us ways to bring the same goodness and help to the spirit of another human being that we would bring to the physical person. They are derived from numerous gospel and epistle passages, with the last work, on prayer, based on a combination of ideas from Old and New Testaments. (See Chapter Twelve for more on the work of prayer.) The seven spiritual works are:

To warn the sinner
To teach the ignorant
To counsel the doubtful

To comfort the sorrowful
To bear wrongs patiently
To forgive all injuries
To pray for the living and the dead.

I got a call once from my young niece, who was given an assignment from her seventh-grade religion teacher to practice all seven of the spiritual works of mercy before the next class! She asked, hopefully, if there was anything she could do for me. I asked for her prayers and also that she remind me that God doesn't hate me just because I'm having a bad week (which I counted as counseling the doubtful). Be grateful that no one is asking you to practice all seven spiritual works of mercy in one go. Just seize the opportunities to practice them as they come.

Social teaching of the church

Apart from traditional lists of moral dos and don'ts, the magisterium of the church provides regular assistance in Catholic discernment on specific issues through a combination of papal letters called encyclicals and bishops' pastoral letters. An encyclical is written by, or under the authority of, the pope and is addressed to the universal church. Although it does not have the infallible weight of doctrine or dogma, it is understood to be written for the serious reflection of the faithful. Encyclicals are published originally in Latin, and even after translation they tend to keep their Latin titles, usually the first words of the letter. Historic documents like *Rerum Novarum* (Of New Things) by Pope Leo XIII in 1891 in support of labor, or *Pacem in Terris* (Peace on Earth) by Pope John XXIII in 1963, which extended and systematized the social teaching of the church, are courageous examples of how a letter from the pope can cause a revolution in vision and purpose in the church and sometimes beyond.

Papal encyclicals are available in Catholic bookstores and on the Internet, but the average Catholic, to be honest, doesn't read them. The "chain of command" in church teaching aims these papal documents primarily at the bishops' conference in a given area, which is responsible for adapting these ideas for their own people. In the United States, we look to the United States Conference of Catholic Bishops (USCCB) to publish their own pastoral letters for our consideration on more immediate matters. Some of the most widely read pastorals in recent years are the bishops' peace pastoral in 1983 *(The Challenge of Peace)* and their economic letter in 1986 *(Economic Justice for All)*. The USCCB's timely, thoughtful examination of currently relevant issues made the influence of these letters stretch beyond the Catholic audience to the arenas of the university, politics and business.

The social teaching of the Catholic church is radical, grounded as it is on the socially disruptive teachings of Jesus. In order to appreciate it, we have to forget for a moment much of what we learned in civics class. We are naturally prejudiced to think of our present social system as the best the world can offer, and that may well be true. But what God intends is far better still. All we have to do is walk through the nearest poor neighborhood to realize that even this society we love so well is only "the dark mirror" of what human society could be.

In the beginning, the teaching goes, God created the world and delivered it over to human stewardship, with all of its rich potential and resources. Creation was intended to be an environment where justice, peace and the fullness of God's blessings would ensure the happiness of all. But the entrance of sin into the world brought division between man and woman, set brother against brother, and the pattern of inequality, survival of the fittest and uncaring competition was branded upon history. The powerful would have more than they need and withhold it from the powerless. We've all become used to the world being this way, since it's the only world we've ever known.

But consider the original proposition that all people are given the world to cultivate and enjoy. The right to private property notwithstanding, the fair and just distribution of goods remains God's intention. This element of the church's social teaching is a revolution in the making: No matter what we've been able to acquire and possess, we can make no claim to any share that is withheld from our sisters and brothers in need.

This is not simply the Catholic church's political or socio-economic statement. Look to the words of Jesus: "Love your neighbor as yourself." "Do not store up treasure on earth, but store your treasure in heaven." "You cannot serve God and mammon." "Do not worry about what you will eat, or what you will wear. Consider the lilies of the field." (See the Sermon on the Mount in Matthew 6.) Our purpose in life is not to acquire and amass possessions for ourselves, our families, our heirs. As Pope Paul VI, one of the architects of the Second Vatican Council, said, "Avarice is the most evident form of moral underdevelopment." If we've set our sights on making a safe, cozy life for ourselves, we've set the standard pitiably narrow and low.

Pope John Paul II, unmistakably not a communist, put the case emphatically: "Private property is under a social mortgage." (See the papal document, *Sollicitudo Rei Socialis* [On Social Concern], 1987.) Whatever we have, we have for the sake of others. What we withhold for ourselves has ramifications for all.

These stirring teachings have consequences for our own moral development as well. We exist within the tension of *being* and *having*. The teachings suggest that if we *have* too much, the less we can *become*. The opposite is likewise true: If we have too little, fewer opportunities to become are available to us. It is necessary, then, for all of God's children to have *enough*. And that will not come to pass so long as some of us are content to become rich at the expense of others.

The marriage of peace and justice

We often talk of peace and justice as if they are two discreet subjects. Some people are politically roused when it comes to matters of war and peace, and others are "into" justice. Pope Paul VI created the first bumper-sticker theology when he declared that "Peace is more than the absence of war." He added, "If you want peace, work for justice." The pope recognized that the development of poor nations was essential to the stability of all nations. He called economic development "the new name for peace."

Peace will never be maintained when the world's wealth is so unevenly distributed. And war, arguably never a desirable event, becomes even more harrowing in the present age of limitless weaponry. War has been dismissed as a political issue, but it is inescapably a moral issue when it reaches the use of the technology of mass destruction. War today is not what it was when both sides were armed with rocks or even guns. Once upon a time, we might talk about a "just" or "limited" war, but in the nuclear age the engagement of arms can end in the widespread killing of innocent bystanders or even in the total annihilation of a nation. When the whole planet is under threat, the question goes beyond politics.

The United States Catholic bishops outlined the historical progression of the moral theory of war in *The Challenge of Peace: God's Promise and Our Response.* In it, they note that in church history three distinct positions on war have been held. The first is the idea that any use of lethal force in incompatible with the Christian vocation. This means we must resist evil nonviolently and cannot justify the taking of human life under any terms. Though this position was not articulated formally until the fourth century, Christians from the time of the early church were in trouble for being unwilling to serve as soldiers. This conscientious objection to war is one of the reasons they were charged as bad citizens in ancient Rome, which was a crime against the state.

The second position on war was the one advanced during the Crusades—not an auspicious time for moral theology. The Crusaders' position was simple: Once you know who the enemy is, go get him any way you can, because he's God's enemy too. The fact that the Crusaders stood to gain greatly in terms of worldly good and power by the routing of "God's enemy" was not a point in favor of this ethical stance.

The *just war theory* is the third and most carefully nuanced of the three positions on war as exercised within the church historically. It states that some, through not all, uses of force are morally justifiable, *if the war is just.* It raises as many questions as it answers: Who determines the justness of a war? What are the criteria under which this war can be fought? Who can be killed, in what manner, under what conditions?

Some moral theologians have suggested that war can never be just, because it can never be shown to be necessary. Alternatives always exist long before people resort to arms. Rather than waiting until war is inevitable, we should move to create a world in which war is obsolete. Or as Pope Paul VI said, "If you want peace, work for justice."

The seamless garment of life

The bottom line of the church's moral teaching is the conviction that *life is sacred,* consecrated to God's purposes. Life is a gift from God, given out of love, to be cherished and cultivated. It is not a "right" that can be bestowed or retracted by human or legal decision. Because we believe life belongs to God and is God's alone to judge, a host of social issues clamor for a Catholic response that upholds the fundamental principle of the sanctity of life.

Cardinal Joseph Bernardin, a former archbishop of Chicago, called for an integrated approach to the life issues facing modern society under the framework of "a consistent ethic of life." He maintained that abortion, capital punishment, modern warfare, euthanasia, medical ethics and socio-economic injustice all challenge the principle of God's sovereignty and life's sanctity. Emotions run high on many of these issues, but this is the basic platform: All the life issues are related, and to champion one and neglect another is to tear at the fabric of the argument of life's sanctity. We can't argue, for example, that new life is valuable but old life is expendable; that healthy people are useful but sick or disabled people are not; that innocent life must be protected but guilty life has forfeited its "sanctity;" that our neighbors should be nurtured and our enemies destroyed; that those who pull themselves up by their bootstraps earn the right to our concern while those who languish in systemic poverty reap only our indifference. As soon as we are willing to admit the argument that one life is not worthy to live, the position in defense of *all* life shatters irreparably. The sanctity of human life is like a seamless garment, and pulling out a single thread causes the entire fabric to unravel.

As adherents to the principles of democracy, most Americans tend to approach these issues primarily in terms of legislation, as though the right laws framed in the right way will save us. Ultimately, however, our hearts must change, as well as our vision, so that any changes in our system will be upheld by the way we view the voiceless, the powerless, the disadvantaged and the enemy.

The teachings of Jesus remain the baseline of the moral formation of Christians. Love your neighbor, he said, and he defined the neighbor to include the one we most prefer to exclude. And when the neighbor becomes the enemy, Jesus added, then love your enemy. It is a scary, challenging, seemingly impossible overwhelming proposition. But it is also what Jesus taught us to do.

The call to moral living

You may be surprised at the contents of this discussion on morality. A thorough reading of the Hebrew prophets and the teachings of Jesus, however, reveals that we will be judged by our capacity to love one another, in terms both broad and concrete. This puts the emphasis squarely on *social sin* and less on the idea of *personal sins*. What these teachings insist on is that sin is an interpersonal affair—something that we build together, much like the Tower of Babel in Genesis. Like the mythical tower, we have built a world out of pride and greed in defiance of God's authority. And like the folks of Babel, we find ourselves at the end of this construction, lost in a maze of nations that do not communicate and cannot live together anymore.

The only way back through the maze and into a future of hope is to embrace again God's original plan for creation: a world of peace founded in justice, with the fullness of blessing for all. In this more global sense of sin and responsibility, personal sins do exist, of course. It is possible for one person to choose to steal, kill or commit sexual infidelity, for example, but these decisions are made within a larger network of greed, violence and infidelity that makes such acts both desirable and profitable. For Catholics, our personal morality and social morality are mutually supportive and can be mutually destructive. We cannot be content to be "good people" living in a "bad world." As our original metaphor of the puzzle demonstrates, all the choices we make must hang together if the good of the whole is finally to emerge.

Questions to Explore

1. Consider the elements of your life—your relationships, work, recreation, responsibilities, values and convictions— as pieces in a puzzle that should fit together. Which pieces presently do not "hang together" with the rest? What can you do to improve the fit?

2. How do you understand the difference between "making a decision" and "Christian moral discernment"? Name some criteria for each.

3. How does our consumer culture affect your efforts to live a moral lifestyle? Which of the images that you "consume"—in advertisements, films, on television, in the arts—most influence your wants and goals? How? Why?

4. Which of the Ten Commandments, in its broadest understanding, offers the most challenge for you? Why? Which of the Beatitudes is your biggest challenge? Why?

5. Look at the list of seven deadly sins: pride, envy, laziness, lust, greed, gluttony and anger. Which root sin is responsible in your life for the most frequent failures to love? What concrete steps can you take to break your bondage to this sin?

6. Review the lists of the corporal and spiritual works of mercy. Think of people you know who have been a model of each of these for you. Reflect on how you might be called at this time to answer the needs of others, both physical and spiritual.

7. Think of a short list of the church's moral teachings (you may browse through the chapter for help) and imagine explaining them to someone who has never heard of the

church's position. How well prepared are you to engage in such a conversation? What steps might you take to become better informed?

8. Reread the three stances on war that Christians have historically taken as outlined in the U.S. Catholic bishops' pastoral letter on peace. Which comes closest to describing your position on war? What is your reaction to the idea that "peace is more than the absence of war"?

9. Which of the life issues that are part of the "seamless garment" argument are most challenging for you to embrace? Do you believe that the sanctity of life can be forfeited under certain circumstances? Explain your position.

10. Name one idea in this chapter that has caused you to reconsider your understanding of morality. What do you think of the distinction between social sin and personal sin?

Faith Response

1. Try rewriting the Ten Commandments in positive terms. For example, the first commandment could be: "I shall obey God and God alone." The fifth might read: "I shall support, nurture and sustain life." Post these affirming commandments on your desk or refrigerator or in another place where you can meditate on them often.

2. Review the works of mercy again. Check off the ones you have satisfied recently. Think of ways you or your parish could meet the demands of those works that are more difficult or intimidating. Be creative in expanding their boundaries. For example, "bury the dead" can also mean starting a ministry to bereaved families in your parish. "Visit the sick" might include providing relief for long-term caregivers and their families.

3. Do some additional research into the social teaching of the church. Go to a Catholic bookstore and pick up a copy of

any recent pastoral letter or papal encyclical. Or call 800-235-8722 to order a title or obtain a catalogue of these publications. Become well versed in at least one social issue that is of particular concern to you. If you're really up for a challenge, read about the one issue on which you disagree the most and see if their publication affects your understanding.

4. Make a commitment to become involved in some aspect of the quest for justice and peace. Your parish or diocese may have a social justice group you can contact for information, or you may choose to support a local, national or international cause with your resources, attention, signature and even vote.

Twelve

Kingdom Coming, All the Time

What are you waiting for? I don't mean right now necessarily, or on this particular day, but in this lifetime. What is it you are expecting? The most disastrous answer you can give is that you aren't waiting for anything. Some people go through life as if it's all "sound and fury, signifying nothing," as Shakespeare said. They live as if they were born for no special reason and intend merely to go on living until they die. End of story. And because the story is so short and random, they settle for immediate gratification in relationships and in the creature comforts of this world. What else is there for them to look forward to?

Those of us who make a commitment to follow Jesus are an Advent people. *Advent* means "coming." We are waiting for "the Arrival from ahead of us," as Protestant theologian Jurgen Moltmann has poetically phrased it. We anticipate the God of the coming. We wait "in joyful hope," in the belief that "Christ has died, Christ is risen, Christ will come again," to use the words of our eucharistic liturgy. This is the defining theology of our faith. We pray as Jesus taught us: "Your kingdom come, on earth as it is in heaven."

Theologians call the study of the "last things"—death, the end of the world, final judgment, heaven, hell and the Second Coming of Christ—eschatology. Because eschatology concerns the part of eternity we can't see—the part after death or at the end of the world—we are naturally very curious about it. We want to know what has happened to the loved ones we have lost, what will happen to us, and where this whole world we love so well is going.

209

Death and what comes after

When I teach the "afterlife" lesson to any church group, people always want to know the facts. "How high is heaven? How hot is hell?" "Under what circumstances do I wind up in purgatory?" "What will happen to my dog?" "If my mother died in her forties and I die an old man, will I be older than my mother in heaven?"

These people are often disappointed by the content of the lesson I offer. Some religious leaders asked Jesus a similar question: If a woman has seven husbands in succession, each one dying before her, and then she herself dies, whose wife will she be in the resurrection? Jesus dismissed the question by saying that the person who asked it didn't understand "the scriptures nor the power of God" (see Matthew 22:23–33). What Jesus was saying is that the issues that concern us now will not concern us in the life of the world to come. We are talking about an existence the likes of which we cannot imagine. Everything in our imagination right now about the afterlife is totally inadequate in comparison to the real thing.

But that doesn't stop us from asking the questions about the afterlife. The first-century Christians in Corinth were as curious as we are about how resurrection works and what life will be like after we die. Since Christians hold firmly to the idea of the "resurrection of the body," as we say in our Creed, the Corinthians wanted to know what kind of body we will have. These are honest questions, considering that the only life we have ever known is an incarnate one, very much related to the condition of our flesh-and-blood selves.

Paul comes down a little hard on the community at Corinth, perhaps because their concern with these matters was out of proportion with the overall agenda of faith. He repeats, firmly, that the teaching of the resurrection is non-negotiable: If Christ has not been raised, our faith is in vain (1 Corinthians 15:12–19). Since Christ has in fact been raised, we are assured of our own resurrected life in the age to come, when God will be "all in all" (1 Corinthians 15:28). But just as the seed does not resemble the tree to come in any respect, we cannot know what our lives, sown in death, will look like in the life to come. What is sown is physical, perishable and humble. What is harvested will be spiritual, imperishable and glorified. Just as "star differs from star in glory," the glory to come is like nothing we have known (1 Corinthians 15:35–41).

As stirring as Paul's words are when we read them today, I doubt that they put the question to rest for the Corinthians. Perhaps they at least put the matter into perspective for us, which is all we can hope for. Paul's teaching echoes what is known about the post-resurrection encounters with Christ. Jesus' own best friends, who loved him deeply, didn't recognize him when he appeared to them after Easter. Each time, Jesus had to say or do something familiar for them to see who he was, as when he called Mary of Magdala by name at the tomb (John 20:11–18) or broke bread with the two disciples on the road to Emmaus (Luke 24:13–35). A glorified body is clearly much different from the one we have now. But those who love us can still recognize us through the intuition of the heart: "Were not our hearts burning within us while he was talking on the road?" (Luke 24:32).

Scripture and afterlife

We now think of the afterlife as a given in Judeo-Christian thought, but it actually came about, like most theology, as an evolution of ideas. The people of the ancient world had a variety of thoughts about what happened after death, mostly coming down to the idea that any existence beyond death was no more than a half-life, a shadow of its former vitality. Unable to produce or influence anything after death, one was reduced to a "shade," with memories of what one had done and failed to do. This half-life was consigned to Hades, or the Underworld, since the dead were placed in the ground. It was, by all accounts, a bleak affair. In Jewish terms, this place was called *sheol*, which has been erroneously identified with hell. It sure may sound like hell to us, but like Hades, *sheol* was an equal-opportunity holding tank for all of history's dead.

For a long time, Jewish thought remained closed on the subject of afterlife. But after the nation was overrun and exiled by the Babylonians in the sixth century B.C., both apocalyptic and wisdom literature from other cultures influenced Jewish reflection on the afterlife. The books of Daniel, Ezekiel and even later parts of Isaiah began incorporating two ideas from those traditions: first, that people will be divided after death according to their deeds; and second, a belief in a coming resurrection began to evolve.

The book of Wisdom gives us the clearest picture of the emerging conversation between the old and new theologies of afterlife. Read chapters 1–3 with this distinction in mind. Chapter 3 is especially of interest, because it is often read at Catholic funerals.

> The souls of the righteous are in the hand of God,
> and no torment will ever touch them.
> In the eyes of the foolish they seemed to have died,
> and their departure was thought to be a disaster,
> and their going from us to be their destruction;
> but they are at peace.
>
> —Wisdom 3:1–3

By the time of Jesus, Jewish thought generally accepted the idea that one's moral status in life affects which pocket of afterlife one is assigned to. But the idea of resurrection was still hotly debated. The Pharisees believed in it, as they did in the reality of spirits, angels and the like. The Sadducees, who controlled the Temple, disparaged the idea. And Jesus, who disliked debating such matters, rose from the dead and settled the issue once and for all—for those who would be his disciples.

Afterlife in contemporary Catholic thought

Catholic theologians today like to distinguish between the *reality* of heaven versus the *possibility* of hell. Heaven exists as the realm of God's perfect will, and hell can be described as a rejection of God's will in favor of one's own. Heaven and hell, then, are not equal-and-opposite territories in the outer cosmos. They are not places at all, so much as states of union with or alienation from God's will. The church, in its canonization of the saints, affirms that there are already human beings "in heaven," that is, in union with God. But it has never been determined

212

that *anyone* is presently "in hell."

God created the heavens and the earth, as scripture points out. But hell is not seen as a distinct creation of God. If hell exists, it is because we choose it. In a real sense we can be said to create it ourselves. Heaven *necessarily* exists, and hell exists only if *we insist* on it. Most biblical descriptions of hell's torments can be read as symbolizing the real suffering into which a sinner descends in the midst of his or her decision to turn from God. Hell is no joke, even if it's not the fiery pit or the icy sea of artistic imagination. Alienation from God, who is love, is a movement into lovelessness and ultimately to despair. Hell is no way to spend an hour, much less eternity.

Our free will means that the choice between heaven and hell is in our hands. In the end, however, time forecloses on our choice. Many of the parables of Jesus reveal that God will give the repentant sinner one more chance, one more season, to repent and turn back to the way of love. But we don't have forever to do this. The time comes when the one who is unprepared to receive love will be forbidden entrance into heaven, as in the tale of the five wise and five foolish bridesmaids (Matthew 25:1–13). The one who comes unprepared to celebrate at the feast will be cast into outer darkness (Matthew 22:1–14). The unyielding fig tree that remains unresponsive to the care of the gardener will be cut down (Luke 13:6–9). As finite, vulnerable mortals, we have no time to lose in turning from sin and choosing love.

We can be certain that many people face death in the "waffle zone" between the full embrace of love and its utter rejection. Theologians speak of purgatory as a period of purification of one's love after death. A person is not dangling between heaven and hell in such a state but rather exists between death and heaven, properly understood. This person cannot be lost, having already made the choice for love, however imperfectly. In post-exilic Jewish tradition, it was perceived that the living could intercede and make amends for the imperfections of those who had died. Prayer and good works on behalf of the dead are in evidence in the century before Jesus (see 2 Maccabees 12:43–46). It has long been the church's teaching that we can assist in the progress of the dead toward perfection with our prayer on their behalf. (For a word on the teaching about limbo, see the discussion of infant baptism in Chapter Six.)

The end of the world

Take a long, loving glance around the world as we know it. What do you love most: ocean, sky, mountains, trees, flowers, birds, the vastness and variety of it all? Is it the sound of music, the laughter of your children, the words "I love you" whispered by one you hold dear? Do you love the gleam of the world's great cities, the hustle and bustle of vigorous humanity at work and play? Is it the face of one particular person or one story that has captured your heart above all others? Is it really possible that everything you have experienced and grown to love will be extinguished one day like a candle flame?

When we read apocalyptic literature, such as the book of Revelation, we get the impression that this huge and wonderful creation of ours is headed for extinction. The earth gets pummeled by plagues, wars and natural disasters until it is destroyed several times over. Meanwhile the inhabitants of heaven wait for it to be over, so that the "new creation" can be ushered in and take up residence in the justice of God.

Many people who read the Bible literally expect things to happen this way. They read in Revelation about wars and famines as if they were reading tomorrow's newspaper. Since apocalyptic literature is literally "hidden" writing, some presume that a close reading will help them to see between the lines the exact date, place and persons involved in the end of the world. Catholic teaching, however, does not promote this view of the world's end.

The writers of apocalyptic literature were mostly interested in speaking to their present circumstances in a hidden and prophetic way. The church was under persecution, the faithful were being seized, and these writings became their consolation in the quest to stand true to Christ until death. Some of the characters in Revelation were references to then current figures, and some events refer obliquely to occurrences of their time. Much of what is said concerns the battle for the soul of the

214

believer and the numbers cited in the text were all used symbolically. It would have been obvious to the intended audience, for example, that the number four meant the whole world, six indicated imperfection, seven stood for completion, and twelve referred either to the tribes of Israel or the apostles. The bottom line of these writings remains pertinent for us: What we know now is passing away, and what is to come will be a marvel.

Jesuit theologian Karl Rahner asked this question: Are we waiting for the termination of history...or its fulfillment? The annihilation of creation...or its transfiguration? According to God's promise, the "new heavens and a new earth" will be established as a final season in which "righteousness is at home" (2 Peter 3:13). If this is what we are waiting for, then maybe it's the coming kingdom—and not the world's end— that compels the closure of time itself.

Now is the time

When I was sitting in religion class in grade school, I heard a lot about afterlife and very little about the kingdom of God. Heaven and hell were described as distant places that were destination points for the saint and sinner, respectively. The rest of us, the vast majority of us, would wind up in purgatory, where our fates sounded far from certain. Heaven, hell and purgatory— not to mention limbo, the place for unbaptized babies and good pagans—were rather definitively described and easily captured the imagination. I could have drawn a picture of each of them if asked. Afterlife was *that* tangibly communicated.

But the kingdom that Jesus described was a lot fuzzier to me. Because the translation "kingdom of heaven" was often used, I presumed Jesus was just using it as a nice metaphor for the heaven I already knew about. Stories about buying the pearl of great price or acquiring the treasure in the field were just fancy ways of talking about getting to heaven. So I continued to equate those stories with the idea of the distant place at the end of time or at the end of my life, whichever came first.

More recent translations of the Bible use the phrase "reign of God" or "kingdom of God" to dispel this confusion and to distinguish these stories from the heaven of the afterlife. As we

215

noted in Chapter Three, in Matthew's gospel alone Jesus speaks of the kingdom nearly fifty times! All of the parables in Matthew, as well as the Sermon on the Mount itself, are for the purpose of fleshing out the meaning of this kingdom. It is not simply a nice metaphor that Jesus likes to use, but it is in fact his central message.

In Mark's gospel, Jesus proclaims at the start of his ministry, "The time is fulfilled, and the kingdom of God has come near" (Mark 1:15). Near? Here? And fulfilled? Now? Suddenly, the idea of the distant and future heaven sounds incompatible with what Jesus is saying. In Luke's gospel, Jesus is even more explicit and personal: "The kingdom of God has come near *to you*" (Luke 10:9). Later in the same gospel, when the Pharisees ask Jesus when the kingdom will come, Jesus responds that its coming cannot be observed in the usual way. "For, in fact, the kingdom of God is among you." Some translators have even preferred, "The kingdom of God is *within you*" (See Luke17:20–21).

It would appear from these sayings that the kingdom is not a future place but rather a present reality. It's more like a verb than a noun. And it's not for later. It's happening right now.

Kingdom coming

All along in religion class, I had been thinking I was supposed to *get* to the kingdom somehow, someday, never realizing that the kingdom was heading *this way,* right smack into the middle of my present life. "The Arrival from ahead of us," we can say, is already at the door. Of course, if I had paid attention to my prayers, I would have known this. Don't we say, in the midst of every Our Father, "Thy kingdom come"? We never say, "May we go to heaven when we die!" And Jesus taught us to pray this way, because the kingdom is coming now, because it is already at hand, among us, even as we speak.

How do we recognize and make room in our lives for a kingdom, whole and entire, being established in the living room, as it were, even as we make our plans for the day? The present and personal kingdom that Jesus described it is not something we Christians can blithely circumvent. We can't put off the kingdom till the afterlife when it's already arrived now, like the unexpected guest, bag in hand, waiting for our welcome. This is the question Jesus puts to each one of us: "Yes or no: Can you make room for the reign of God or not?"

Theologians of eschatology have written much about the "last things" that remain tucked beyond the borders of this life: final judgment, the end of the world, the coming of the new creation when God will be "all in all." But the kingdom, which refuses to be tucked away for tomorrow, is both a reality for the end of time *and* a present event to be reckoned with. Some theologians have come to talk about a "realized eschatology," a kingdom already planted here and not yet fully known to us. This kingdom of "already and not yet" suggests that God, who exists outside of time, does not feel compelled to move in a linear fashion. We can imagine that these "last things" of which the church speaks are not simply waiting up ahead as we progress in a vertical movement toward eternity but are thrusting into history and bringing eternity to bear upon us in the present hour. Or, as a priest I know often says, "Don't wait until you die to get to heaven!"

You may be wishing at this point that "kingdom come" would stay put in eternity and leave you to your humble plans for the day. You may have a sinking feeling that, if the kingdom is coming right now, something will be required of you. You would be right.

Consider it an invitation
Back to idea of the kingdom as the unexpected guest with bag in hand, awaiting our decision. Yes or no: Can we welcome this surprise or not? We can view the arrival of the kingdom as a problem to be solved, a burden to be borne, or an intrusion to be rejected if we so choose. This guest brings *change*, and that can mean upsetting our plans and interrupting our current direction, which most of us would deem intolerable. Or we can open our arms and change our hearts, inviting this guest into our homes, our lives, into the center of our day. We can see the arrival as a surprise, a gift, a new possibility for what will happen. We can let go of our agenda and wait upon what will

217

come. This new attitude is what Jesus invites us to entertain. This is what living for the kingdom means.

Kingdom living is an invitation to take a risk. It involves a new way of seeing what is happening all around us. Life chugs along in a predictable pattern, but the kingdom, breaking into time and into our midst, asks us to "think different" about business as usual. The kingdom is a kind of universal translator, taking every event of our lives and giving it a new meaning, bringing good out of it. "All things work together for good" as Paul says (Romans 8:28). The kingdom interprets all of human history as *salvation history,* opening our eyes to God's redemptive power operating in every episode of our lives. Kingdom embraces the sacramental worldview that common things hold sacred realities. In fact, the sacraments are merely concrete moments when we can see clearly the kingdom breaking into time. For this reason, Karl Rahner has called the Eucharist "the sacrament of eschatology." It is the ultimate moment of consummation between what *is* and what *shall be,* when the new creation is realized in its fullness and God is truly all in all.

And yes, seeing through the lens of the kingdom does disrupt our plans for the day and our world as a whole. Making room for the kingdom turns our world upside down. Suddenly the last are first, the least are the greatest, the way of the child is better than the way of the adult, the self-righteous are turned away and notorious sinners are chosen to enter, the rich carry too much baggage to get through the needle's eye, and the poor ones are given cause to rejoice. To live in this kingdom, we have to stand on our heads, priority-wise, and we will be judged ridiculous by all kinds of sensible people.

A while ago I met a man at a party who admired my conversation until he heard that I was a Christian. Distressed and disgusted, he demanded, "Why? Don't you know that Christianity is a religion for losers?"

"Exactly," I assured him. "Of course, the difference between you and me is that I hear that as good news."

The communion of saints

Just how are we supposed to go about making room for this

218

kingdom of God breaking into our lives? What will our lives look like if we do? Have no fear: The church has supplied a veritable army of examples for us in the canonized saints. These folks belong to a roster of faithful ones whose example was so remarkable to those around them that they were recommended to the whole church for imitation. The canonized saints are part of what is known as the communion of saints, another name for the community of faithful living in this world and the next. The communion of saints, however, is also full of interesting characters like Martin Luther King, Jr., Mother Teresa, your favorite aunt Florence, and ... you. You may feel a little hushed by that idea, but get used to it. Everyone in the communion of saints has the kingdom in common.

The communion of saints is not a static reality. We have already noted the Catholic practice of praying for the dead. We believe we can influence the affairs of souls on the other side of death who are heading toward the perfection of love we call heaven. In the same way, Catholics believe that the saints beyond death can assist us. Those whose love has already been perfected and who presently enjoy union with God can influence our affairs as well. We can ask for their intercession, or prayer of petition, on our behalf. We pray for the souls who need help, and the saints pray for us when we need help. The communion of saints shares a local economy of grace that draws us all deeper into the heart of God.

The word *saint* comes from the Latin *sancta*, or "holy." In the Old Testament, the holy ones are variously described as those who are faithful to God or those who are "separate" from the world. This isn't to imply that holy people should be "otherworldly," unconcerned with the realities of society. To be indifferent to ecological disaster, homelessness or violence, for example, would be incompatible with the call to holiness. To be "separate" from the world means to hold spiritual gain as more desirable than material wealth. Even the desert fathers, those Christians of the early centuries who saw society as a shipwreck from which each person ought to escape with his or her life, retreated to the desert to live lives of solitude, penance and prayer for the *sake* of the world, not to abandon it.

219

We are God's holy ones, part of the communion of saints. Though we may not always make holy decisions—in tune with God's will—our vocation is a common call to holy living. We have the companionship of other present-day saints who are struggling to live out this vocation as we do, as well as the help of those who have "gone before us, marked with the sign of faith," as we pray during the Mass.

Role models for the kingdom

The saints who have "made it" by perfecting their love can help us through their intercession, but they also give us the gift of their example. The canonized saints are the heroes of the church, whose stories inspire and motivate us to heroic acts of service and love. Though formal canonization was not recorded until the tenth century, those who gave their lives as martyrs for the faith from the first generation of Christians were remembered by name in the church's liturgy. When martyrdom became less common, one could pursue spiritual perfection by becoming a "living martyr," one who had "died to the world" as a hermit or monastic. Later, exemplary leadership or tireless service could place a person in the ranks of the saints. Being a miracle-worker, in any age, was a sure sign that a person's heart was in close union with the God of love.

What it means to be officially recognized as a saint of the church has evolved over time, as the community's need to be edified has changed. That is why Catholics have not stopped adding to the canon of saints, making sure that along with popes, priests, kings and queens, there are plenty of peasant girls, parents and ordinary people from every culture, race and tongue, whose examples continue to inspire a new generation of the church.

Some saints have become the particular patrons of a country, trade or circumstance. The patron saint of the United States, for example, is Our Lady of the Immaculate Conception. The patron saint of nurses is Elizabeth of Hungary, and the newly appointed patron of computer users is Isidore of Seville, a sixth-century bishop and genius who was as remarkable in his age as the inventors of the computer and the Internet are today. Francis of Assisi is, of course, the patron saint of animals, while the one to turn to in prayer for ailments of the throat is fourth-century martyr Blaise. Anthony of Padua remains the go-to guy if you've lost something.

Devotion to the saints may seem like a medieval thing to someone outside of the church, and it is one of the most frequently lampooned aspects of Catholicism. I admit, some of the biographies of the saints go over the top in drawing an explicit halo around their heroes' lives, and most certainly some depart from fact to legend rather quickly. Some stories of saints give honor to someone for things we would not find admirable today, like acts of self-mortification or pole-sitting (you'll just have to trust me on this one). Christina the Astonishing flew, and that was not the most astonishing thing about her. Reading some saints' biographies can be better than anything on television, but most of us would find such lives neither edifying nor imitate-able.

For every surreal account of sanctified behavior on the shelf, however, there are many that command our attention and admiration for their courage and love. We may honor Francis today for his love of animals, but his challenge to the wealth and privilege of the institutional church of the twelfth century was nothing short of breathtaking. Katharine Drexel, a Philadelphia heiress, was a pioneer of human rights, investing her fortune and energy into the education of African American and Native American children in the late nineteenth century. Camillus de Lellis was an Italian gambler in the sixteenth century who literally lost his shirt before he turned his life over to God and spent the rest of his years tending relentlessly to the needs of the sick poor. Through the stories of the saints, we see how people in many different times and circumstances opened their lives to the kingdom and made it real for others.

And the saints keep coming. The last century produced folks like Thomas Merton, Dorothy Day, Cesar Chavez, Oscar Romero and Mother Teresa, to name only a handful whose stirring example showed us how to welcome the kingdom into the world. Who will join the canon of saints of the twenty-first century? *Your* name is on the list of candidates.

Encouraging words

Vincent de Paul, the patron saint of charitable societies, was a pastor to the peasants of France in the seventeenth century. (The society that bears his name was actually founded a century later by a layman, Frederic Ozanam.) Vincent's life was a remarkable witness for the rich to whom he gave direction as well as to the poor he served. Toward the end of his life, Queen Anne of Austria tried to persuade him to rest. "Monsieur Vincent," she said, "you have lived your life well; you have fed the hungry, clothed the naked, healed the sick, visited those in prisons, comforted the afflicted. Tell me, is there anything left for you to do?"

"Yes, Madame," old Vincent replied.

"Tell me, what is it?" the Queen asked, much troubled.

The old man said simply: "More."

Words like these challenge us not to retire from good works when we feel we've paid our dues for the kingdom's sake. In the same way, when we begin to wonder if our prayer life is going anywhere, we can find strength in the words of fifteenth-century Joan of Arc. When the tribunal accusing her of heresy asked her if the so-called voices she heard could perhaps be in her imagination, she fumed at them: "Of course they're in my imagination! How else might God speak to me?"

It also helps to know that holiness doesn't preclude one's humanity, as in the example of Teresa of Avila, a sixteenth-century mystic and one of four women who are Doctors of the Church, those honored as eminent teachers of the faith. Teresa was a Spanish noblewoman who had little patience with hardship, even after she became a cloistered nun. When she found prayer or the company of others to be boring, she said so. When she felt angry, she was not above expressing her rage. One day, caught in a rainstorm, her carriage foundered in the mud and she shook her fist toward the heavens. "No wonder you have so few friends," she railed at God, "if this is how you treat them!"

The simplicity of Augustine's advice is appealing, sounding so timely from across sixteen centuries: "Love, and do what you will." Bernard of Clairvaux, Cistercian abbot and spiritual writer of the eleventh century, argued the case that there are only four virtues leading to holiness: "Humility, humility, humility, and humility." It would be hard to miss his point.

The words of the saints, as much as the record of their deeds, are as comforting as a conversation with a friend who has stood in our shoes. The saints know what it's like to hesitate on the brink of a decision, afraid of the cost. "All will be well," fourteenth-century anchoress Julian of Norwich counseled. Her confidence is infectious.

You are here

We started this conversation a dozen chapters ago with a dose of humility, contemplating the mystery inherent in human reality. There are things we don't know, and perhaps can't know, given our finite perspective as creatures restricted to space and time. We have considered what can be known of God through the created world, the person of Jesus, and the gifts of the Holy Spirit. We have spent time examining our relationship to the teaching and tradition of the church. We have viewed our humanity through the seven windows of the sacraments, trying to see the world as God sees it. We have asked what it means to pray, what Mary's role in salvation history has to say to us, and how to live morally. Finally, we wind up contemplating the end of time and realizing that eternity is not as linear as the sense of time we have. God is the One who is, who was, and who is to come. God is also the One whose divine name, spoken to Moses, is "I AM." God, the omnipresent, is always here; and to God, the eternal, it is always now.

We who are grounded in time and space find it hard to conceive of a kingdom that at the same time has both already arrived and is still to come. We might think of it as "arrived" insofar as our lives are faithful conduits of God's love. It is "coming" in the sense that we are not yet perfect lovers, still making mistakes, still fearful of our vulnerability, still wanting to cling to some fierce sense of self that does not admit the Other. The kingdom *comes*, as the Lord's Prayer tells us, when *God's will is done*...and not a moment before. We only have to do God's will to experience kingdom coming, all the time.

So here we are, at this particular X on the map, in this generation, on this patch of planet, with a handful of years belonging to us. What will *you* do with *yours*? And whom, finally, will you serve?

Questions to Explore

1. What people or events are you waiting for with great anticipation? With great trepidation? What does waiting teach you about the value of who or what is coming?

2. What were your thoughts about death and afterlife before reading this chapter? Did any of the ideas in this chapter strike you as helpful or disturbing? Why? What unanswered questions do you still have about what comes after death?

3. Read from the book of Wisdom, chapters 1-3, about afterlife. What new insights does this scripture passage offer you? Why do you suppose a part of chapter 3 is included at most funerals?

4. Heaven has been described as perfect union with God's love and hell as alienation from that love. Give some examples how people might choose heaven or hell, as defined in relationship to God's love, in their daily lives.

5. Do you think history has to come to an end in order to be fulfilled? Do you think the world has to be destroyed in order to be transfigured in glory? Defend your answer.

6. What makes the kingdom of God different from the heaven of afterlife? How comfortable are you with the idea that the kingdom is coming this very moment and is already partially realized?

7. If the kingdom comes and inverts the present order of society, so that those on the top will end up on the bottom and vice versa, where will you be when the "new world order" is established? In what concrete ways does the coming of the kingdom turn your life upside down?

8. Is it easy or difficult to think of yourself as a saint? Why?

Do you believe your prayer can affect the circumstance of those who have died? Do you believe prayer of the saints can assist you in your present circumstances? Explain your answer.

9. Name three saints with whom you are familiar. What might attract someone to their example? Name some contemporary people whose example attracts or inspires you. Explain why they do.

10. Which sayings of the saints, quoted in the chapter or elsewhere, are helpful to you in welcoming the kingdom into your life? What other wise sayings have you heard that have made an impact on your worldview and way of living?

Faith Response

1. Read a biography of a saint who interests you. You may want to choose the saint for whom you are named or under whose name you were confirmed. Or get a copy of Butler's *Lives of the Saints* or a page-a-day saints book and become more familiar with the saints of the church.

2. Obtain a biography of a modern hero who is not (yet) in the canon of the church's saints. Compare his or her words and example to the stories of canonized saints. Consider how your own words and example could be a model of heroism for those around you.

3. Make a conscious decision to welcome the kingdom of God into your life. Pray the Our Father deliberately and often, and look for ways that the upside-down, disruptive presence of the kingdom may be trying to break into your daily life.

4. Resolve to be one of the saints of the twenty-first century! Make heroic choices for good, champion the lowly, risk being foolish for the kingdom, aim for downward mobility. Be brave, be prayerful, be joyous, knowing that you rest always in the heart of God.

Afterword

If you have made it this far in our conversation, you may get the sense that it is now your turn to say something. What do you make of this invitation into the life and vision of the Catholic church? As I said near the beginning, the voices we most frequently hear regarding what it means to be Catholic are the bemused or disgruntled ones: Hollywood, the press and those alienated from the church. Practicing and believing Catholics are not heard above the din. Their quiet witness of loving, faith-filled lives glides beneath the radar of what the world calls news. I hope this discussion has been a kind of celebration of what is good and true and hopeful in the church. Certainly these beliefs that I hold and teach bring joy to my life and have changed it beyond imagining. I believe, in the dawning light of a new millennium, that Catholicism brings its beauty—"ever ancient and ever new," to paraphrase Augustine—to a world in need of such vision.

If you have read this book as a Catholic, I hope you have found in these pages confirmation for your own faith. May God continue to lead the church, correct us in error, challenge us in complacence, humble us in arrogance, forgive us our sins and teach us to love with the passion of Jesus.

If you have come to this book as an individual seeker on a journey or more communally as an inquirer in the RCIA, I wish you blessings on the road ahead. It is my prayer that you have found here some clarification and answers to questions you may have had. May the breath of the Holy Spirit blow through you in your discernment and give you courage to become the person God created you to be. If you are looking for a community of faith to share your journey, we Catholics could use your company.

If you picked up this book in pain, angry with the Catholic church or absent from it, let me say thank you, first of all, for giving me a chance to speak. I realize you wouldn't still be here if you didn't love the church even in your hurt. I know that it is love that makes the pain so deep. When love disappoints us, we wonder where we can turn for consolation. In the Desiderata, an early writing found on an old church wall, an anonymous author wrote: "With all its sham, drudgery, and broken dreams, it is still a beautiful world." Considering our spotty and sometimes misbegotten history, I have often felt that the same words could fairly be applied to the church. The church, a divine idea wrapped in human freedom, is far from a perfect entity. Even as I love my life as a Catholic, I too have been seared by official church pronouncements that contradict my conscience, disappointed by the cowardice sometimes exhibited by church leaders or members, ashamed of the wrongs that have been perpetrated in the name of God. I love the church, and yet I am not blind to the human weakness that can and does confound the good news it was originally commissioned to bear. For those of you who are not sure you can accept such a community, I ask your forgiveness and pray for your healing. We are less without you.

For all of us, meek or bold, sure or unsure, notorious sinners or saints-in-training, the church has an invitation to offer. It is the message of Christ, radically opposed to business as usual in the world. It is good news in the midst of the bad news blared by the media or the dreary sameness of the story of our culture. If you become a part of the story of the church, you will embrace an adventure like nothing you have imagined it to be when peering over the edge of it. When the disciples asked Jesus where he was staying, he answered mysteriously, "Come and see." It is the most wonderful invitation of all.

Appendix

Sign of the Cross
> In the name of the Father, and of the Son, and of the Holy Spirit. Amen.

Our Father
> Our Father, who art in heaven, hallowed be thy name; thy kingdom come; thy will be done on earth as it is in heaven. Give us this day our daily bread; and forgive us our trespasses as we forgive those who trespass against us; and lead us not into temptation, but deliver us from evil. Amen.

Hail Mary
> Hail Mary, full of grace, the Lord is with you; blessed are you among women and blessed is the fruit of your womb, Jesus. Holy Mary, Mother of God, pray for us sinners now and at the hour of our death. Amen.

Doxology
> Glory to the Father, and to the Son, and to the Holy Spirit: As it was in the beginning, is now and ever shall be, world without end. Amen.

Blessing Before Meals
> Bless us, O Lord, and these your gifts
> which we are about to receive from your bounty,
> through Christ our Lord. Amen.

Act of Contrition
> My God, I am sorry for my sins with all my heart.
> In choosing to do wrong and failing to do good,
> I have sinned against you whom I should love above
>   all things.

I firmly intend, with the help of your grace,
to do penance, to sin no more, and to avoid the near
occasion of sin.
Our Savior Jesus Christ suffered and died for us.
In his name, my God, have mercy.

Prayer to the Holy Spirit

Come, Holy Spirit, fill the hearts of your faithful.
And kindle in them the fire of your love.
Send forth your Spirit and they shall be created.
And you will renew the face of the earth.
Lord, by the light of the Holy Spirit
you have taught the hearts of your faithful.
In the same Spirit, help us choose what is right
and always rejoice in your consolation.
We ask this through Christ our Lord. Amen.

Memorare

Remember, O most gracious Virgin Mary,
that never was it known that anyone who implored
your help,
or sought your intercession, was left unaided.
Inspired by this confidence, I fly to you,
O virgin of virgins, my mother!
To you I come; before you I stand, sinful and
sorrowful.
O Mother of the Word Incarnate, despise not my
petitions,
but in your mercy hear and answer me.

Hail, Holy Queen

Hail, Holy Queen, Mother of mercy!
Hail, our life, our sweetness and our hope!
To you we cry, the children of Eve;
to you, we send up our sighs,
mourning and weeping in this valley of tears.
Turn, then, most gracious advocate,
your eyes of mercy toward us;

lead us home at last and show us the blessed fruit of
   your womb, Jesus.
O clement, O loving, O sweet Virgin Mary!

Angelus

   Leader: The angel of the Lord declared unto Mary.
   All: And she conceived of the Holy Spirit.
   Hail Mary…

   Leader: I am the handmaid of the Lord.
   All: Be it done to me according to your word.
   Hail Mary…

   Leader: And the Word was made flesh.
   All: And dwelt among us.
   Hail Mary…

   Leader: Pray for us, O holy Mother of God.
   All: That we may be made worthy of the promises of
      Christ.

   Leader: Let us pray.
   All: Pour forth, we beseech you, O Lord,
   your grace into our hearts,
   that we to whom the incarnation of Christ, your son,
   was made known by the message of an angel,
   may by his passion and cross be brought to the glory
      of his resurrection,
   through the same Christ our Lord. Amen.

The Holy Rosary

   The Five Joyful Mysteries:
      The Annunciation
      The Visitation
      The Nativity
      The Presentation
      The Finding of the Child Jesus in the Temple

The Five Mysteries of Light:
  The Baptism of Jesus
  The Miracle of Cana
  The Proclamation of the Kingdom of God
  The Transfiguration
  The Institution of the Eucharist

The Five Sorrowful Mysteries:
  The Agony in the Garden
  The Scourging at the Pillar
  The Crowning with Thorns
  The Carrying of the Cross
  The Crucifixion

The Five Glorious Mysteries:
  The Resurrection
  The Ascension
  The Descent of the Holy Spirit
  The Assumption of Mary
  The Crowning of Mary Queen of Heaven

Way of the Cross (Stations)
Traditional
  1. Jesus is condemned to death.
  2. Jesus takes up his cross.
  3. Jesus falls the first time.
  4. Jesus meets his sorrowful mother.
  5. Simon of Cyrene helps Jesus carry the cross.
  6. Veronica wipes the face of Jesus.
  7. Jesus falls the second time.
  8. Jesus meets the women of Jerusalem.
  9. Jesus falls the third time.
  10. Jesus is stripped of his clothing.
  11. Jesus is nailed to the cross.
  12. Jesus dies on the cross.
  13. The body of Jesus is taken down from the cross.
  14. The body of Jesus body is placed in the tomb.

Scriptural
1. Jesus prays in the Garden of Olives.
2. Jesus is betrayed by Judas and arrested.
3. Jesus is condemned by the Sanhedrin.
4. Jesus is denied by Peter.
5. Jesus is condemned by Pontius Pilate.
6. Jesus is scourged and crowned with thorns.
7. Jesus is made to carry the cross.
8. Simon of Cyrene helps Jesus carry the cross.
9. Jesus meets the women of Jerusalem.
10. Jesus is crucified.
11. Jesus promises the kingdom to the repentant thief.
12. Jesus speaks to his mother and John.
13. Jesus dies on the cross.
14. Jesus is laid in the tomb.

Nicene Creed

We believe in one God, the Father, the Almighty, maker of heaven and earth, of all that is seen and unseen. We believe in one Lord, Jesus Christ, the only Son of God, eternally begotten of the Father, God from God, Light from Light, true God from true God, begotten, not made, one in being with the Father. Through him all things were made. For us and for our salvation he came down from heaven: by the power of the Holy Spirit he was born of the Virgin Mary, and became flesh. For our sake he was crucified under Pontius Pilate; he suffered, died, and was buried.

On the third day he rose again in fulfillment of the Scriptures; he ascended into heaven and is seated at the right hand of the Father. He will come again in glory to judge the living and the dead, and his kingdom will have no end.

We believe in the Holy Spirit, the Lord, the giver of life, who proceeds from the Father and the Son. With the Father and the Son he is worshipped and glorified. He has spoken through the prophets.

We believe in one holy catholic and apostolic Church. We acknowledge one baptism for the forgiveness of sins. We look for the resurrection of the dead, and the life of the world to come. Amen.

Apostles Creed

I believe in God, the Father almighty, creator of heaven and earth; and in Jesus Christ, his only Son, our Lord; who was conceived of the Holy Spirit, born of the Virgin Mary, suffered under Pontius Pilate, was crucified, died and was buried.

He descended into hell; on the third day he rose again from the dead. He ascended into heaven, and is seated at the right hand of the Father. From thence he shall come again to judge the living and the dead.

I believe in the Holy Spirit, the holy catholic Church, the communion of saints, the forgiveness of sins, the resurrection of the body, and life everlasting. Amen.